VIETNAM STUDIES

LOGISTIC SUPPORT

by

Lieutenant General Joseph M. Heiser, Jr.

DEPARTMENT OF THE ARMY
WASHINGTON, D.C.   1974

Library of Congress Catalog Card Number: 72-600389

Reprinted 1975

Foreword

The United States Army has met an unusually complex challenge in Southeast Asia. In conjunction with the other services, the Army has fought in support of a national policy of assisting an emerging nation to develop governmental processes of its own choosing, free of outside coercion. In addition to the usual problems of waging armed conflict, the assignment in Southeast Asia has required superimposing the immensely sophisticated tasks of a modern army upon an underdeveloped environment and adapting them to demands covering a wide spectrum. These involved helping to fulfill the basic needs of an agrarian population, dealing with the frustrations of antiguerrilla operations, and conducting conventional campaigns against well-trained and determined regular units.

Although this assignment has officially ended, the U.S. Army must prepare for other challenges that may lie ahead. While cognizant that history never repeats itself exactly and that no army ever profited from trying to meet a new challenge in terms of the old one, the Army nevertheless stands to benefit immensely from a study of its experience, its shortcomings no less than its achievements.

Aware that some years must elapse before the official histories will provide a detailed and objective analysis of the experience in Southeast Asia, we have sought a forum whereby some of the more salient aspects of that experience can be made available now. At the request of the Chief of Staff, a representative group of senior officers who served in important posts in Vietnam and who still carry a heavy burden of day-to-day responsibilities has prepared a series of monographs. These studies should be of great value in helping the Army develop future operational concepts while at the same time contributing to the historical record and providing the American public with an interim report on the performance of men and officers who have responded, as others have through our history, to exacting and trying demands.

All monographs in the series are based primarily on official records, with additional material from published and unpublished secondary works, from debriefing reports and interviews with key participants, and from the personal experience of the author.

To facilitate security clearance, annotation and detailed bibliography have been omitted from the published version; a fully documented account with bibliography is filed with the Office of the Chief of Military History.

The reader should be reminded that most of the writing was accomplished while the war in Vietnam was at its peak, and the monographs frequently refer to events of the past as if they were taking place in the present.

The author of this monograph, Lieutenant General Joseph M. Heiser, Jr., has been engaged in planning and directing logistical support to the U.S. Army soldier, other U.S. Services, and the Armed Forces of Allied Nations since his commissioning as an officer in the Ordnance Corps in 1943. Having served in the Southern Base Sector Command of the European Theater of Operations from 1943 to 1945, he became a staff officer of the Office of the Chief of Ordnance. He later served as the Executive Officer of the Ordnance School and Division Ordnance Officer, 7th Infantry Division, Korea. He was designated Commanding General, U.S. Communications Zone Europe in 1965. He then became, successively, Assistant Deputy Chief of Staff Logistics (Supply and Maintenance), Headquarters, Department of the Army, Commanding General of the 1st Logistical Command, Vietnam, and Deputy Chief of Staff for Logistics of the U.S. Army.

Washington, D.C.   VERNE L. BOWERS
15 December 1972   Major General USA
                                                       The Adjutant General

iv

Preface

During World War II, Admiral Ernest J. King is alleged to have said, "I don't know what the hell this logistics is that Marshall is always talking about, but I want some of it." It's pretty well known that before that war ended, everyone knew in general terms what it was that General Marshall was talking about and that Admiral King had plenty of it.

Knowing in general terms what logistics means is not enough. The purpose of this monograph is to relate in specific terms what logisticians did and how they did it in supporting combat forces in Vietnam. Not only were American soldiers supported, but at the height of hostilities, in addition to U.S. Forces, the U.S. Army in Vietnam also provided support to the military forces of the governments of South Vietnam, Republic of Korea, Thailand, Australia, New Zealand, and other allied countries.

Probably the best balanced assessment of logistics support in Southeast Asia is provided in the final report by the Military Operations Subcommittee of the Committee on Government Operations, House of Representatives (Holifield Committee) wherein, after approximately four years of surveillance of supply support in Southeast Asia by Congress and the Government Accounting Office, it was reported that, ". . . supply support in Vietnam has been a truly remarkable achievement, but the question must be asked, did it entail unnecessary, hence avoidable, costs? . . ." The Army, in cooperation with Congress, the Government Accounting Office, Office of the Secretary of Defense, and the other military services, began a program called the Logistics Offensive (so named by General Abrams, the Commander, United States Military Assistance Command, Vietnam, in early 1969) to immediately reduce the cost of providing logistics support and yet increase combat effectiveness. This program is a continuing one and up through September 1972, has yielded benefits estimated at 9.3 billion dollars. Of this total, 6.9 billion dollars have directly impacted on the preparation of the Army's budget submissions. The difference is considered to be a bonus, taking into account reduced requirements for facilities, personnel, equipment, transportation, and utilities to support a more efficient logistic system. These savings have been accompanied with dramatic increases in logistics readi-

v

ness for that part of the Army not in Vietnam. Based upon unit reports, equipment on hand increased 44 percent from fiscal year 1968 to fiscal year 1972, while equipment deployability, or operability, increased 41 percent during the same time period. In addition, the fine logistics support of the forces in Vietnam was maintained.

In most human endeavors, history shows a mixture of good and bad results. Combat support of Vietnam is certainly no exception. As Congress noted, supply support has been a remarkable achievement. Also among the good are many overlooked facets, including the unpublicized constructive efforts which contrast with the publicized destructive ones. For example, construction efforts by U.S. servicemen on behalf of the Vietnamese in 1968 and 1969 include:

Schools	1,253	Churches	263
Hospitals	175	Dispensaries	422
Market Places	153	Bridges	598
Roads (km.)	3,154	Dwellings	7,099

Much of this was accomplished by American soldiers in their non-duty time—showing again the humanistic qualities of the American soldier displayed in other wars.

In addition, because of the vast experience gained, the American Army has a larger group of professional military logisticians than ever in its history—many of them junior officers and enlisted personnel—which bodes well for the future. However, we must insure that lessons learned of what to do are adopted and that lessons learned of what not to do will result in corrective action so that those experiences will not recur. It is with this specific thought in mind that this monograph has been prepared.

Finally, in Vietnam, there was a close and wonderful relationship between the man doing the fighting and the man providing the support. In part, this was due to the fact that both were exposed to the same dangers and, that unlike World War II and Korea, there were no safe rear areas in Vietnam. In August 1968, Sergeant William W. Seay, a truck driver—a logistician—won the medal of honor by breaking up an ambush against his convoy on the road to Tay Ninh. This man gave his life to save the lives of his comrades and supplies for the men fighting in the Tay Ninh border area. Logisticians are proud of Sergeant Seay and are proud too of the collective achievements in providing the quality and quantity of support furnished to the combat forces in Vietnam.

To perpetuate the great support provided the combat soldier and in memory of the heroic tasks performed by logistics soldiers such as Sergeant Seay, the "LOGISTICIAN'S CREED" has been

published and distributed to serve as a lasting reminder of what
has been done and as a challenge to what needs to be done by all
Army logisticians serving in the defense of their country.

Washington, D.C.   JOSEPH M. HEISER, JR.
15 December 1972   Lieutenant General, U.S. Army

Acknowledgments

The story of logistic support in Vietnam is one of thousands of logisticians who worked tirelessly to provide that support. This volume relates their accomplishments and attempts to do justice to all the many facets of that complex support operation. Even documenting their story was not a one man job, and so I wish to extend my appreciation to all those who participated in this effort with special thanks to:

The Logistics Monograph Review Team. This "murder board" was composed of General Frank T. Mildren, Lieutenant General Jean E. Engler, USA (Ret.), Lieutenant General Oren E. Hurlbut, USA (Ret.), Lieutenant General John Norton, Lieutenant General William R. Peers, Lieutenant General Carroll H. Dunn, Major General Clarence J. Lang, Major General Henry A. Rasmussen, Major General Richard J. Seitz, Brigadier General Robert W. Duke, USA (Ret.), and Mr. Joseph P. Cribbins. Their collective knowledge and first-hand experience were invaluable in providing background and insight into the logistics story as it unfolded in the early drafts of the Monograph.

Colonel John M. Miller and Colonel William H. Hoffmann who analyzed and assessed the historical significance of the wealth of information contained in the early drafts and provided day-to-day guidance to the Monograph Team.

Lieutenant Colonel Albert F. Boll who developed the initial detailed topical outline for the Monograph to direct the efforts of the staff members of the Office of the Deputy Chief of Staff for Logistics.

The members of the Office of the Deputy Chief of Staff for Logistics team who painstakingly researched and prepared the many papers which formed the basis for the Monograph.

The Monograph Team. This team was composed of Colonel James R. Wilson, USAR, Lieutenant Colonel John B. Crockett, Jr., USAR, Major Willard A. Newman, USAR, Major Felix G. Porter, USAR, and SP5 Felix Ramos, who performed the yeoman task of researching historical information and editing the separate staff papers into a single comprehensive volume.

Lastly, I commend all the logisticians who participated in or supported operations in Vietnam, for they accomplished the deeds that are recorded herein.

Washington, D.C.   JOSEPH M. HEISER, JR.
15 December 1972   Lieutenant General, U.S. Army

Illustrations

Charts

Maps

Tables

Contents

Illustrations are from Department of Defense files. The painting on the front cover is "Welcome Relief" by Specialist Kenneth J. Scowcroft; on the back cover "Convoy on the Mang Yang Pass" by E. C. Williams.

LOGISTIC SUPPORT

CHAPTER I

Introduction

This monograph on logistic support to Vietnam is an historical account of significant actions and events, and includes discussions of the logistic environment, decisions, techniques, accomplishments, and lessons learned during the years 1965 through 1970 and, in some cases, early 1971.

The monograph describes selected logistic events in order to assist the Army in its development of future operational concepts and provides reference material for a comprehensive historical record.

This document traces the evolution of logistics operations beginning in the period before the extensive U.S. buildup in early 1965. Environmental factors influenced the manner in which the logistician had to perform his mission—overcrowded ports, lack of warehousing and storage areas for unloaded supplies, poor security conditions at existing facilities, and insufficient and inadequately trained personnel to perform the monumental task of support for combat operations.

Supply support in Vietnam is discussed from the management viewpoint, including the particular or significant experience gained in various types or classes of supply services provided by the logistician such as maintenance, construction, real estate procurement and management, and transportation support including aviation. Each is illustrated to present a better understanding of techniques used and concepts developed which may influence future logistic support doctrine. A discussion of graves registration, property disposal, bath, laundry, bakery, and food services is also included.

In addition to the support of U.S. Forces, this monograph includes information on the logistics support to Army of the Republic of Vietnam, Free World Military Assistance Forces, logistic responsibilities relative to the Pacification Program, and the effects on the total logistics efforts throughout the world.

To understand the events and decisions related to logistics in the Republic of Vietnam, one must evaluate them against a backdrop of the conditions and problems which prevailed at the time. Fundamentally, none of the background is new or unique to the history of combat logistics. Nonetheless, each condition and each event had its own impact and posed its own problems. Never before had the Army's logistic system been tasked with the mission of supporting large numbers of ground combat troops operating in a counterguerilla role with a pipeline 9,000–11,000 miles long. The logistics doctrine developed as a result of years of experience in conventional ground warfare was not always applicable in the Vietnam environment. Many of the techniques and assumptions which were accepted as valid in conventional warfare did not apply in the harsh, primitive, jungle environment and the isolated support enclaves. Even so, Vietnam is a story of remarkable logistics achievement. At no time was logistic support a constraint on a major tactical operation. This record was made despite the conditions which imposed a fantastic strain on logistics operations and which offered an enormous challenge to all logisticians.

Bordered on the west by Cambodia and Laos and on the east by a seacoast of approximately 1,500 miles on the South China Sea and the Gulf of Thailand, the Republic of Vietnam extends in a crescent shape along the southeastern side of the Indochina peninsula. The land area is dominated by a mountain chain, extending southward from the republic's northern border to within 60 miles of Saigon, with peaks ranging in height from 2,000 to 8,000 feet. The overall topography of Vietnam comprises jungles, deltas, swamps, plains and mountains. The Mekong Delta, southwest of Saigon, is a vast alluvial plain fed by the many mouths of the Mekong River and criss-crossed by a dense network of canals. The Delta is one of the major rice producing regions of Southeast Asia. The topography of Vietnam created many difficulties for U.S. Forces, hindering such activities as construction, transportation and communications while, at the same time, facilitating the enemy's type of operations.

The climate of Vietnam is tropical and subject to monsoon rains. There are two seasons: hot and dry, and hot and rainy. Highest temperatures and humidity are experienced in the southern delta in April and May, with the rainy season beginning in late May and continuing through September. In the coastal and highland areas the highest temperatures and humidities are experienced during the months of July and August, with the rainy season beginning in October and continuing through March. In the highland areas the nights are cool regardless of the season. Overall, the climate of Vietnam severely hampered all logistical operations.

The population of the Republic of Vietnam totals approximately 18 million. The bulk of this population has subsisted throughout the years by the cultivation of rice on lands irrigated through the use of primitive pumps and sluices. The majority of the population lives in the open lowland plains and the rice bearing deltas. The uplands region has been left to the ethnically alien and primitive mountain tribes. Although the majority of the population is ethnically and culturally Vietnamese, there are significant minorities. This minority population is comprised of approximately 1 million Chinese (mostly living in the Saigon area), 500,000 Cambodians, and approximately 1 million Montagnard mountain tribesmen. Buddhism is the predominant religion in Vietnam, although there are approximately 2 million Roman Catholics.

Saigon, the capital of the Republic of Vietnam, is the largest city in the Republic and is located approximately 50 miles inland from the South China Sea on the west bank of the Saigon River. At the time the U.S. buildup began in Vietnam, this city was a busy commercial port, and the only port of significance in the country. As the population has increased from 2 million people in 1964, to approximately 3.5 million in early 1971, Saigon (including the twin city of Cholon) became overcrowded. With the overcrowding came many problems which impaired facilities for health and sanitation, transportation, and security. These problems weighed heavily in the October 1967 decision to move most of the military facilities located in Saigon to Long Binh which was approximately 20 miles northeast of Saigon.

In 1965, Vietnam was primarily an agrarian country with a very low level of industrialization. The few industries established by the French were located in North Vietnam. By the end of 1970, there were only 82 large or medium manufacturing operations in all of South Vietnam. Public utilities and services were wholly inadequate by western standards. Facilities vital to a modern logistics base such as ports, terminal facilities, warehouses, communications, transportation, storage, and maintenance facilities, were either limited or nonexistent. The lack of industry was naturally accompanied by a shortage of technicians and skilled labor. For the most part, all necessary supplies, equipment, and skills to support military operations had to be imported, and all necessary facilities had to be built.

In accordance with the obligation as a member of the South East Asia Treaty Organization the U.S. supplied military matériel and equipment at the request of the Republic of Vietnam. A Military Assistance and Advisory Group was established to supervise and coordinate this support program. This commitment for support was made by President Dwight D. Eisenhower on 10 October 1954. In the following year, the Military Assistance and Advisory Group effort was given authority to organize and train as well as to equip the armed forces of South Vietnam.

In 1956 the communist organization in South Vietnam (the Viet Cong) initiated a campaign of terror to undermine the authority of the central government. This campaign included the assassination and kidnapping of government officials and supporters. By 1960 the number of assassinations had reached 1,400 and over 700 kidnappings had occurred. President John F. Kennedy approved requests for additional aid in 1961. As communist pressure increased and military requirements increased, the Military Assistance Command, Vietnam, was created in February of 1962.

By the end of that year, U.S. advisers were in operational control of U.S. helicopter missions transporting and supporting South Vietnamese Army operations. Overall operational authority was vested in the U.S. Ambassador, with the Embassy handling the pacification program and Military Assistance Command, Vietnam, directly responsible to the ambassador for support in all other fields. In 1963 President Diem was assassinated. A series of coups followed the assassination. These happenings, in addition to assassinations and kidnappings by the Viet Cong, seriously weakened the Vietnamese government. The South Vietnamese Army sustained a series of defeats. Pacification of the countryside was nearly stopped and the enemy was found everywhere. By 1965, it became obvious that a rapid buildup and employment of U.S. combat forces were needed to prevent the complete collapse of the Government of South Vietnam.

General William C. Westmoreland, Commander, U.S. Military Assistance Command, Vietnam, stated that as late as March 1965 no decision had been taken on U.S. intervention with ground forces, other than the limited Marine Security force deployed to protect the Da Nang Airfield. Consequently there was no logistic system in being, and no development of secure logistic bases, except the totally inadequate installations associated with South Vietnamese forces. There were inadequate ports and airfields, no logistic organization, and no supply, transportation, or maintenance troops. Due to the grave tactical situation, President Lyndon B. Johnson directed the deployment of U.S. combat forces. Because of force level ceilings and the decision not to mobilize the reserves, the logistical buildup lagged behind the combat force buildup. That this procedure succeeded, is a tribute to the imagination, determination, and energy of those officers and men in all the services who were charged with this almost impossible task.

The Vietnam conflict was quite different from that for which the Army had trained, and, for that matter, was at variance with combat dynamics upon which the Army's logistic doctrine was based. Vietnam was a war fought essentially by small units (maneuver battalions, companies, and similar forces) in constant pursuit of an elusive enemy. In stark contrast to World War II and Korea, Vietnam was characterized largely by small, isolated actions consisting of ground and air assaults mounted from the numerous isolated base camps dotting the countryside. There were no fixed terrain objectives. Even when some key terrain feature was at issue, it was usually for a limited purpose and a designated time.

There was no neat, linear division between enemy and friendly forces; no front line; and no rear boundaries. Consequently, there was neither an Army service area, nor a communications zone. In fact, the combat zone and the communications zone were one and the same. At no time were there really "secure" ports, depots, storage facilities, service areas, or supply routes. The relative degree of security varied from time to time and place to place. Attacks on logistic facilities and operations at all levels were common, even in the later years of the war. These attacks included major ambushes of supply convoys; harassment by small arms fire; rocket and mortar bombardment; and vicious sapper attacks against general depots, ammunition pads, and petroleum tanks. Later in the war there were some more or less "cleared areas." In 1965, there was quite literally no "friendly" territory.

CHAPTER II
Logistics Environment

To understand the problems and conditions that characterized the logistical effort in Vietnam, one must keep in mind the sequence of events during the early buildup period. The speed and magnitude of the escalation of U.S. combat troop deployments in response to enemy action and pressure proceeded faster than a logistic base could be developed to support these units. The Republic of Vietnam had a low level of industrialization. Modern logistic facilities were limited or nonexistent. The in-country logistic system supporting the South Vietnamese Armed Forces was incapable of supporting major U.S. forces. The small, highly fragmented system supporting the U.S. advisory effort could do no more than provide the skeleton for a later logistical system. The enemy controlled the major part of South Vietnam, either by direct occupation or through terror tactics. The principal terrain features as well as land and water arteries were either under enemy control, or subject to the constant threat of interdiction.

Logistics planning was further complicated by the fact that logistic troops and units were deployed at about the same rate as tactical forces rather than in advance of them as desired for the timely establishment of an adequate logistic base. The chronology of U.S. unit arrivals in the Republic of Vietnam shows a continuous inflow of detachment- and company-size logistical support units during practically every month of the period spring 1965 to summer 1966. In addition, logistics units were deployed on a Technical Service basis (Table of Organization and Equipment) whereas the new Combat Service to the Army doctrine had already been approved, thus causing much agony. Meanwhile, major tactical forces, to include the bulk of the 1st Infantry Division; the 1st Cavalry Division (Airmobile); the 173d Airborne Brigade; the 1st Brigade, 101st Airborne Division; and the 3d Brigade, 25th Infantry Division (which was later to become the 3d Brigade of the 4th Infantry Division) were in-country and engaged in battle by January 1966. The major part of the 25th Infantry Division had arrived by April of that year and brigade-size elements arrived practically every month during the period August–December 1966, to include elements of the 4th, 25th, and 9th Infantry Divisions, as well as the 11th Armored Cavalry Regiment, and the separate 19th and 199th Light Infantry Brigades. The remaining brigade of the 9th Infantry Division arrived in January 1967. Meanwhile, further deployment decisions were made, and the Americal Division, the 101st Airborne Division (-), and other units appeared in Vietnam during the period September 1967 to March 1968.

Logistic Concept (1965) and In-Country Planning

As early as 1962, the need for a centralized U.S. logistical organization in South Vietnam was foreseen by Commander U.S. Military Assistance Command, Vietnam, Lieutenant General Paul D. Harkins. The proposal was disapproved, however by Commander in Chief U.S. Army Pacific and Commander in Chief Pacific, who felt that the requirement was not justified at that time. The idea was revived in August 1964 by the Military Assistance Command, Vietnam, J–4, who believed that the current and future situation would require a logistical command to support activities in South Vietnam. Accordingly, he saw that a plan was prepared which included the prompt introduction of a logistical construction capability. On 21 December 1964, the Joint Chiefs of Staff endorsed the Military Assistance Command, Vietnam, plan and recommended that 230 men be initially dispatched to South Vietnam to form a logistical command as soon as possible. Secretary of Defense Robert S. McNamara approved the plan in principle, but stated that additional justification was needed, particularly for the engineer construction group. However, he felt that the subject was of sufficient importance to send a special representative to South Vietnam, and on 31 January 1965, a group from the Office of the Secretary of Defense arrived in Saigon. After four days of conferences, this group recommended the establishment of a logistical command with an initial strength of 350 men. The establishment of an engineer construction group, not recommended initially, was approved in April as planning for a further buildup developed.

On 25 February 1965, the Secretary of Defense approved the introduction of a logistical planning group in the Republic of Vietnam consisting of 17 officers and 21 enlisted men. Colonel Robert W. Duke was enroute to take command of the 9th Logistical Command in Thailand. He was intercepted in Hawaii and ordered to the Republic of Vietnam to take charge of the planning group. He arrived in Saigon on 6 March 1965. The balance of the officers and enlisted men for the planning group arrived in Saigon during the last two weeks of March 1965. On 1 April 1965, the 1st Logistical Command was activated in Saigon by Commander in

Chief U.S. Army Pacific General Order, using the personnel of the logistical planning group as its initial strength.

Prior to this time, logistical support in Vietnam had been fragmented, with the Army providing only Class II and IV items which were peculiar to the Army, Class V items used by the Army aviation units, and maintenance of vehicles, armament, and instrument calibration by a small Direct Support shop in Saigon. The rest of the support was provided by the Navy through Headquarters Support Activity, Saigon because the Navy had been designated as the executive agency responsible for supporting the Military Assistance and Advisory Groups and missions in Southeast Asia.

The mission of the 1st Logistical Command as developed by Colonel Duke and the initial small planning group was, in broad terms, that the 1st Logistical Command would assume responsibility for all logistical support in Vietnam, less that which was peculiar to the Air Force or Navy. This initial mission included procurement, medical, construction, engineer, finance and accounting of all U.S. Army forces in-country, except Military Assistance Command, Vietnam, advisors; and excluded communications, aviation, and military police support which were retained by U.S. Army Vietnam (the Army component command under Military Assistance Command, Vietnam, and over the 1st Logistical Command). Requirements beyond direct support and general support maintenance capability were to be retrograded to Okinawa. Subsequent add-on missions were planned to be put into effect as the capability became available. These add-on missions were to: assume support of Military Assistance Command, Vietnam, advisors from Headquarters Commandant, Military Assistance Command Vietnam, a task accomplished on 1 September 1965, phase-out the Navy supply activity in Saigon—The 1st Logistical Command started assuming Headquarters Support Activity Saigon functions in September 1965, and completed the mission in March 1966—and assume common item support for all U.S. forces in South Vietnam.

The 1st Logistical Command was authorized direct communications with U.S. Army Ryukyu Islands (Okinawa) on logistic matters. Logistic requirements were placed there. After screening, requirements were filled or passed to U.S. Army Pacific. It either filled them or passed them to Army Materiel Command. This proved to be very unsatisfactory due to inadequate electrical communications with Okinawa, lack of adequate stocks and personnel resources in Okinawa as well as U.S. Army Pacific, and the many headquarters in the logistic chain. Through this chain there was a loss in excess of 40 percent of all requisitions submitted in the initial stages of the buildup. A combat area should be able to submit requisitions directly to Continental U.S. Continental U.S. could then direct shipment to the combat area from the nearest source to that area having the required items in stock.

The 1st Logistical Command, in coordination with Military Assistance Command, Vietnam, operational planning, developed its own logistic concept for South Vietnam. The plan provided for two major base depots and five support commands. (Map 1) The seas and rivers were initially to be the main supply routes within Vietnam. However, a change over to road and rail would take place when the tactical situation permitted. Each support command would provide all logistic support on an area basis and have a 15 day stockage. Depots would have a 45 day stockage. The Saigon Depot would support the Vung Tau and Can Tho Support Commands. The Cam Ranh Bay Depot would support the Nha Trang, Qui Nhon and Da Nang Support Commands.

A two depot concept was considered essential due to the vulnerability of the Saigon River and port to Viet Cong action and the limited port capacity. Vung Tau was considered an alternate to the Saigon port in the event of loss of Saigon or blockage of the Saigon River. Cam Ranh Bay was selected as the other base depot and port due to its excellent deep water harbor, the existing pier, its central location, and U.S. capability to secure the area from Viet Cong attack.

This plan by the 1st Logistical Command was implemented with only two changes; the Marines were landed at Da Nang and, by Commander in Chief Pacific direction, the Navy was given the responsibility for both tactical and logistical operations in I Corps. The Da Nang Support Command was eliminated from the 1st Logistical Command plan. It was reinstated in 1968. The anticipated scale of tactical operations in the Delta area of IV Corps did not materialize, so the Can Tho Support Command was not activated. The IV Corps was supported by the Vung Tau Support Command by sea and air.

The original plan for the refinement of a logistical plan in an orderly fashion followed by a deliberate and orderly implementation never came to pass. Instead it quickly turned into a concurrent planning and implementation process. The Secretary of Defense approved at the 9–11 April 1965 Hawaiian Conference an Army Combat force of over 33,000 troops with the first combat troops (173rd Airborne Brigade from Okinawa) to arrive in South Vietnam on 21 April 1965. This was just the beginning of the ac-

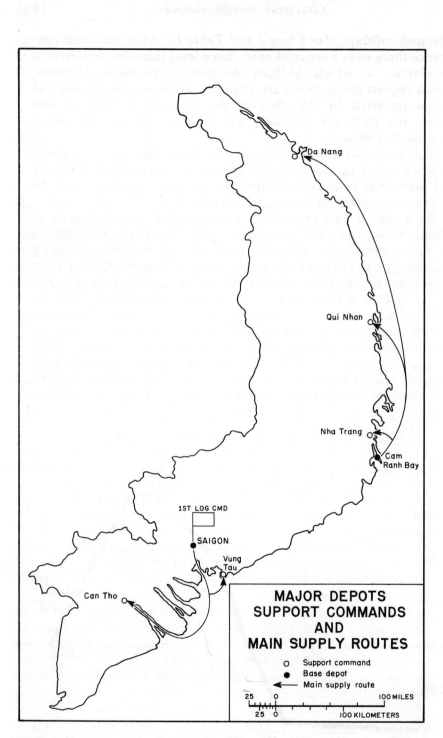

MAJOR DEPOTS
SUPPORT COMMANDS
AND
MAIN SUPPLY ROUTES

MAP 1

celerated buildup. (*See Chart 1 and Table 1.*) After the April conference there were a series of other force level planning conferences in Hawaii, at which Military Assistance Command, Vietnam, would request forces that were required. However, the number of troops approved by the office of the Secretary of Defense was always less than the number requested by Military Assistance Command, Vietnam.

U.S. Forces were built up in an imbalanced manner. Continued enemy pressure on the beleaguered government of South Vietnam and manpower ceilings combined to cause the logistics base to be inadequate in relation to the total force level.

Each time a new ceiling was established it was announced as a final ceiling and could not be changed. Therefore, all planning for future operations had to be based on this number, including requests by the Office of the Secretary of Defense to Congress for supporting funds. This series of "final ceilings," and the decision not to call up a large number of Reserve Component units, established a pattern of "too late planning," and "too late determination of requirements" that affected every facet of the military establishment from draft quotas to administration, training, equipping, procurement by Army Materiel Command, Defense Supply Agency, and Government Services Administration. This resulted in a drawdown of reserve and project stocks to an unacceptable level.

CHART 1—AUTHORIZED TROOP LEVEL IN SOUTH VIETNAM

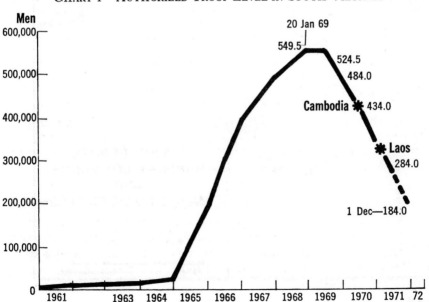

TABLE 1—U.S. ARMY AND TOTAL U.S. MILITARY PERSONNEL
IN SOUTH VIETNAM

Date	U.S. Army Personnel	Total U.S. Military Personnel
31 Dec 1960	800	900
31 Dec 1961	2,100	3,200
31 Dec 1962	7,900	11,300
31 Dec 1963	10,100	16,300
31 Dec 1964	14,700	23,300
31 Mar 1965	15,600	29,100
30 Jun	27,300	59,900
30 Sep	76,200	132,300
31 Dec	116,800	184,300
31 Mar 1966	137,400	231,200
30 Jun	160,000	267,500
30 Sep	189,200	313,100
31 Dec	239,400	485,300
31 Mar 1967	264,600	420,900
30 Jun	285,700	448,800
30 Sep	296,100	459,700
31 Dec	319,500	485,600
31 Mar 1968	337,300	515,200
30 Jun	354,300	534,700
30 Sep	354,200	537,800
31 Dec	359,800	536,100
*31 Jan 1969	365,600	542,400
31 Mar	361,500	538,200
30 Jun	360,500	538,700
30 Sep	345,400	510,500
31 Dec	330,300	474,400
31 Mar 1970	321,400	448,500
30 Jun	297,800	413,900
30 Sep	295,400	394,100
31 Dec	250,700	335,800
31 Mar 1971	227,600	301,900
3 Jun	197,500	250,900

*Indicates peak strength in South Vietnam
Between 1954–1960 U.S. Military Strength averaged about 650 advisors

The first US Army combat unit to arrive in South Vietnam
(173rd Airborne Brigade) was employed in the Saigon area to
insure retention of Bien Hoa Airfield and to assist in securing
Saigon. It was initially supported directly from Okinawa by a daily
C–130 aircraft flight. Later the support was assumed by the 1st
Logistical Command.

The second combat unit to arrive was the 2d Brigade of the 1st Infantry Division. Plans called for their employment at Qui Nhon to secure that area for future use. From the meager logistic resources in South Vietnam some were deployed to Qui Nhon to support that unit. Due to the buildup of enemy pressure on Saigon, Commander, U.S. Military Assistance Command, Vietnam, made the decision two days before the arrival of the 2d Brigade of the 1st Infantry Division that the 2d Brigade would be employed in the defense of Saigon. This resulted in a scramble to relocate the few U.S. supplies and ammunition in South Vietnam from Qui Nhon south some 250 miles to Saigon. Numerous changes were made in tactical plans in the initial stages of the buildup due to Viet Cong pressure. Such changes were necessary, but had an adverse effect on orderly logistical planning and implementation.

As logistical units arrived in South Vietnam they were assigned to appropriate depots or Support Commands as the tactical situation directed. In all Support Commands small units and detachments arrived ahead of the command and control units. As a result officers from the seventeen-man officer staff of the 1st Logistical Command had to be sent to the Support Command areas to receive, organize, assign missions, coordinate efforts, and command these small units and detachments pending arrival of a command and control headquarters. As an example, a U.S. Army major with a jeep and a brief case was the complete command and control unit for the Saigon area. This included finding and securing living areas and work areas for arriving units. Prior to June 1965, the 1st Logistical Command operated on a very thin shoestring. As more staff officers and command and control units arrived in June the command and control situation improved greatly.

On 11 May 1965, the Commander U.S. Military Assistance Command, Vietnam, and his staff were briefed on the logistic plans of the 1st Logistical Command. This briefing included real estate requirements and requirements for tactical troops for depot and support command areas at Qui Nhon, Nha Trang, and Cam Ranh Bay. The plan was approved on 12 May 1965. The first ship unloading operation at Cam Ranh Bay took place on 15 May 1965. Since Army stevedores had not yet arrived in South Vietnam, and the South Vietnam stevedore union refused to send civilian stevedores to Cam Ranh Bay, the first ship was unloaded by a U.S. transportation lieutenant and a small group of enlisted men assembled through levies on units for anyone with any stevedore or small boat experience. From such a start Cam Ranh Bay was built up to a major and efficient port.

With the arrival of combat forces and the 1st Logistical Command becoming operational, its small staff could not accomplish all the planning that was required. A request was placed on U.S. Army Pacific for assistance. U.S. Army Pacific then provided five officers on a 90 day temporary duty tour. These officers reported to the 1st Logistical Command on 23 April 1965 and were given the task to make a study of the Qui Nhon enclave, Nha Trang enclave, and the Cam Ranh Bay area, to determine the tactical security requirements and the feasibility of utilizing these areas as included in 1st Logistical Command's concept, and to refine the logistics planning for each area to include base development.

These planners prepared a study which proved to be of great value in base development and the expansion of the 1st Logistical Command's capabilities. This study with appropriate recommendations and requests for tactical troops for security of desired areas was presented to the Commanding General U.S. Army Vietnam and Commander U.S. Military Assistance Command, Vietnam, in May 1965. Approval was received and security was provided as requested at each location, except Qui Nhon. General Westmoreland approved the security plan for Qui Nhon, but due to Viet Cong pressure and a shortage of U.S. forces the implementation of the plan was delayed over a month. Even then the forces available were not able to push out and secure all of the originally planned areas. This left the ammunition depot at Qui Nhon exposed to enemy action.

Upon completion of the enclave study, a new problem faced the planning group. It was recognized that the continued influx of troops into the city of Saigon (10,000 in the next 4 months) would soon exceed its capability to absorb. It was also recognized that usable real estate and facilities were not available in the Saigon area. A threefold mission was given to the planning group: develop a short range plan to absorb the influx of troops into the Saigon area, develop a long range plan that would ultimately move the bulk of U.S. Army personnel out of the Saigon area, and develop detailed plans for the security and logistical development of the Can Tho areas.

A thorough reconnaissance was made and chosen areas were selected. In order to relieve the pressure on Saigon facilities, the Long Binh area was selected for the establishment of a major logistical and administrative base. A master base development plan was prepared which provided areas for all activities in Saigon.

General Westmoreland (who was both Commander U.S. Military Assistance Command, Vietnam, and Commanding General

U.S. Army Vietnam) was briefed on the study and approved it in principle, except he elected to move Headquarters U.S. Army Vietnam to Long Binh (Headquarters Military Assistance Command, Vietnam, remained in the Saigon area). The 1st Logistical Command immediately began implementing the study by locating the ammunition depot, hospital, engineers, plus direct support and general support supply and maintenance support at Long Binh. The movement of headquarters type activities was delayed by the requirement for $2 million to develop an adequate communication system in the area and by the time required for installation of the system.

The study on Saigon proved to be of great value. Long Binh became a major installation in the Republic of Vietnam. The study on Vung Tau and Can Tho resulted in the elimination of Can Tho as a support command. The delta area was supported from Vung Tau and Saigon. The Vung Tau portion of the study included plans for the development of Vung Tau as a deep draft port utilizing De Long piers.

Major Logistics Constraints

To the logistician, it is extremely important to have an early decision establishing theater standards of living. These standards should determine the basic authorization for post, camp, and station property, PX stockage of merchandise, whether base camps are to be constructed, construction standards, the degree of permanency for fixed installations, and utilities and services to be provided. Obviously, such a decision has a tremendous impact on the logistic system. Construction materials alone constituted some 40 percent of total tonnage of materials coming into South Vietnam in 1965 and 1966.

Without such established standards to use as terms of reference, it was impossible to realistically determine requirements for such items as real estate, supply, storage, maintenance, construction, electricity and other utilities, as well as the resultant port unloading capability required. Without such standards, the logistic system has no grounds for challenging requirements placed upon it. Such a decision was never made in the early days of Vietnam. Therefore, every unit independently established its own standard of living, ordering from supply catalogs as if they were Sears and Roebuck catalogs. Commanders desiring to give their personnel the very highest possible levels of comfort and quality of food, requisitioned air conditioning and refrigeration equipment far in excess of that authorized by Tables of Organization and Equipment. This had a mushrooming effect. Requirements for electrical power generating equipment were in turn increased to the point that demand exceeded the capability of Tables of Organization and Equipment authorized equipment. As the requirement for this equipment increased, the numbers of makes and models proliferated (as suppliers of standard makes and models were unable to keep up with the rapidly increasing demands). As the quantities of equipment increased, so did the requirements for repair parts and qualified maintenance personnel. The repair parts were a problem because of the many varied makes and models and the resultant lack of interchangeability among their parts. It was difficult to maintain full Tables of Organization and Equipment authorized maintenance strength much less the numbers of personnel required to maintain the excess equipment. Therefore, because these personnel were not readily available in sufficient quantities, back-up equipment was requisitioned (for emergency use) further burdening an already heavily taxed logistic system. Finally decisions were made on a piece-meal basis on such things as construction standards. But even with established standards, there was flexibility in interpretation. More often than not, the interpretation did not favor the most austere construction or equipment requirements. This not only put a heavy burden on the logistical system, but it also taxed the Continental U.S. troop base which was not structured in numbers or skills to support the construction or equipment installation and subsequent maintenance requirements which evolved from the Vietnam buildup.

War Reserve Stocks

The stocks available in March 1965 were totally inadequate. For example, only one DeLong pier was available while a dozen could have been used. The timely availability of these piers would have saved the government large sums of money in ship demurrage and speeded up the buildup of forces.

Logistical Management Organizations

Logistical management organizations were not available. As an example, it was a year before a supply inventory control team arrived in South Vietnam. By the time it had become operational, its equipment was found to be inadequate and had to be upgraded. This same situation was common in other areas of logistical management. In a new theater of operations under combat conditions, there is a pressing need early in the operation for management organizations to be completely mobile, automated, and self-supporting. Further, these early logistics management organizations and units were Technical Service oriented even though the Combat Service to the Army functional doctrine had been approved. Difficulties were experienced in fitting the Technical Service organizations into the new doctrine that had not been fully tested before Vietnam.

Engineer Construction

As the buildup progressed, it became apparent that the engineer construction program was becoming so large it required a special command to oversee it. In July 1965, the decision was made to deploy an engineer brigade to the Republic of Vietnam, and upon its arrival the engineer construction functions were transferred from the 1st Logistical Command to the Engineer Brigade.

With increased combat requirements, the priority for logistics construction projects declined for a period and the construction of essential port and depot facilities fell behind schedule, adversely affecting the capability to handle incoming troops, equipment, and supplies. However, in December 1965, Commander in Chief Pacific directed that the highest priority be given to port and beach clearance and depot construction. After this the capability to handle incoming cargo steadily improved.

Logistic Support Principles

The organization for supply support followed the area support, "logistical island," concept with the sea being the main supply route. Field depots were established in each support command to receive, store, and issue Classes II, IV, VII and IX items, less aviation, avionics, medical, and missile peculiar items. The depots provided area support as indicated below:

1. The 506th Field Depot, Saigon (later US Army Depot, Long Binh) was responsible for III and IV Corps.

2. The 504th Field Depot, Cam Ranh Bay (later US Army Depot, Cam Ranh Bay) was responsible for the southern part of II Corps.

3. The 58th Field Depot, Qui Nhon (later US Army Depot, Qui Nhon) was responsible for the northern part of II Corps.

4. The US Army Field Depot, DaNang was established on 25 February 1968 with the mission of supplying Army peculiar items

in I Corps. This depot operated as a field depot of the Qui Nhon base depot.

Virtually all Army tactical operations received logistics support from 1st Logistical Command elements operating logistical support activities located at major base camps such as Tay Ninh, Bearcat, Phuoc Vinh, Can Tho, Pleiku, An Khe, and Chu Lai. When forces beyond the reach of these facilities required additional support, temporary forward support activities were deployed.

Initially, medical services and medical supply were organic to the 1st Logistical Command mission. As the buildup progressed, the magnitude of the medical mission became greater. A decision was made to transfer this function from the 1st Logistical Command to a medical brigade. The 44th Medical Brigade assumed this function upon arrival in South Vietnam in 1966.

Aviation logistic support was initially provided by the U.S. Army Support Command, later U.S. Army Vietnam. The 34th General Support Group (aviation supply and maintenance) was deployed to South Vietnam in mid-1965 to manage this function.

The Logistical Support Activity was a continuing provisional activity composed of 1st Logistical Command elements and generally located in a fixed base camp to provide direct and general supply, maintenance, and service support to U.S. and Free World Military Assistance Forces on an area basis. The type and number of units comprising a Logistical Support Activity was dependent upon the scope of the support mission. Many of these operations involved substantial portions of either a supply and service battalion, direct support maintenance battalion, or elements of both with the senior officer present serving as the Logistical Support Activity commander. Stockage levels of all classes at a Logistical Support Activity were determined by the densities of personnel and equipment supported, considering replenishment capabilities. Stockage objectives for the various classes of supply varied from 5 to 45 days depending upon the commodities being stocked.

A Forward Support Activity was a provisional organization, temporary in nature, and deployed in the vicinity of a supported tactical unit's forward operating base to provide direct supply, maintenance, and service support. It was deployed to support a specific tactical operation, when the tactical organic support capability was not sufficient to provide the support required. Upon completion of the operation, it was withdrawn from the area of operations, and its assets and personnel returned to their parent unit. Personnel and equipment comprising a Forward Support Activity were drawn from Tables of Organization and Equipment and Tables of Distribution and Allowances units assigned to the parent Support Command of the 1st Logistical Command. Forward Support Activities could stock Class I, III, V, and limited, fast moving Class II and IV, if the tactical unit was unable to provide their own support. Stockage levels were set at a minimum level consistent with operational requirements (based on troop and equipment densities, resupply rates, capacity and consumption experience). Throughput was used to the maximum extent possible to replace stocks consumed at Forward Support Activities. Maintenance and services were provided as required depending upon the supported unit's organic capabilities, tactical deployment, and densities.

If a Forward Support Activity became a continuing activity, it was usually redesignated as a Logistical Support Activity. Normally, a Forward Support Activity which continued operations over six months was redesignated as a Logistical Support Activity.

The concept of using a Forward Support Activity to provide combat service support was developed due to the particular environment in South Vietnam and the manner in which tactical units operated. Brigade-size units were engaged in search and destroy operations which in many cases were conducted in areas located a considerable distance from their base camp and major support installations.

The 1st Logistical Command did not have separate authorization for the personnel and equipment required to operate Forward Support Activities, although the need for such authorization existed. Personnel and equipment were drawn from Tables of Organization and Equipment and Tables of Distribution and Allowances units assigned to the parent support command or were provided by the other support commands when the requirement exceeded the parent support command's capability. The initial Forward Support Activity concept envisioned the organization and fielding of Forward Support Activities in support of tactical operations of short duration. Experience showed, however, that some Forward Support Activities were required for extended periods of time resulting in a degradation of the capability of the units from which personnel or equipment were drawn.

Establishment of permanent brigade base camps and the deployment of non-divisional Tables of Organization and Equipment supply, service, and maintenance units to these areas reduced the requirements for Forward Support Activities. In many locations where Forward Support Activities originally provided support, it was possible later to provide logistical support by a Logistical

Support Activity with composite support organizations providing tailored supply, service, and maintenance support on an area basis. Then when brigades were deployed outside of their normal area of operations, in most cases, it was possible for the tactical units to obtain support in their new area from combat service support units in that area. When required, augmentation of Tables of Organization and Equipment support units in forward areas enabled a direct support maintenance battalion, for example, to provide across-the-board logistical support to all divisional and non-divisional units in its area of responsibility. Although the requirement for operation of Forward Support Activities was significantly reduced, each Support Command maintained on-call a Forward Support Activity (by specifically designated personnel and equipment) capable of rapid deployment when a Forward Support Activity was required by tactical units. The implementation of the Forward Support Activity and Logistical Support Activity concept enabled tactical commanders to concentrate on their primary mission while ranging deep into enemy territory. These commanders knew that the required logistical support would be available whenever and wherever required.

As the buildup progressed, the technology for the management of supplies improved and new and imaginative concepts and procedures were developed. The period 1965–1966 was characterized by fifteen months of unprecedented growth and development. Inheriting a fragmented logistics structure consisting of some 16 different systems managed by separate component services, U.S. Army Vietnam and the 1st Logistical Command pulled these systems together to form a unified structure. However, even then it was not feasible to combine all aspects of support into one command. In this period, the 1st Logistical Command managed all logistics and support functions for U.S. Army Vietnam except for aviation supply, maintenance support, and engineer construction. The logistics island concept and Logistics Support Activity and and Forward Support Activity support concepts were developed, and three major support commands were established at Saigon, Cam Ranh Bay, and Qui Nhon. Major port and depot construction was undertaken in each area to support the hundreds of thousands of combat and logistics troops entering the country. In late 1965, the control of stocks in storage and on order was accomplished by a laborious manual process. Each depot was considered a separate entity and requisitioned replacement supplies directly through 2d Logistical Command in Okinawa. Under this system, there was no practical accountability of total in-country supply levels. In less than three years, this process was replaced by a complex control system involving the large-scale use of electronic computers. Coincidentally, procedures were evolved to provide continuous and up-to-date inventory accounting of all stocks within Vietnam. In late 1967, a fully automated central inventory control center was established at Long Binh (handling all type of supplies, except ammunition, aviation, medical and special forces items), and was known as the 14th Inventory Control Center.

Modern computer equipment was installed in the 14th Inventory Control Center to attempt to bring some order to the supply chaos in the depot stock inventory. The major problem encountered was the tremendous influx of supplies which were over the beaches and through the port flooding the depots under a massive sea of matériel and equipment much of which was unneeded. Push supplies and duplicate requisitions of thousands of tons of cargo piled up in the depots, unrecorded and essentially lost to the supply system. In the latter part of 1967, control was slowly established over the requisitioning system through the use of automation and the flow of unneeded supplies abated somewhat. Through these improvements in control and accountability, in-country requirements could be tabulated, interdepot shortages and excesses balanced, and requisition priorities evaluated.

Port Situation in Vietnam

In the pre-buildup stage, most cargo destined for Vietnam was shipped directly from Continental U.S. depots and vendors to west coast military sea or aerial ports. From these ports it was loaded aboard ships or aircraft and moved either to Vietnam directly or to Okinawa which provided backup support. Cargo shipped directly to Vietnam, for the most part, was initially received at the Saigon water port or the Tan Son Nhut airport. Military cargo was treated very much as commercial or Agency for International Development cargo, with little emphasis on specialized development of surface or air distribution methods, facilities, or equipment.

Between mid-1965 and late 1966, cargo continued to move primarily by ship. Airlift was used to move the great majority of troops and priority cargo, which accounted for only a small part of the total tonnage moved. Surface cargo, during this period, continued to flow to Okinawa, Vietnam and Thailand causing multiport discharging, although efforts were made to direct shipments to the final destination port.

Initially, most waterborne cargo arriving in South Vietnam was received at the Saigon Port, the only port with deep draft piers except for a small two-berth pier at Cam Ranh Bay which had been constructed in 1964 under the Military Assistance Program. The Saigon Port was a civilian port under the management control of the Republic of Vietnam's governmental port authority. It consisted of ten deep draft berths. U.S. Army cargo was unloaded by Vietnamese civilian stevedores at berths assigned by the civilian port authority. Coordination of military cargo unloading and port clearance was handled by the Navy's Headquarters Support Activity Saigon.

When the buildup began, the port continued to operate in this fashion. Headquarters Support Activity Saigon never knew from day to day how many berths or which berths would be made available to them for the unloading of U.S. cargo. In addition, customs at the Saigon port dictated that cargo discharged from ships be placed on pier aprons to await port clearance by the cargo owner. It was up to the consignee to remove the cargo from the port. Cargo not consigned to U.S. forces remained on the piers for weeks and sometimes months, creating undesirable and crowded working conditions which adversely affected port operations. Repeated efforts to get South Vietnam to clear the piers were unsuccessful. Some of the cargo being received by South Vietnam was U.S. Military Aid equipment which became South Vietnam equipment as it was unloaded. U.S. forces were accused many times of improper port clearance because this equipment was olive drab in color. But such equipment frequently proved to belong to South Vietnam and the U.S. Army had no authority to move it.

The overloaded port facilities and the operational necessity to selectively discharge cargo to get high priority cargo ashore before less urgently required items resulted in excessive ship turn-around time which increased the total number of ships required. This situation was complicated as cargo was manifested by broad categories only, for example, general cargo, making it impossible to locate specific items. Holding the ships for lengthy periods resulted in demurrage charges of from $3,000 to $7,000 per day per ship. Also the inadequate and insecure railroads and highways forced the distribution system to rely heavily on shallow draft vessels for transshipment of cargo between the Saigon Port and other locations, and intratheater airlift between Tan Son Nhut air terminal and other locations. The problem was further aggravated by a shortage of shallow draft vessels both military (LCMs and LCUs) and civilian assets, which were used for offloading cargo from deep draft vessels at ports not having adequate berthing facilities for the larger ships. Civilian lighterage as well as military landing craft, primarily LCMs and LCUs were used for this purpose.

The U.S. Army's 4th Transportation Command arrived in South Vietnam on 12 August 1965. It was given the mission of assisting Headquarters Support Activity Saigon in U.S. port operations and assuming that function completely as soon as possible, which it did in September 1965. In addition, it was charged with providing technical assistance to port and beach operations at Cam Ranh Bay and the support commands being established throughout South Vietnam. As U. S. Army terminal service companies were received, they were initially employed in unloading of ammunition at Na Bhe, the central ammunition receiving point just south of Saigon, and were later employed in Saigon proper. In May 1965, a request was made to the government of the Republic of South Vietnam to acquire the three Maritime Marine piers adjacent to the Saigon port facilities for the exclusive use of U. S. Forces. These facilities were owned by a French shipping firm. This request ran into financial and political difficulties, but was finally approved in December 1965 after the personal intervention of General Westmoreland and the U. S. Ambassador. With the exclusive use and control of these facilities, port operations improved in efficiency and volume. The delay in obtaining these piers plus the shortage of yard and storage space and the lack of a depot structure and accounting procedures prevented the early establishment of adequate port facilities.

Nevertheless, it was apparent that additional port facilities would be required in the Saigon area. The 1st Logistical Command made this known to Commander U.S. Military Assistance Command, Vietnam, who directed his staff to develop plans for the facilities now known as Newport. Construction began on this fifty million dollar facility in early 1966. In April 1967, the first deep draft vessel was discharged at the Newport facility. Also, during this period, several other ports throughout Vietnam were in the construction phase.

By the end of December 1967, the ports in use by the Army numbered 10; Saigon, Qui Nhon, Cam Ranh Bay, Vung Ro, Vung Tau, Cat Lai, and Nha Trang were the deep draft ports; Dong Tam, Phan Rang and Can Tho were the shallow draft ports. These improvements in port capabilities brought about a reduction in the average time a deep draft ship waited for a berth in Vietnam ports from 20.4 days during the most critical period of 1965 to the 1970 average of less than two days.

Warehousing and Storage Facilities

Prior to the buildup, warehouses and storage areas were literally nonexistent, except for limited facilities in the Saigon area. Supplies were scattered in several locations throughout Saigon, all of which were substandard and overcrowded; some were only open storage. At the time the 1st Logistical Command became operational, there was a construction backlog for the troops already incountry. Construction of logistics facilities competed with many other requirements. Since there was never more than $300 million in annual capability to apply against a total theater program of close to $2 billion, the construction effort took almost six years to accomplish.

To initially offset this shortage of facilities, negotiations were initiated with the United States Overseas Mission to obtain 13 Japanese built warehouses with dirt floors and no electrical wiring in the Fishmarket area in Saigon. Three of these buildings were obtained by the end of 1965 and the remaining 10 during 1966. A contract was also let to construct an added 210,000 square feet of covered storage and to fill an area behind the warehouses that would serve as hardstand for open storage and a troop cantonment area. This area housed the 506th Field Depot until a new depot was constructed in Long Binh in 1968 and the move to the new facilities was completed 1 July 1969.

By way of comparison, the new depot facilities at Long Binh provided 1,869,000 square feet of black-topped hardstand and 1,458,000 square feet of covered storage, whereas the depot facilities at the Fishmarket in Saigon had a total of only 670,000 square feet of covered storage space as late as March 1967.

Additionally, agreement was reached with the United States Overseas Mission on 16 March 1965 to provide and erect some prefabricated buildings owned by the United States overseas mission for use as warehouses in the Qui Nhon, Da Nang, Cam Ranh Bay, Nha Trang, and Saigon areas. These buildings were finally available for occupancy in February 1966, almost one year after the agreement. The same basic situation prevailed at Qui Nhon where substandard and overcrowded facilities were occupied until completion of the new depot at Long My in 1968.

The United States constructed a major depot and port complex at Cam Ranh Bay costing over $145 million, $55 million of which came from Army appropriations. Cam Ranh Bay was an undeveloped area located at an excellent natural harbor which when completed had over 1.4 million square feet of covered storage, 1.2 million square feet of open ammunition storage area, and bulk storage facilities for over 775,000 barrels (42 gallons per barrel) of petroleum products. Construction of this complex was started early in the buildup period when it was envisioned that the main war effort would be along the Cam Ranh Bay–Ban Me Thuot–Pleiku axis. Since the war activity took place to the North (Qui Nhon and Da Nang) and South (Saigon), the depot was not utilized to the degree the planners originally anticipated. As a result, there are some who claim that the war passed Cam Ranh Bay by. When taken in that particular context, there is some truth to the claim.

Even though war activity took place in areas different from those expected, Cam Ranh Bay played an important role in the logistics picture. A U.S. Army Support Command was established there as a major logistical command and control element, the Korean forces were supported almost exclusively from Cam Ranh Bay throughout the time they were in the II Corps Area, transshipping supplies from ocean going vessels to coastal type shipping was accomplished there, and marine maintenance was done there. The excellent and secure ammunition storage areas permitted keeping large stocks of needed ammunition in-country relatively safe from enemy attack and the cold storage facilities permitted fresh vegetables to be brought down from Dalat and stored properly till distributed to our forces. Also having a major storage and shipping facility close to the major air base operated by the Air Force was a distinct advantage. At one time it was planned to move the Headquarters of the 1st Logistical Command there (it was later decided that the 1st Logistical Command and Headquarters U.S. Army Vietnam should remain near Headquarters U.S. Military Assistance Command, Vietnam) and until fairly late in residual force planning, Cam Ranh Bay was going to remain as a major U.S. logistic complex. This too was dropped in favor of the Saigon-Long Binh area.

Continental U.S. Production Base

At the time the Vietnam buildup began, the Army's industrial base was operating at a relatively low level. This can be seen from a comparison of the Procurement of Equipment and Missiles for the Army contracts awarded before and after the buildup began. (Chart 2)

Procurement and receipt of equipment lagged behind the increase in Army strength during the buildup. The lag in production resulted in inadequate quantities of equipment being available to supply all worldwide needs. Extraordinary actions and management techniques were used to obtain the maximum benefits from the 1965 inventory and assets being produced. These are covered

CHART 2—PROCUREMENT OF EQUIPMENT AND MISSILES FOR THE ARMY
CONTRACT AWARDS

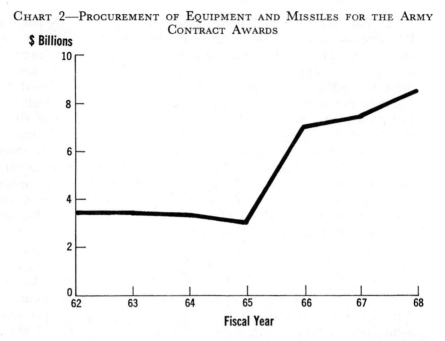

in greater detail in other sections, but in general, items critically needed in Southeast Asia were taken from reserve component units and active Army units not in Southeast Asia, and new issues of certain items of equipment in short supply were centrally controlled by Headquarters, Department of the Army.

There were four main reasons for production lagging behind equipment and supply requirements:

1. A planning assumption that all hostilities would end by 30 June 1967. During 1965, President Johnson announced the build-up of forces in South Vietnam. The Army immediately updated its existing studies to ascertain the ammunition posture—both the availability of world-wide assets and the U.S. Army Munitions Command's capability to support combat operations from industry production. These updated studies became the basis for the supplemental fiscal year 1966 budget programs. The fiscal year 1967 Army budget was restated on the assumption that Vietnam support would continue only through June 1967. Because of this assumption, many planned mobilization producers were not interested in bidding. Due to production lead times involved, they would be reaching peak rates at the time production supposedly would be cut back. Also more profit could be derived from the manufacturer's production of consumer goods.

2. The lack of a full mobilization atmosphere precluded the full employment of the Defense Production Act of 1950 (as amended). Since the U.S. itself was not imminently threatened, it was not felt appropriate to create a crisis situation among industry and the populace. Therefore, the powers granted by Congress in the Defense Production Act of 1950, which permit the Government to direct civilian industries to manufacture those items needed for national defense in preference to civilian oriented items, were used very sparingly. This meant that in many cases civilian industries were unwilling to undertake the manufacture of defense oriented items at the sacrifice of interrupting their supply to a flourishing civilian market. However, in the cases where it was deemed necessary to employ provisions of the Defense Production Act, the problems were resolved effectively.

3. The "No Buy" restriction placed on the procurement of major items of equipment for temporary forces (units that were to be manned only for the duration of the Vietnam conflict) by the Office of the Secretary of Defense constrained Procurement of Equipment and Missiles for the Army programs. These procurement restrictions actually made it necessary for certain of these units to borrow equipment that had been purchased for other units or for reserve stocks. This resulted in a lessening of the readiness posture of the unit or reserve stocks for which the equipment was originally purchased.

4. For some specialized and often high priced items there was frequently only one source of procurement. This "sole source" was a hindrance to rapidly increasing the quantities of the items available. The production facility manufacturing a particular item, in some cases, could not increase its production fast enough to meet the rapidly rising military requirements. Also, some manufacturers did not deem it feasible to expand their production facilities, at great expense, to meet temporarily increased sales to the government. In addition, for the same reason, new sources of supply were not easily convinced to enter into production of these items.

The industrial base utilized by the Army consists of both government owned and privately owned production facilities including real estate, plants, and production equipment. Private industrial facilities are of primary importance and are only supplemented by the Army's resources. However, Army owned facilities are required to produce military items having no significant commercial demand. Accordingly, the Army has throughout its history maintained varying capabilities for production, mostly in the munitions area.

Prior to the buildup for Southeast Asia, only eleven of twenty-five Army owned munition plants were operating. Immediate actions were taken to activate whatever additional ammunition plants were required to support the anticipated consumption. Six ammunition plants were activated in fiscal year 1966; six more were activated in fiscal year 1967; and the last plant required to meet production requirements was activated in fiscal year 1968. Only one government owned munition facility remained inactive.

One important factor in the rapid improvement of the ammunition production base was the special emphasis given to munitions. During the latter part of 1965 when the increased tempo in Vietnam made it apparent that ammunition was going to be required in larger quantities than the post-Korea stocks would support, the Secretary of Defense established a relatively small organization to control air munitions. Shortly thereafter it was suggested to the Secretary of the Army that he establish a similar organization to control ground munitions. The organization was activated in the Army Secretariat and staffed by requesting people with the required expertise. On 15 December 1966, the Office of Special Assistant for Munitions was established in the Office of the Deputy Chief of Staff for Logistics and at that time the Army Secretariat relinquished the responsibility and the authority to the Army staff. However, a close relationship existed between Office of Special Assistant for Munitions, the Army Secretariat, and the Ground Munitions Office in the Office of the Secretary of Defense because of the intense interest in the ammunition program. This interest stemmed from the high dollar value of the program and congressional concern over ammunition matters. Eventually the Office of the Special Assistant for Munitions became a Directorate within the Office of the Deputy Chief of Staff for Logistics known as the Office of the Director of Ammunition.

Logistic Personnel and Training

During the period 30 June 1965 through 30 June 1967 a total of 1,057,900 personnel entered the Army and losses totaled 584,500. The resulting numerical turnover of personnel exceeded the Army's peak strength. Of the total gains, 977,000 were new accessions with no prior military experience (616,600 draftees; 360,400 first term enlistees). Another 80,900 were procured from other sources such as reenlistees within 90 days of discharge. While the Army's total strength was expanding by almost 50 percent, its monthly loss of trained personnel averaged over 24,000. These losses created turbulence, denied the Army the use of immediately available trained skills, and required that over one million men and women be brought on duty to achieve an increase in overall strength of less than 474,000. Replacing skilled individuals with personnel of like skills was a serious problem. The Army was faced not only with the problem of training thousands of personnel with entry-level skills, but also had to provide additional training in lieu of skill progression normally acquired by on-the-job experience.

One of the most significant factors contributing to the personnel turbulence throughout the Army was the one-year tour for personnel assigned to South Vietnam. In late 1965, to avoid 100 percent rotation of men in a unit in Vietnam at the end of their 12 month tour, the Army applied personnel management techniques to insure that not more than 25 percent of a unit would be rotated in any one month. These techniques included tour curtailments, short extensions, exchanges of troops with other similar units, and voluntary extensions of individuals.

The rapid buildup, coupled with the twelve-month tour of duty, made the replacement program a problem of great magnitude. The regular replacement of personnel in the short-tour areas came close to representing a complete annual turnover. Rotation after a year boosted individual morale, but it also weakened units that had to send experienced men home. Further, personnel turnover often invalidated training previously accomplished by a unit. A large portion of the Army's enlisted requirements is in skills that are not self-sustaining because the requirements for them in long-tour areas are inadequate to provide a rotation base for short-tour areas. The advantages in morale outweighed the disadvantages cited, but the drawbacks to short tours were there and cannot be glossed over.

In many cases, support personnel assigned to Vietnam did not have the essential experience in such areas as depot operations, maintenance, and supply management. There was a shortage of junior officers and senior non-commissioned officers who had the logistics experience necessary to supervise "across the board" logistics for brigade size tactical units at isolated locations. Many of the supervisory personnel did not have any experience or training outside of their own branch and were assigned duties and responsibilities above that normally expected of their grade.

Logistic support units deployed to Vietnam were deficient in unit training. Of significant impact upon mission accomplishment was the method by which the support units were trained in the early 1960s. With reorganization from the technical service concept to the Combat Service to the Army concept, functional training of units was decentralized in the Continental Army Command to post, camp and station level. There were no Quartermaster, Ordnance, or other titular heads looking after the training of their units. This condition fostered a haphazard incorporation of current doctrine and procedures in training which was already decentralized.

A program was initiated at Atlanta Army Depot to provide on-the-job training in depot operations for selected enlisted personnel enroute to U.S. Army Vietnam. From 1967 through 1970, 4,619 enlisted personnel received this training.

Other special training programs were established to provide orientation and training for selected officer personnel at the Defense Supply Agency Depot at Richmond and at the U.S. Army Electronics Command, Fort Monmouth, New Jersey.

Beginning in June 1968, the 1st Logistical Command initiated some fairly extensive training courses in South Vietnam. Project SKILLS was introduced to provide orientation, indoctrination, specialist training, and on-the-job training on a recurring basis at all levels of command. SKILLS I ALPHA was a detailed orientation and indoctrination of newly assigned colonels and higher key staff officers and commanders at battalion or higher level, Department of the Army civilians of equivalent grade, and command sergeants major. SKILLS I BRAVO was a formal orientation and indoctrination for enlisted specialists newly assigned to elements of the command.

SKILLS I CHARLIE was an orientation, indoctrination, and formal continuing on-the-job training of all enlisted personnel. With the increasing role of local nationals in the 1st Logistical Command, the need for a local national training program was recognized and Project SKILLS II was initiated. This program was designed not only to help get a job done, but also to contribute to the self-sufficiency of the Republic of Vietnam in the future.

The trained personnel shortage was also alleviated somewhat by the arrival in-country of Program Six units which were force packages consisting of Army, Reserves, and National Guard combined by Department of Army and containing many highly educated personnel who possessed critical skills.

Strategic Army Forces were tapped to meet Vietnam personnel requirements. The primary mission of Strategic Army Forces is to maintain combat readiness to respond to contingencies on a worldwide basis. In April 1965, a substantial drawdown of Strategic Army Forces personnel began. At that time approximately one-third of the command was composed of logistic and administrative personnel. This was not a balanced force, and under the impact of drawdowns, the percentage of logistic and administrative personnel remaining in Strategic Army Forces units was reduced further to approximately one-fifth by the end of Fiscal Year 1966. Unit readiness was further degraded by drastic imbalances in enlisted grades and military occupational specialties. Logistical activities in South Vietnam often experienced shortages of personnel with specific skills and technical training. In some cases, skill categories were deficient in the numbers required because of the civilianization of Continental U.S. military activities and the constant decline in the retention rate of experienced military personnel. Concurrent with the decision not to call the Reserves was the determination to continue normal separations. Consequently, discharges at the end of periods of obligated service, resignations, and retirements were continued as in peacetime. The Army was most severely restricted by this policy. There were shortages of officers in all grades except lieutenant. U.S. Army Europe was also called on to provide many trained troops and specialists with critical skills in the combat service support for South Vietnam. As a result, combat unit personnel in U.S. Army Europe were diverted from their intended assignments to perform maintenance, supply, and housekeeping tasks. Tour length policies and worldwide distribution of structure spaces caused an enlisted skill imbalance between short tour areas and the rotation base. For certain skills (for example helicopter mechanics, electronic maintenance, and supply personnel) the preponderance of structure spaces was in short tour areas.

The percentage of support personnel versus combat personnel in South Vietnam fluctuated. Early in 1965 the percentage of support personnel was estimated by some authorities to be as low as 25 percent. At that time supply lines of communication were not as long as they later came to be. In 1966, as supply lines of communication had lengthened and a major effort was underway to alleviate the congested ports and depots, the percentage increased to approximately 45 percent. By 1969, at the height of our troop strength, the percentage of support personnel had dropped to 39 percent. However, this percentage rose again as our strength reductions continued and a greater percentage of combat forces were withdrawn. For example, by the end of March 1971, the ratio of personnel had changed to 53 percent combat and 47 percent support due to the requirement for support personnel to retrograde matériel of the departing combat units. These support percentages include only military personnel. In addition to

these personnel, civilian workers and contracting firms were employed for many support services throughout the Vietnam operation.

In viewing the above percentages, it is important to remember
that the classification of Army units as either combat or support is
not clearcut, and the definitions of these categories are subject to
varying interpretations. For example every infantry unit includes
administrative personnel whose mission is something other than
combat with the enemy; and every supply company contains truck
drivers or helicopter pilots who travel daily to the combat zone
where they are subject to hostile operations and contacts. With
these qualifications in mind, we generally classify the total strength
of each division, plus all other infantry, armor, artillery, and
certain aviation, engineer, and signal units as combat forces. All
other types of units (for example maintenance, supply, military
police, medical, and transportation) are classified in the support
category.

The force structure of the active duty components of the Armed
Forces must be designed to permit adequate logistic support of
ready forces in quick reaction to emergency situations. During
peacetime, emphasis was in some cases placed on the maintenance
of combat and combat support forces without adequate combat
service support units and trained technical personnel. As a consequence, when contingency operations are undertaken and the
Reserves are not called up, serious deficiencies in logistic units and
trained logistic personnel may be expected. There is a need, therefore, to enhance readiness to respond promptly to limited war of
scope comparable to the Vietnam conflict without reliance on
national mobilization or callup of Reserves to conduct logistic operations.

Security

Logistic security, including the physical protection of logistic
personnel, installations, facilities, and equipment was one of the
more critical aspects of the logistic effort in Vietnam. Ambushes,
sapper and rocket attacks and pilferage caused logistics commanders to be constantly aware of the necessity for strict security
measures. The tactical situation was not always evident or given
consideration during the installation construction planning phase.
There were no "secure" rear areas. Often planning personnel did
not fully appreciate the tactical situation, and some installations
were constructed at the base of unsecured high ground, making

the dominant terrain feature a prize for the enemy for observation purposes as well as offensive action.

Personnel and equipment authorizations for logistic organizations were inadequate for the additional mission of security. Radios and field telephones were in short supply. These items were essential to the security of the installation perimeter, including the bunkers, towers, patrols, "sweep teams", and reaction forces. Night vision devices helped but were not available in adequate quantities.

Pilferage and sabotage were prevalent at many installations. Some of the means utilized by commanders to minimize these actions are listed below:

1. Frequent inventories were taken.

2. Continous employee education was conducted.

3. Physical barriers with intrusion delay devices and detection aids were employed.

4. Employee identification badges were used to control access to various controlled areas, as well as the installation itself.

5. Access to storage areas for highly sensitive items were strictly controlled.

6. Management techniques such as spot inspection, spot searches of personnel, and bilingual signs warning personnel against infractions of rules or theft were used to insure understanding by workers.

7. Strict controls were implemented on receipts and transfers of cargo between ports and the first consignees. Transportation Control and Movement Documents were used extensively for the transfer of cargo from one storage area to another.

8. On sensitive items such as those highly desired by the enemy, markings were subdued or obliterated, to prevent identification by the enemy, and in their place "U.S. Government" was stenciled. In subdued or obliterated markings, the federal stock number had to remain visible and legible.

9. Twenty-four-foot-high anchor fences were used around petroleum, oils, and lubricants tank farms to improve security from sapper attacks and other sabotage efforts by the enemy.

10. Practice alerts were conducted frequently to assure that all personnel were familiar with their defensive assignments within the perimeter in case of an enemy attack.

Convoy commanders were continually faced with security problems in the movement of cargo from one location to another over the insecure highway system in Vietnam. Support from artillery fire support bases and medical units, and military police escorts were arranged when such was available.

The compelling need to move cargo dictated the "do it yourself" principle. To help combat the lack of security in this type of operation, and to monitor the shipments in an effective way, many safeguards were initiated. Military drivers and trucks were used to haul post exchange and other sensitive supplies or readily marketable commodities. Trip ticket controls, road patrols, check points, radio reports of departures and arrivals, and strict accounting for loading and offloading times were used. Close liaison with Vietnamese law enforcement agencies along the truck route was established. Armed security guards were utilized to reduce the effectiveness of enemy ambushes.

To offset the shortage of armored vehicles available for convoy escort, transportation units devised the expedient of "hardening" some cargo type vehicles. The beds of 5-ton trucks were usually floored with armor plate and sandbagged. The sides and front of the trucks were also armor plated. The trucks were usually equipped with M60 and 50 caliber machine guns. One gun truck was assigned to accompany about ten task vehicles in a convoy. In 1968 the V–100 armored car was sent to South Vietnam and was exceptionally useful when available for convoy security. Helicopter gun ships were used to maintain aerial surveillance of convoy columns. In addition to providing the surveillance function and a rapid means of response to an enemy attack, these gun ships presented a visible deterrent to the enemy. Clearing of roadsides and paving road surfaces to make mining more difficult and mine detection easier increased security.

Of special help to the logistic commanders were the combat arms officers on the U.S. Army Vietnam and the Support Command staffs who advised and assisted them on security matters. With their guidance, logistic commanders were able to improvise within their own resources and provide an acceptable degree of security.

Despite the various obstacles involved, the logistic security mission was in most cases effectively accomplished. Convoys delivered their cargos, and defensive measures at logistic installations repeatedly frustrated enemy attacks.

CHAPTER III

Supply Support In Vietnam

For the first time in modern history, the U.S. Army was required to establish a major logistical base in a country where all areas were subject to continuous enemy observation and hostile fire, with no terrain under total friendly control. There was no communications zone; in fact, combat and communications zones were one and the same, and the logistics soldier was frequently and quite literally right with the front line tactical soldier. There was no meaningful consumption and other experience data upon which to base support estimates. As a result, there was an initial influx of huge quantitities of supplies of every description to support the tactical troop buildup. This occurred well before the availability of either a logistic base or an adequate logistical organization.

Adding to the difficulties in 1965 was the fact that the supply systems then being used in the United States were either automated or in the process of being automated. Personnel were being trained in automated supply procedures. But going into Vietnam the way we did meant going in with light, non-automated logistic forces. Actually the Army didn't have the computers and technological skills to support the buildup with an automated supply system. Initial operations in Vietnam involved the use of a manual system for in-country support. The interface between these systems, which relied heavily upon punch card operations, and the more computerized wholesale systems, posed difficulties until in-country mechanization was expanded.

During the initial year and a half of manual operation, the sheer volume of traffic and the inability to interface with the automated Continental U.S. systems resulted in an almost insurmountable backlog of management problems that required two years to untangle. Even though UNIVAC 1005 card processors were installed in the depots in 1966–67 and replaced with IBM 7010/1460 computers in 1968, the lead time associated with the approval process, construction of facilities, writing and debugging computer programs, and making the system operational was such that, by the time a new system was on line, it was barely adequate to cope with the continually increasing requirements.

Automatic Data Processing System capability for logistic management must be introduced in a combat theater as soon as possible with adequate communications support and with the capability of interfacing with Automatic Data Processing Systems outside the combat area.

By 1968 there was an automated supply system operating in Vietnam. Even at the direct and general support level there was automation to some degree. At this level there were NCR 500 computer processors to compute repair parts requisitioning objectives and dues-in and dues-outs.

Repair Parts Supply

Repair parts (Class IX) supply was especially interesting due to the fact that the number of items authorized for stockage mushroomed from an insignificant number in 1965 to 200,000 in October 1966 and then was reduced to 130,000 in May, 1967 and to 75,000 by March 1971. Besides a monumental bookeeping exercise, there were other dynamics in the system. We had to automate so that we could manage.

To get items in-country that would be needed by the arriving forces, Push Packages were used initially. The purpose of this method of supply was to provide a form of automatic resupply to meet the anticipated consumption and to support the prescribed load lists, and the authorized stockage lists of committed units until normal requisitioning procedures could be established. In June 1965, when the use of Push Packages began, all types of supply items were included, but by January 1966 Push Packages contained only repair parts.

Among the factors entering into the decision to use Push Packages were:

1. Theater prestockage had not been effected when the Vietnam buildup commenced except for limited U.S. Army Pacific war reserve prepositioned equipment in Okinawa and elsewhere.

2. The long order and shipping time from Continental U.S. to Vietnam precluded the use of normal requisitioning procedures.

3. The rapid introduction of a large number of combat units into Vietnam was accompanied with an entirely inadequate number of supply support units and logistic supervisory personnel. Supply support units, such as Direct Support Units and General Support Units which would normally have carried the authorized stockage for supporting the combat units were not available in South Vietnam.

4. The tactical concepts of air mobility to be employed in Vietnam dictated the immediate availability of repair parts for the great density of helicopters and other types of equipment.

5. Engineer and service type units that were initially employed anticipated an early need for repair parts due to the primitive areas in which they would be operating and the resultant high intensity of equipment usage.

6. Procurement of military supplies was not possible on the Vietnamese economy.

Packages were made up for all large units and for small units when combined troop strengths reached approximately 5,000. These packages were shipped to Vietnam in various increments. The supplies included in each incremental package were developed from National Inventory Control data. The first two increments were shipped directly to the designated unit or force, while the remaining increments were intercepted at the depots responsible for supporting the unit or force. The composition of each supply package was of necessity determined from data not associated with Southeast Asia operations. World War II and Korean experience was all that was available. As a result, in some cases the packages proved to be unbalanced in relation to demand, causing overages in some items and shortages in others.

Nevertheless these automatic resupply packages served a very definite and useful purpose in supporting the initial buildup of combat troops in Vietnam, particularly during 1965 and early 1966. Without this form of resupply, we would not have been able to support our combat troops within the time frame that we did. The success of the Push Packages is attested to by the fact that no major combat operation was ever delayed or hampered by a lack of supply. A number of problem areas were encountered, however, which included:

1. The inability of inexperienced unit supply personnel to sort, identify, and properly issue the volume of items received. In many cases, the original Push Packages and their individual contents were identifiable only by shipment numbers and Federal Stock Numbers. Therefore, highly skilled supply personnel were required for placing these items in the proper bins to make them readily available for use.

2. A lack of secure warehouse and storage space and sufficient logistic units at depots. The size of individual Push Package increments arriving in Vietnam initially was too large for the discharge capacity, storage facilities available, and the capabilities of the supply units at the unloading areas.

3. In some cases, unit destinations were changed without changing the destination of the Push Package causing a delay in the receipt of the package by the intended unit.

4. Inexperienced personnel became accustomed to the "push" philosophy and failed to evaluate measures for transition to the normal "pull" system. As a result of the dependence upon external assistance, units failed to maintain effective demand data or to initiate measures which would permit stockage at intermediate support levels.

Because of the problem areas encountered, supplies in many cases were available in-country, but could not be identified or located. For example, in mid-1966 (even in 1968) some of the original Push Package supplies still remained in the depots, unbinned, unidentifiable and unusable for the purpose for which they were shipped. This factor together with the overagest resulting from unbalanced packages had the net effect of generating excess supplies in various locations in Vietnam.

In future operations, Push Packages may again be required for initial or special supply support. These packages, as proven by experience, must be developed on an austere basis and include plans which permit transition to normal supply support. Push Packages should be based on the latest experience factors available and should be scrubbed to exclude those items which are "nice to have." Push Packages should make maximum use of standard containers with stocks prebinned and accompanied by locator cards. These packages should also contain prepunched requisitions to be introduced into the system in order to establish support stocks at theater level. Push Packages should be approved only as an interim relief measure which permits the pull system to again respond to the unit's needs.

On 10 June 1966, as a result of conferences, communications, and experience gained during the buildup, Department of the Army dispatched a message to U.S. Army Pacific and Army Materiel Command setting forth an automatic supply policy and procedure which stopped Push Packages and started the process of normalizing supply support. Essentially supply support of all forces was to be provided through normal requisitioning procedures within U.S. Army Pacific, and Army Materiel Command was to provide equipment density data for projected deployments to provide an order-ship lead time in excess of 195 days.

Exceptions to the above, were a 90 day package of high mortality repair parts for the 11th Armored Cavalry Regiment, support for new items of equipment introduced into Vietnam,

and for any unscheduled arrivals. These exceptions were considered on a case-by-case basis. Falling into the latter category were
the 9th Infantry Division and the 196th and 199th Infantry
Brigades. However, by January 1967 their stockage position and
supply management capability had improved to such a level that
U.S. Army Vietnam advised that Push Packages were no longer
required for these units. U.S. Army Vietnam requested that any
further preparation on movement of such packages be discontinued unless they specifically requested or concurred in such
shipment.

TABLE 2—PUSH PACKAGES DATA

Packages	Incre- ments	Line Items	Units	Days of Supply	$-Value
1–A	8	51,000	Log Sup	120	8,745,664
2	15	24,000	Inf Bde	240	21,066,321
3	15	24,000	Airborne Bde	240	19,629,691
4–A	15	75,000	Airmobile Div	240	89,329,697
4–B	15	78,000	Airmobile Sup	240	26,956,335
4–C	15	59,000	Corps Sup	240	12,367,475
5	14	133,000	Inf Div	210	73,182,715
8	14	115,000	Combat Sup Log & Adm	210	47,163,539
9	14	156,000	Combat Sup Log & Adm	210	59,397,912
10	14	50,000	Combat Sup Log & Adm	210	10,194,865
11	4	16,000	Combat Sup Log & Adm	210	3,497,674
12	4	21,000	Combat Sup Log & Adm	210	4,461,050
15	1	12,335	25th Div—1st & 2d Bde	60	611,414
16	1	11,279	25th Div—3rd Bde	60	588,039
17	1	16,904	25th Div (Minus)	60	1,546,430
18	1	8,253	4th Inf Div	60	1,047,092
19	1	3,732	11th Arm Cav Div	90	931,187
20	1	2,823	196th Bde	90	253,840
21	1	5,430	9th Inf Div	90	1,342,413
22	1	2,950	199th Inf Bde	90	215,897
Total	155	865,706			382,529,250
			Cam Ranh Bay		
XZJ	1	50,321	Depot Stocks	60	6,411,744
YUH	1	15,200	Hawk Missile Bn	90	1,500,000
	2	65,521			7,911,744
Grand Total	157	931,227			*390,440,994

*Equivalent of 195,220 short tons.

The above tabulation (*Table 2*) of Push Packages shipped
to Vietnam indicates packages shipped, number of line items,
and dollar value of each package. Also shown are two special

applications of Push Packages—the Cam Ranh Bay Depot Stock package and the special package for a Hawk battalion.

As a result of Vietnam experience, U.S. Army Materiel Command automatic supply procedures have been revised. The selection of support items is equipment oriented, rather than force oriented and employs the principle of repair by replacement of components and modules (Contingency Operations Selection Technique). Also, a technique has been developed for the pre-determination of austere, essential requirements for automatic supply support of type units to permit effective planning for receiving, storing, and handling matériel incident to unit deployment. Another procedure has been adopted which provides for the computation of requirements for support stocks based upon existing deployable divisions rather than type forces (Contingency Support Stocks). Still another technique, under continuing review and refinement, calls for the containerization of minimum essential items of matériel needed to support specific quantities of an end item for a specific period (Container Integrated Support Package). The matériel included in such support packages would be identified and binned within the containers to facilitate receipt, storage, issue, and replenishment actions.

Short Supply Items

Earlier it was noted that equipment to support our forces was produced after the need or requirement was apparent. Naturally there were shortages. And the lag between the establishment of requirements and the availability of sufficient assets existed right up to 1971 for some items. To satisfy the requirements for forces being sent to Vietnam and for the replacement of combat and other losses, equipment was withdrawn from and denied to the rest of the Active Army and Reserve components. Some items became so critical that their allocation was controlled by the Department of the Army through the application of intensive management techniques.

Satisfying the need for items in short supply was a different process for each item. Eight situations for eight different classes or types of equipment follow for illustrative purposes.

Armored Personnel Carriers

It wasn't easy to satisfy the requirements before 1967, but from 1967 through 1969 the demand for armored personnel carriers in U.S. Army Vietnam jumped dramatically. Tables of Organization and Equipment requirements increased approximately 124 percent, while at the same time new operational uses were causing greater exposure and increased battle losses. To reduce losses, overhaul was increased; and to minimize shortages, assets were withdrawn from lower priority units worldwide. Early in 1967, Army Materiel Command began developing a belly armor for armored personnel carriers to reduce damage and casualties caused by mines. A mine protection kit was developed consisting of belly armor, rerouted fuel lines kits, and non-integral fuel tanks. By mid-March 1969, U.S. Army Vietnam had tested the first belly armor and it was enthusiastically accepted by commanders and crews. U.S. Army Vietnam asked for expedited procurement to equip all their armored personnel carriers, since high battle losses were projected and the kits had proven to be effective in reducing losses.

In August 1967, it was decided that conversion of the armored personnel carrier fleet from gasoline to diesel power was necessary to reduce the danger of fire after suffering enemy caused damage. At that time, 73 percent of the armored personnel carrier fleet in U.S. Army Vietnam was gasoline powered. An intensive effort was made to equip the entire U.S. Army Vietnam fleet with diesel engines. All new diesel production was allocated to Southeast Asia; however, high losses and increased deployments exceeded the production rate. It was 1 July 1968 before the total armored personnel carrier fleet in U.S. Army Vietnam was equipped with diesel engines.

Beginning in April 1967, a Closed Loop Support program was developed to retrograde armored personnel carriers needing repairs, repair them, and return them on a scheduled basis. New techniques were developed in the repair of battle damaged vehicles in which damaged sections of hulls were cut out and replaced. Plans were made to expand Sagami Depot, Japan to cover the requirements of the Eighth Army, U.S. Army Vietnam, and the Republic of Vietnam Army. Production schedules were increased and a maximum effort was exerted to recruit additional personnel. Starting in 1969 Sagami was able to support the U.S. Army Vietnam rebuild requirements thereby enhancing supply performance.

Ground Surveillance Radars

The AN/TPS–25A ground surveillance radar became a critical combat support item in 1968. It had proven to be very successful in locating personnel moving at night in the rice paddies of the Mekong Delta. Since it had not been produced since 1959, the withdrawal of the assets from other major commands and Reserve Components was necessary. The overhaul and shipment of the radar sets to meet U.S. Army Vietnam's total requirements was completed in August 1969.

In order to maintain the inventory of radars in Vietnam at a high state of operational readiness, they too were included in a Closed Loop Support Program reducing total requirements through the integration of transportation, supply management, and maintenance.

Engineer Construction Equipment

The Line of Communications Program was undertaken in Vietnam by the 18th and 20th Engineer Brigades. It soon became apparent that there was not sufficient standard military design engineer construction equipment to complete the road construction program within the allotted time frame. Engineer construction equipment is normally associated with long lead times so if the program was to be accomplished by the desired time not only would large quantities of equipment be needed, but more operators and maintenance personnel would be required. Therefore, it was decided to acquire 31 different types of commercial items, totaling 667 pieces at a total acquisition cost of $23,860,000. A plan prepared by U.S. Army Vietnam called for the procurement of the equipment with Military Construction Army funds and included extra major components plus a one-year supply of repair parts. Deliveries covered the period January–September 1969. Maintenance above the operator level and repair parts beyond the one-year overpack quantities were provided by civilian contracting firms.

The M16A1 Rifle

Initially U.S. and allied forces were equipped with either the M14 or M1 rifle. When the decision was made to equip all forces in Southeast Asia with the M16A1 rifle, we were faced with a limited, but growing, production capacity and ever increasing requirements. In country, it was merely a matter of establishing priorities to distribute the rifles as they were received and providing for the turn in of the M1 and M14 rifles for reissue or retrograde. In the Continental U.S. however, a central point of contact was established in the Department of the Army in December 1967, specifically the Office of the Deputy Chief of Staff for Logistics, to monitor and control funding, procurement, modification, distribution, and maintenance of this rifle. This office functioned through December 1970.

Electric Generators

The increased usage of electrically powered equipment by the Army in Vietnam resulted in the requirements for electricity far exceeding that required during World War II. During that war, the average consumption per soldier was 1/2 kilowatt hour per day. In Vietnam the average consumption was 2 kilowatt hours per day, a four fold increase.

Large capacity generating equipment was needed, because the Vietnamese local power sources were incapable of supplying our requirements. Some of the power requirements were satisfied by converting eleven T-2 petroleum tankers to power barges and by erecting fixed plants throughout Vietnam. The fixed plants were operated by contractors (either the Vinnel Corporation or Pacific Architects and Engineers) since military personnel are not trained in the operation of such commercial type equipment.

Other requirements were met through the diversion of small tactical generators from their normal use. This meant that many small generators were used to perform a task better accomplished with a single large capacity piece of equipment.

With increased requirements came many procurement actions resulting in an extensive number of makes and models in the theater. At the peak of the buildup, there were about 145 makes and models in the 1.5 kilowatt to 100 kilowatt range.

Because of the around-the-clock utilization, age of the assets, lack of parts, lack of an adequate maintenance float, and the numerous makes and models, requirements were generated so rapidly that authorizations documentation could not keep pace, resulting in difficulty in accounting for actual assets on hand. With time and strong management efforts the situation improved. Power requirements were met through additional inputs, a reduction in requirements, and the washing out of some of the non-standard equipment. However, complete standardization will not be possible until the introduction of the Military Standard Family which is programed for fiscal year 1973.

The M107 Self-Propelled Gun Tube

The M107 Self-Propelled Gun, mounting the 175-mm M113 gun tube, was introduced into South Vietnam by artillery units arriving in late 1965. This weapon posed significant operational readiness problems in early 1966. Due to inadequately trained maintenance personnel and a shortage of manuals, there was a 30 percent deadline rate. The rate of fire of these weapons was consuming tubes on the average of one tube per gun every 45 days. Since this far exceeded the planned consumption rate, the Commanding General, U.S. Army Matériel Command initiated a worldwide cross leveling action to provide the U.S. Army Vietnam requirements. At the same time, he advised U.S. Army Vietnam of the results of a test utilizing a titanium dioxide additive, supplied in a cloth sleeve, which had doubled the 175-mm gun tube life expectancy. This increased tube life was expected to ease the critical supply posture in the 175-mm gun tubes. However, in July 1966 a catastrophic failure of a 175-mm gun occurred in U.S. Army Vietnam and the Commanding General, U.S. Army Materiel Command, directed that no tubes, even with the additive, would be fired beyond 400 rounds at equivalent full charge.

The supply situation on gun tubes remained critical and Continental U.S. airlift was employed to satisfy most of the U.S. Army Vietnam requirements of this item through July 1967. In September, gun tube shipment by surface transportation was begun. The U.S. Army Vietnam stockage objective was attained in December 1967 and in January 1968 the U.S. Army Vietnam tube consumption stabilized.

Tropical Combat Uniforms and Combat Boots Under FLAGPOLE

During the period August 1965 to August 1966, the Office of the Secretary of Defense originated a system for reporting items considered essential to the Army Buildup by U.S. Army Vietnam field commanders under the code name FLAGPOLE. This was a technique used by Secretary of Defense McNamara to be kept advised of the status of selected critical items.

Two of the items which came under FLAGPOLE were tropical combat uniforms and tropical combat boots because at the onset of the conflict these items were in short supply. Procurement and distribution of these items was controlled by the Joint Materiel Priorities Allocation Board established by the Joint Chiefs of Staff who allocated monthly production to the services.

During the period of critical short supply, all Army deliveries of tropical combat uniforms and boots, relatively new items in the supply system, were airlifted from producer to U.S. Army Vietnam without the need for the command to requisition on the Continental U.S. Automatic air shipments continued through May 1967. Pending availability of tropical combat uniforms and boots in the Continental U.S., Department of the Army established a policy in September 1965 whereby personnel deployed from the Continental U.S. with four utility uniforms and two pairs of leather combat boots. The tropical combat items were subsequently obtained by the individual in Vietnam. This policy continued until a sustained supply position was reached. Effective 1 July 1967, units deployed were equipped at home station with five combat uniforms and two pairs of combat boots. On 1 August 1967, personnel replacements enroute to Vietnam (excluding E–9s, W–4s, and field grade) were issued four tropical combat uniforms and one pair of combat boots at the Continental U.S. Personnel Processing Centers; E–9s, W–4s, and field grade, because of direct call to aerial port, received these items in Vietnam. The distribution of lightweight tentage, lightweight ponchos, collapsible canteens and canteen covers was also controlled by Joint Materiel Priorities Allocation Board. Air deliveries were made from contractor source to U.S. Army Vietnam without the need for the command to requisition on the Continental U.S. The "push" method of supply for these items ended in May 1967, at which time the availability was adequate for U.S. Army Vietnam to requisition on the Continental U.S.

Dry Battery Supply and Storage

The supply system provided dry batteries designed with the assumption that adequate refrigerated space would be available to prevent deterioration in the extreme temperatures common to Vietnam. However, there was not enough refrigerated space available in Vietnam to provide the protection for the required stock levels. The combination of the lack of refrigerated storage space, the temperatures in Vietnam, and an overtaxed supply system resulted in a system of expedited battery resupply out of Japan known as Project "Orange Ball." It was initiated in 1968 and involved the use of 20' x 8' x 8' refrigerated containers delivered in frozen condition every ten days to U.S. Army Vietnam depots. Project "Orange Ball" was designed to modify the supply system so that smaller quantities of batteries were provided to the user at more frequent intervals. To provide the batteries faster under Project "Orange Ball," units that required batteries handcarried requests for a two or three days supply to their Class I supply points. On their next scheduled visit to the supply point, two or three days later, they drew the batteries they had requested on their previous visit along with their rations, and at the same time submitted another request for two to three days supply of dry batteries which they would pick up on their next scheduled visit. From this specialized system, a direct delivery system of dry batteries from Continental U.S. to U.S. Army Vietnam was instituted. Exclusive dedicated transportation by refrigerated container vessels (Sea and Land) was utilized. By this method, dry batteries for U.S. Army Vietnam were shipped direct from the Continental U.S. contractor plants to Oakland Army Terminal on a bi-weekly basis. Dry batteries were then shipped by the refrigerated vessels to depot facilities in U.S. Army Vietnam. Upon their arrival in Vietnam, established "Orange Ball" procedures were used.

Management Techniques

There were three main phases of the conflict in Vietnam: buildup, sustaining, and phasedown. Each phase required special management techniques.

During the buildup phase, emphasis was placed on getting equipment and supplies into Vietnam without regard for the lack of a sufficient number of logistic units in-country to account for and effectively manage the incoming items. This of course was necessitated by the rapidity of the buildup and the tactical requirement to increase the combat strength in South Vietnam as rapidly as possible. As a result, supplies flowed in ahead of an adequate logistics base, preventing the orderly establishment of management and accounting operations.

The sustaining and drawdown phases can be considered together. During the sustaining phase, there were enough logistics units to start managing the supplies in Vietnam, to identify excesses, to retrograde unnecessary stocks, and to create order out of chaos. What was started during the sustaining phase was not only carried over in the drawdown, but was intensified and added to. Interestingly enough some of the management devices used to support the buildup were useful in the latter two phases and were adopted for worldwide use.

To support the buildup, many intensive management systems were employed. Eight of the most significant are described in the following paragraphs. They are as follows: the HAWK Stovepipe, Red Ball Express, the Department of the Army Distribution and Allocation Committee, Quick Reaction Assistance Teams, EN-SURE, Closed Loop Support, Retrograde of Equipment—KEY-STONE, and the Morning Line of Communications Briefings, Vietnam.

Hawk Stovepipe

The 97th Artillery Group (Air Defense), equipped with the Hawk missile system, was deployed to Vietnam in September 1965. This was the first occasion for the Army to deploy a complex missile system into an active theater, and much attention was given to its support. Since there was no Army Hawk logistic support system in Vietnam at the time of deployment and since this was the only Army using unit, an opportunity existed to establish a logistic system to support this weapon with operational readiness being the paramount consideration (the U.S. Marines had Hawk and a logistic system which was later changed to rely on the Army for parts support).

The support system developed for the Hawk battalions used a logistic line from the United States supplier directly to the using Hawk organization, thus the name Hawk Stovepipe. The Vietnam end of Stovepipe was the 79th General Support Unit which stocked all repair parts, both common and peculiar, required for support of Hawk. The United States end of the Stovepipe was the Army Missile Command's National Inventory Control Point. All echelons between the inventory control point and the 79th were bypassed. The inventory control point was the single point of control over all requisitions received. Requisitions flowed from a Hawk battery to its battalion direct support platoon, to the 79th, then daily via U.S. air mail to the National Inventory Control Point. Usually within two hours after receipt, the inventory control point took action and matériel release orders were issued. Requisitions for other Continental U.S. National Inventory Control Points of the Army Materiel Command, Defense Supply Agency, or Federal Supply Service (General Services Administration) were sent to the Missile Command National Inventory Control Point for rerouting to the supplying National Inventory Control Point. Follow-up action was taken by the Missile Command National Inventory Control Point on all requisitions, relieving the 79th General Support Unit of this administrative burden. Transportation was coordinated by a Missile Command transportation officer within the terminal areas at Fort Mason and Travis Air Force Base, California. The majority of shipments were flown to the Tan Son Nhut Air Base, located a short distance from the 79th General Support Unit's Hawk support element.

As a result of this system, high priority requisitions for parts were filled within eight days of receipt and lower priority requisitions were filled within 17–18 days of receipt. Another measure of the success of the Stovepipe system in Vietnam was the Hawk system's operational readiness rate which averaged 90 percent. This was well above the readiness rate of Hawk units in the rest of the world. The Hawk Stovepipe's success in Vietnam prompted its adaptation to missile systems in other theaters.

Red Ball Express

Red Ball Express was a special supply and transportation procedure established by direction of the Office of the Assistant Secretary of Defense (Installations and Logistics) on 1 December 1965. Red Ball Express was designed to be used in lieu of normal procedures exclusively to expedite repair parts to remove equipment from deadline status. Reserved and predictable airlift directly responsive to General William C. Westmoreland was made available for this purpose.

Weekly reports were provided to Secretary of Defense Robert S. McNamara, on the not operationally ready-supply rates of specific critical items that he selected for review. The Red Ball Express system, as described below, was highly successful in reducing and maintaining deadline rates to acceptable levels.

A Red Ball Control Office was established in Saigon with the Logistics Control Office, Pacific designated as the focal point in the Continental U.S. for system control. Travis Air Force Base was used as the Aerial Port of Entry for all Red Ball Express shipments. Special Red Ball sections were established at each Continental U.S. supply source.

Red Ball Express requisitions were prepared by the using units and placed on the nearest Direct Support Unit for supply. If the Direct Support Unit could not fill the requirements, the requisition was forwarded to the supporting depot. If the depot could not satisfy the request, it was forwarded to the Red Ball Control Office in Vietnam, where in-country assets were searched for available stocks. If the requisition could not be satisfied in-country, it was then forwarded to the Logistics Control Office, Pacific for forwarding to the appropriate Continental U.S. supply source. The Logistics Control Office, Pacific also contacted U.S. Army Vietnam for additional information, verification of stock numbers, quantities, or other missing or incorrect information to preclude the requisition from being rejected. Continental U.S. supply sources furnished the Logistics Control Office, Pacific with shipping information on Red Ball Express requisitions. All Red Ball Express shipments were sent to Aerial Port of Entry, Travis Air Force Base, California, via premium transportation or air parcel post depending on the size and weight of the shipment. At Travis Air Force

Base, Red Ball Express shipments were segregated according to their intended destination. When Red Ball Express matériel was air lifted, the Logistics Control Office, Pacific was furnished copies of aircraft manifest pages together with the tail numbers of the aircraft and in turn these data were furnished the Red Ball Control Office, Vietnam via telephone or teletype.

The final report submitted as of 31 July 1970 indicated approximately 927,920 net requisitions were processed from inception. Of this total, 98.1 percent or 909,998 requisitions representing 66,985 short tons were airlifted to Vietnam. The Red Ball Express Hi-Pri requisition rate in relation to the Army's worldwide demands placed on Continental U.S. sources averaged 2.2 percent for the period fiscal year 1968 through fiscal year 1970.

In 1968–69, Department of the Army objectives were reoriented toward a streamlined system designed to improve response to the customer. Department of the Army Circular 700–18, published in November 1969, advanced these objectives by providing guidance on an INVENTORY-IN-MOTION principle of non-stop support direct from Continental U.S. to the Direct Support Unit level. The circular tasked Army Materiel Command to position stocks in theater oriented depot complexes and to develop the logistics intelligence to control the system. The circular laid the ground work for the Army's current worldwide Direct Support System. Red Ball program characteristics, to include the integration of supply, transportation, and maintenance activities into a single system, the positive control of requisitions from inception at the Direct Support Unit until matériel is delivered to country and the generation and application of management data were applied in the design of the Direct Support System. Since July 1970, Direct Support System has been changing the image of large overseas depot operations. It is supporting the Army in the field directly from the Continental U.S. wholesale base, bypassing theater depots and break bulk points. The overseas depots have gradually assumed the role of advance storage location for War Reserve, Operational Project Stocks as a safety level.

Department of the Army Distribution and Allocation Committee

It was clear in 1965 that depot stocks of major items and assets coming from production would be inadequate to satisfy the demands of the buildup and other worldwide requirements. If everything were to go to Vietnam (as its priority would have permitted), the readiness posture of the rest of the Army could have been degraded to an unacceptable degree. For this reason, the

Department of the Army Distribution and Allocation Committee was established to control the distribution of short-supply end items. This was to insure that the Army's available assets would be allocated in such a way that the Army would realize the maximum benefits.

The committee was chartered under Army Regulation 15-9 which established it as an agency of the Department of the Army staff and gave it sole responsibility for the items under its control. It was chaired by the Assistant Deputy Chief of Staff for Logistics (Supply and Maintenance) and had as participants members of the Department of the Army staff, U.S. Army Materiel Command, National Inventory Control Points, and major Army commands such as U.S. Army Pacific, U.S. Continental Army Command, and U.S. Army Europe. Participation by major commands was helpful in that the asset situation and distribution options could be understood and appreciated by all concerned at the same time.

Since its founding the concepts and functions of the committee have undergone an evolutionary change. While insuring that the requirements of Vietnam were satisfied, it was at the same time instrumental in restricting and stopping the influx of excess equipment to that theater in 1969. This was possible because of visibility of unit status and authorizations at the Department of the Army level. Other uses of the Department of the Army Distribution and Allocation Committee were to monitor long range distribution plans, to provide data available within Department of the Army for response to quick reaction queries concerning the Army's capability to support alternative organizational concepts or assistance programs, and to override procedures that would normally be correct but that would be unwise for a particular situation.

Quick Reaction Assistance Teams

To provide prompt response to requests for assistance from Vietnam, the Department of the Army directed the Army Materiel Command to form quick reaction assistance teams. By mid-February 1966, Army Materiel Command had established a roster of Department of the Army civilian specialists who were prepared to depart from the Continental U.S. on 48 hours notice and remain in the theater up to 90 days to provide the expertise the undersized logistics force lacked. The roster consisted of over 300 personnel in various grade and skill levels within approximately 40 functional areas of supply and maintenance operations. These individuals were issued passports and visas for Vietnam (required at that time). They also received the necessary medical inoculations, so when their particular skills were required, they were able to provide quick reaction assistance.

ENSURE

The ENSURE project encompassed procedures for *Expediting Non-Standard Urgent Requirements for Equipment* and was initiated on 3 January 1966. The purpose was to provide a system to satisfy operational requirements for non-standard or developmental matériel in a responsive manner and bypass the standard developmental and acquisition procedures. Matériel items were developed and procured either for evaluation purposes (to determine suitability and acceptability) or for operational requirements. The procedure was applicable to matériel required by either U.S. Army forces or allied forces, or both. The Assistant Chief of Staff for Force Development was designated the principal Department of the Army staff member to control the ENSURE project. All ENSURE requests were sent to his staff for initial evaluation. Concurrently these requests were also provided Commanding General U.S. Army Materiel Command, Commanding General U.S. Army Combat Developments Command, and Commander in Chief U.S. Army Pacific for their evaluation as well.

A total of 394 ENSURE projects have been initiated since the beginning of the program in 1966. As of February 1971, 44 of this total were in the process of being evaluated, 159 had been cancelled and 191 were completed. Completion of an ENSURE project is accomplished when the equipment is type classified as either Standard A or Standard B.

Logistic support of an ENSURE item, after type classification, follows the normal support procedures associated with any other standard piece of equipment. During the period an ENSURE item was under evaluation, logistic support was provided by the appropriate National Inventory Control Point using the development and procurement support package developed when the items were approved for acquisition and evaluation.

Closed Loop Support

During December 1966 another special intensive management program was developed to control the flow of serviceable equipment to Vietnam and the retrograde of unserviceable assets to repair facilities. Closed Loop supplements the controls inherent in the normal supply and maintenance system. In January 1967, the program was initiated for management of selected Materials Handling Equipment, Communications and Electronics Equipment, the M48A3 Tank, the M113 and M113A1 Armored Personnel Carrier and related major assemblies and components.

The objectives of Closed Loop Support were to insure timely response to the needs of operational units, to exert more effective control of critical serviceable and unserviceable assets in the logistics pipeline, to reduce the backlog of unserviceables at all levels, to insure the timely availability of reparable assets at depot maintenance overhaul facilities, and to improve asset control of the flow of controlled items throughout the system. This integrated program provided better asset visibility for the Army matériel managers to plan, program, fund, and operate the Army logistic system more efficiently.

Closed Loop Support is a totally integrated and controlled special management program in which Department of the Army designated major end items of equipment and secondary items are intensively managed through the supply, retrograde, and overhaul process to and from respective commands providing positive control and prescribed levels of logistics readiness.

Fundamental to the Closed Loop Support system is the Closed Loop Support network, an Army-wide functional grouping of controlled activities, supply, maintenance, and transportation elements through which the Closed Loop Support system is operated and controlled. (*Chart 3*)

The following criteria governed the selection of items nominated for intensive management under the Closed Loop Support system: items whose high unit cost and/or complex nature limits normal logistical support; items essential to a particular mission; items in short supply that impact most severely on operational readiness of a given command; items in a critical worldwide asset position; and items considered critical by a major Army commander. Some of the criteria were the same as those used in selecting an item for Department of the Army Distribution and Allocation Committee control. Indeed many Closed Loop items were controlled by Department of the Army Distribution and Allocation Committee. Therefore, at the Deputy Chief of Staff for Logistics level, Department of the Army Distribution and Allocation Committee and Closed Loop staff responsibilities were in the same staff element.

Within Department of the Army Distribution and Allocation Committee the new or repaired assets are the "managed" items.

CHART 3—CLOSED LOOP SUPPORT NETWORK

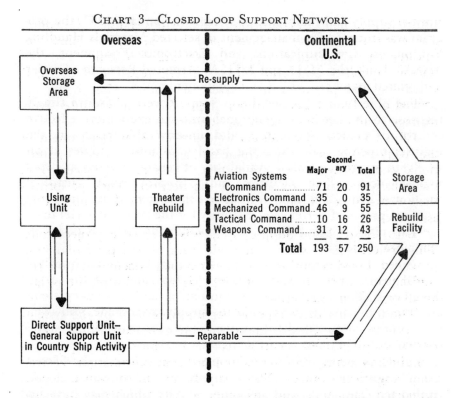

Closed Loop differs in that the repairable assets constitute the life blood of the system. Army management, at all levels, gave special attention to predicting and controlling the flow of unserviceable items to and from repair and overhaul facilities. To provide incentives for local commanders to turn in operating equipment scheduled for repair, it was necessary to have a replacement item available for direct exchange. The concept was simple and basic, but smooth operation of the concept in a system as large as the Army's requires more than routine controls.

Once an item was selected as a candidate item, a detailed review process was conducted at a Closed Loop Support Conference. Representation at the Closed Loop Support Conference included representatives from the interested commands and activities, for example Department of the Army, Army Materiel Command, Major Commands, National Inventory Control Points, National Maintenance Points, Project Managers, Defense Supply Agency and others as appropriate. Conferees analyzed the allowances for equipment (Tables of Allowances and modified Tables of Allowances, Special Authorizations, Tables of Organization and Equipment and Modified Tables of Organization and Equipment); stock status of equipment on hand by condition code previous transaction history; maintenance capability of direct and general support units, in-country depots, in-theater depots, Continental U.S. depots and contractor capability and availability; current repair and overhaul schedules; and procurement delivery schedules. After being approved as a Closed Loop Support item, the item was intensively managed and controlled at all logistic levels.

Closed Loop project officers were appointed at Department of the Army and in each major command, agency, or activity by functional commodity or weapons system. These project officers were the principal points of contact in the network. They performed their Closed Loop Support duties in addition to their other duty assignments.

Each Closed Loop Support item was assigned a project code. This project code was then the trade mark of that particular item providing a ready identifier for that item on all documentation (including transportation and handling) , in all communications, and on all packaging and crating.

The following three types of reports were used by the system:

1. A monthly Closed Loop Support summary which was a resumé of programed versus actual performance. This report was compiled by Army Materiel Command from information received from Logistical Control Offices, supply and maintenance depots, supported commands, and any other activity which may have had an assigned function in carrying out the Closed Loop Support program.

2. Problem Flasher messages which provided warnings of potential deviations from the scheduled movements of serviceable input, retrograde matériel, and matérial to be overhauled. Problem Flashers also described actions being taken to compensate for program deviations, gave the anticipated recovery date, and information as to any assistance required.

3. Real-Time reports were dispatched by priority message by transceiver for each serviceable item shipped from or received by Continental U.S. and overseas air and water terminals. These reports provided notification of lift and receipt data to interested activities. The Closed Loop concept was initiated to provide critical item management for U.S. Army Vietnam. However, from this origin, the system has been expanded to the remainder of the U.S. Army.

Retrograde of Equipment—KEYSTONE

In mid-June 1969, the President of the United States announced the first incremental withdrawal of U.S. Forces from the Republic of Vietnam. This initial redeployment withdrawal phase was given the project name KEYSTONE EAGLE.

The initial KEYSTONE increments identified problem areas in the classification and disposition of equipment generated by redeploying units. The standard technical inspection required extensive technical expertise and was time-consuming. Concurrently, the KEYSTONE processing points were experiencing a large backlog of equipment while requests for disposition and/or claimants were processed.

Two management techniques evolved in support of KEYSTONE Operations. The classification of matériel was modified to reflect the level of maintenance required to upgrade the matériel for issue. SCRAM was the acronym used to identify Special Criteria for Retrograde of Materiel. SCRAM 1 matériel can be issued "as-is" or requires minor organizational maintenance. SCRAM 2 matériel requires Direct Support or General Support maintenance prior to issue. SCRAM 3 matériel must be evacuated for depot maintenance. SCRAM 4 is unserviceable or economically unrepairable and is processed to property disposal.

The second technique provided the KEYSTONE processing centers with disposition instructions in anticipation of equipment being turned in. The "predisposition instructions" were prepared based on estimates of quantities of equipment as well as estimates of the condition of equipment to be released by redeploying units. This asset projection was matched against other claimants for the serviceable equipment; unserviceable equipment was reviewed against approved maintenance programs. Generally, available items were used first to satisfy Southeast Asia requirements, then other U.S. Army requirements. The primary considerations in the preparation of these instructions were to preclude the transshipment of equipment, to reduce shipping costs wherever feasible, and to preclude the retrograde of matériel not required elsewhere.

Morning Line of Communications Briefings—Vietnam

Major General Charles W. Eifler, who was the Commander of the 1st Logistical Command in Vietnam from January 1966 to June 1967, developed a system for reviewing the status of stockage for Classes I, III, and V types of supply. The system involved the daily review with his seven Directors and three staff officers along with their senior advisers of the stockage status for these classes of supply. The review utilized charts which covered every Depot, Supply Point, and every Supply Area in support of combat operations in Vietnam. The daily review covered significant data for the number of troops supported and established stockage objectives which were compared with the Receipts and Issues for the preceding twenty-four hours. An analysis of the stock balance was made each day and management action was taken on the spot when any area appeared to be in a critical position. It was an extremely effective management tool and there was seldom a day without a significant management action being taken on one of these classes of supply.

Other areas that could be critical were also reviewed at the same morning sessions. Examples are: the number of artillery pieces deadlined with the reasons and actions being taken, and the status of port facilities with particular emphasis given to number of ships awaiting discharge and the number programed for the next thirty days. To put the logistic picture in the proper perspective a detailed review of the tactical situation was conducted every morning.

Project for the Utilization and Redistribution of Matériel

During late 1967, after the Vietnam buildup had been largely completed, excess began to attract serious attention. Secretary of Defense McNamara took unprecedented action and directed that action begin immediately to redistribute excesses prior to the conclusion of the conflict, so as to assure their application against approved military requirements elsewhere in the military supply system. This action was designed to preclude a recurrence of the history of excesses and surpluses following past conflicts. In his memorandum of 24 November 1967, establishing the Project for the Utilization and Redistribution of Materiel, the Secretary of Defense designated the Secretary of the Army as the executive agent for the Department of Defense and further directed that an Army general officer be designated as the Project Coordinator. The Commander-in-Chief, Pacific was directed to establish a special agency to maintain an inventory of excess matériel, supervise redistribution or disposal of such matériel within his area, and report the availability of matériel which could not be utilized in the Pacific area to other Defense activities in accordance with procedures developed by the Project Coordinator.

The Commander in Chief, Pacific established the agency directed under the 2d U.S. Army Logistical Command on Okinawa. The agency was known as the Pacific Command Utilization and Redistribution Agency.

Pacific Command Utilization and Redistribution Agency initiated operation on 1 April 1968 on a semi-automated basis which continued until 30 June 1968 at which time it was fully automated.

Pacific Command Utilization and Redistribution Agency has undergone some major improvements to increase utilization of the excess matériel. In July 1968, a special off-line teletype screening procedure was developed and implemented in the Pacific Command Utilization and Redistribution Agency operation to expedite the screening of bulk-lot items by Continental U.S. inventory managers and supply activities in the Pacific Command in 21 days. This procedure provided rapid disposition instructions to the owning service in order to open up critically needed storage space. In November 1968, the funding policy was revised to permit the transfer of specific categories of service excesses between Pacific Command component commanders on a nonreimbursable basis at field level. In December 1968, a team of merchandising specialists was sent to Okinawa to develop an intensified merchandising program. The task was to produce a catalog on high dollar value items which could be distributed to the Pacific Command Utilization and Redistribution Agency customers. The catalog provides visibility, interchangeability and substitute capability. In May 1969, a controlled free issue program was implemented in Pacific Command Utilization and Redistribution Agency, whereby matériel designated by Defense Supply Agency and Government Services Administration as not returnable to the Continental U.S. wholesale level could be issued without charge to the Pacific Command military customers. The free issue program was expanded in July 1969 to include selected expendable and shelf-life items.

In July 1969, Commander in Chief Pacific initiated a study to redesign the Pacific Command Utilization and Redistribution Agency operations and Office of the Assistant Secretary of Defense (Installations and Logistics) directed implementation of some of the major concepts included in the Commander in Chief Pacific study, which were designated as Quick Fix improvements. These improvements included increased military service and other Federal agency participation, Closed Loop status reporting, up-grade of the Pacific Command Utilization and Redistribution Agency automatic data processing equipment, and a reduced screening time concept. The Pacific Command Utilization and Redistribution Agency Quick Fix improvements were implemented on 1 October 1970. These improvements had a significant impact in the Department of Defense excess screening cycle by reducing the screening time from about one year to about 75 days.

During the period 1 April 1968 through January 1972, the Military Services nominated $2.1 billion worth of excess to Pacific Command Utilization and Redistribution Agency for screening.

Of this $306 million worth was redistributed in the Pacific Area and other overseas commands and $710.3 million worth was returned to the Continental U.S. wholesale system, resulting in utilization of $1.03 billion, or approximately 48 percent utilization. The balance of this material was declared Department of Defense excess and returned to the owning Services.

Managing the Logistics System

During the buildup and into the Spring of 1967, management emphasis was on getting the supplies to the combat units. The influx of logistics units to Vietnam; the need to establish depots, ports, and organizational structures; and just coping with a rapidly expanding system needing more resources than were available relegated anything not related to the top priority effort to the status of a back burner project. Excesses accumulated, but were not recognized, and requisitions continued to be submitted to Continental U.S. for items that were already in excess in Vietnam.

The nature of operations was such that authorizations did not necessarily represent the needs of units. Units often needed more or different items than were authorized and the requisitioning system honored such requisitions. The Army Authorization Document System was not able to keep up with the needs. Equipment a unit had in excess of its authorization was not reported in its inventory reports (Army Regulation 711–5).

Frequently documentation on incoming supplies was either lost or illegible upon arrival of the supplies and the contents of containers was unknown. Unqualified supply personnel set aside these containers to be identified later, which frequently extended beyond the rotation date of the individual who had knowledge of the circumstances.

Failures of the supply system to locate, identify, and provide a required item undoubtedly degraded supply discipline at the using unit level which in turn made a substantial contribution to further breakdown in control and to increasing excesses. Rather than using normal follow-up procedures, it was common for the requesting unit to re-requisition the needed items one or more times, thereby bringing unneeded items into country as well as creating inflated demand data at the supporting units and depots.

In the spring of 1967, concern about the numbers of high priority requisitions being received from Vietnam caused a number of National Inventory Control Points, U.S. Army Pacific Headquarters, and other commands in the requisitioning channel to challenge requisitions. Later the program was formalized under the name

Project CHALLENGE, which required unit commanders to verify the priority of the requirement. Project CHALLENGE reduced premium transportation and handling costs and started to reinstate some degree of control on the requisitioning process.

In addition to the excesses created by the Push Packages arriving in-country prior to the arrival of adequate logistics units, the deterioration of identification markings on packages added even more excesses as the unidentified items on hand were re-requisitioned.

The personnel assigned as warehousemen were generally untrained and inexperienced in supply operations which added to the confusion. To attempt to rectify this lack of experience and training, the Department of the Army instituted Project COUNTER.

Early in 1967 a group of supply assistance personnel from U.S. Army Materiel Command organizations went to Vietnam on temporary duty, under the code name Project COUNTER. These people provided formal instruction in supply procedures and assisted in-county personnel in performing location surveys, conducting inventories, identifying and classifying matériel, reviewing and improving prescribed load lists and authorized stockage lists, and generally assisted in supply management activities. In all, a total of four Project COUNTER teams were provided during 1967–1968 and proved extremely helpful in upgrading the technical competence of supply personnel in Vietnam.

In order to direct attention and effort to the many tasks that had to be performed once there was a satisfactory logistic base in Vietnam, the Commanding General of the 1st Logistical Command established an extensive command and control program for logistics management in 1968. The program was formalized into a number of objectives, performance statements, and progress reports, which were incorporated in a command publication referred to as the Pink Book. This was given wide distribution within the 1st Logistical Command and tied together short and long range projects in all logistics areas to increase efficiency, to bring stock levels down, and to identify and reduce excesses.

Early in 1969, during a meeting at Phu Bai including General Abrams, Commander U.S. Military Assistance Command, Vietnam, the Commanding General of the 1st Logistical Command and others, General Abrams used the term Logistics Offensive to describe what was required of the Army logistics system in Vietnam. While General Abrams meant it as a compliment for the progressive improvement being made in all areas of logistics, in reality he had issued a resounding challenge to all professional Army logisticians to institute a series of actions with follow-up attention, similar to those employed by tactical commanders in launching offensive operations.

Soon after this, the 1st Logistical Command's Pink Book became known as the Logistics Offensive Program. This program was adopted by Department of Army for Army-wide application in September 1969. By 31 March 1971 this program had grown to include over 130 different projects. The following list contains some of the projects contained in the Logistics Offensive Program.

Sample Projects of the Logistics Offensive Program

1. Inventory in Motion
2. VERIFY
3. STOP/SEE
4. CONDITION
5. CLEAN
6. Vietnam Asset Reconciliation Procedures (VARP)
7. SEE MOVE
8. KEYSTONE

The concept of *Inventory in Motion* was first applied to ammunition and is discussed in some detail in the ammunition chapter. As applied across the board, inventory in motion was a supply management program that had as its goal integrating supply and transportation to reduce the requirement for stock levels in Vietnam and other storage areas.

Integrated planning and control of the movement of supplies resulted in responsive resupply and smaller local inventories. Having fewer supplies on hand meant reduced care and preservation efforts, smaller storage areas to protect, and easier inventory management. Basically stocks in transit or in the pipeline were considered as being part of the inventory.

The use of the inventory in motion concept for ammunition and bulk petroleum was facilitated by the relatively small number of different items and predictable consumption rates. Likewise, consumption of subsistence was relatively stable, being pretty much in proportion to troop strength. The effectiveness of applying inventory in motion procedures to other supplies such as repair parts, clothing and individual equipment, administrative and housekeeping supplies and equipment, principal items, and packaged petroleum products was more difficult because of the large number of items and varying demand rates. One of the major problems was the lack of data announcing that truck convoys, airplanes, or vessels were scheduled to arrive on given dates. Consequently, advance planning at storage activities was limited and matériel actually in transit could not be considered as assets.

It became apparent that an interface between supply and transportation data was necessary to achieve the desired asset visability of intransit matériel. A conference was held in September 1969 with representatives of U.S. Army Pacific, U.S. Army Vietnam, 1st Logistical Command, and the U.S. Army Logistics Control Office Pacific which resulted in creating a Logistics Intelligence File. Through the Logistics Intelligence File, U.S. Army Vietnam and the Central Financial Management Agency, Ft. Shafter, Hawaii, were able to have daily updated information on each open requisition. This gave U.S. Army Vietnam the capability to determine where any requisition was at any time, e.g., in process at the Continental U.S. National Inventory Control Point depot, intransit to the terminal, or in the terminal awaiting lift, as well as the lift data (such as transportation control number, carrier, and estimated time of arrival). Through use of the Logistics Intelligence File, the concept of inventory in motion has been applied to most commodities in Vietnam.

Another management program, Project VERIFY, was established in Vietnam to study the management procedures and statistical data used by the 1st Logistical Command to describe and evaluate its logistic efforts. The aim of Project VERIFY was to produce standardized management procedures, statistical terms, and usable standards that could be expressed as management objectives.

The project concerned itself with the movement of supply items through the depots. It also was concerned with the flow of paperwork pertaining to these supplies—noting the paths of the various copies in order to determine the control measures used. Data were sought to determine the time frames involved in the various processes. These data were analyzed and corrective actions were taken when deficiencies or inefficiences were found. This helped to implement other projects designed to speed up the movement of supplies to the requesting units.

During 1968 it was becoming apparent that items were being requisitioned on a routine basis that were not actually needed in Vietnam. What the situation needed was some degree of personal attention to prevent the shipment of these items. In June 1968, Project STOP was initiated in U.S. Army Vietnam for the purpose of preventing shipping of supply items from Continental U.S. that were not needed in Vietnam. All possible actions were taken from cancelling requisitions not yet filled to stopping shipments up to the point where items were loaded on board ship. In addition, related procurements were terminated, stretched out, or diverted to other uses. Stops on requisitions started with the 1st Logistical Command's submission of requests for cancellation of specific items by Federal Stock Numbers. Items stopped were either stocked in Vietnam in quantities excess to the requirements there, or in quantities exceeding the depot system's capacity to handle and store.

In September 1968, Project SEE began with teams established at each major post in U.S. Army Vietnam to devote full time to physically examining (seeing) bulk items in storage at depots, on the piers, and being unloaded from ships. These teams initiated immediate action to determine whether the items aboard ships should continue to be unloaded, or whether they should be diverted elsewhere (in country or out of country). When an item not desired was located, action was initiated to have the appropriate Federal Stock Number broadcast to all supply agencies involved including Army Materiel Command, Defense Supply Agency, and 2d Logistical Command in Okinawa, so that action could be taken throughout the system to stop movement of this item to Vietnam.

In late September 1968 Project STOP and Project SEE were merged into one project which was given the code name of Project STOP/SEE. Under this concept 1st Logistical Command designated items on a STOP/SEE listing by Federal Stock Number and nomenclature which were in long supply, items deleted from the theater authorized stockage list, or luxury and convenience items. When an item appeared on one of these listings, 1st Logistical Command suspended requisitioning by blocking the computers in country and sending copies of these listings to Continental U.S. Inventory Managers. These Managers then took steps to locate and cancel all open requisitions for these items and to frustrate shipments through STOP procedures.

Project STOP/SEE EXPANDED was a further extension of Project STOP/SEE and was initiated 19 November 1968. The Commanding General U.S. Army Vietnam, in accordance with Project STOP procedures, requested blocking action by Federal Supply Class with Federal Stock Number exceptions. Under this program, the majority of Federal Stock Numbers within a Federal Supply Class were blocked at the Defense Automatic Addressing System Office and all low priority requisitions (IPD 09–20) for Vietnam were cancelled and the shipments were frustrated. High priority requisitions (IPD 01–08) continued to be honored. The U.S. Army Inventory Control Center Vietnam (formerly the 14th Inventory Control Center) then provided a standardized list of Federal Stock Numbers, by Federal Supply Class in card deck format, to the Logistics Control Office,

Pacific for use in completing Project STOP actions. By the end of February 1971, $644 million of requisitions had been cancelled through the use of STOP/SEE techniques.

Project CONDITION was first implemented in the 1st Logistical Command in February 1969. It was implemented because of conditions found to exist when Project COUNT I (reliability of the location system and inventory) and Project COUNT II (100% cyclic inventory) were conducted during the period September 1968 to January 1969. The intent of Project CONDITION was to purify condition data of matériel assets at each depot. It consisted of two basic phases. Phase I was the separation of all stock counted into two categories; first, that stock which was obviously condition A, and second, all other stock which was designated as Code J. Phase II consisted of the condition coding of all incoming depot stocks as either Code A or K. Code K identified all receipts which were obviously not Code A. Quality control technicians inspected and determined the requirements and recommended priorities for care and preservation.

Project CONDITION was extended to Army Materiel Command and other major commands as an integral part of the Logistics Offensive. The objectives were to provide visibility of the actual condition of the inventory worldwide (not in the hands of troops) and to identify and monitor progress on that portion which required care and preservation.

Project CLEAN was established as an integral part of the inventory-in-motion concept to eliminate excess supplies from the Army supply system by determining what supplies were on hand in the field but were no longer required for mission accomplishment, and then to redistribute them to where they were required, retrograde them to maintenance activities, or dispose of them through disposal channels. During fiscal year 1970 and 1971, supplies valued at almost $1.5 billion were eliminated from oversea stocks. In these years, U.S. Army Vietnam alone retrograded over 671,000 short tons of supplies. The authorized stockage list for Vietnam was reduced from a high of 297,000 different items in July 1967 to 74,900 items in March 1971, without any loss of the high quality of support provided to the combat forces.

The Vietnam Asset Reconciliation Procedures was a program developed in December 1969 to cope with the problem of excesses. A bit of background data reveals that during the buildup and sustaining phases, U.S. Army Vietnam was given first priority for the fill of all major item requisitions. U.S. Army Vietnam requisitions were processed and filled with little regard as to whether formal authorization existed. In general, U.S. Army Vietnam requirements were not questioned and requisitions on the wholesale supply system were accepted at face value. This policy was necessary because formal authorization documents could not keep pace with the rapidly changing situation. As a result of this policy, U.S. Army Vietnam developed excess positions for many items. While some of these excesses were real, others were only apparent in that the items on hand were actually required for mission performance, but the need for them had never been recognized in an authorization document. Vietnam Asset Reconciliation Procedures was intended to establish control over excess assets in the hands of U.S. Army Vietnam units, obtain visibility over the actual requirement situation in U.S. Army Vietnam, and reconcile differences between U.S. Army Vietnam recorded quantities and National Inventory Control Point shipped quantities.

Vietnam Asset Reconciliation Procedures was unique and constituted a departure from conventional asset control and accounting procedures. Under Vietnam Asset Reconciliation Procedures, units reported to U.S. Army Vietnam those assets on hand which were in excess of written authority; however, there was no penalty for reporting these excesses. Reporting units were allowed to retain them on loan provided they were required for mission accomplishment. U.S. Army Vietnam reviewed the loans every 180 days as a minimum. Assets on loan to units were accounted for through the depot reporting system (Army Regulation 711–80)) rather than the unit reporting system (Army Regulation 711–5). Assets within unit tabular authority continued to be reported through the regular unit reporting system. As of 31 December 1970, approximately $160 million (at budget costs) of previously unreported assets had been accounted for under Vietnam Asset Reconciliation Procedures.

Project SEE/MOVE was begun in July 1969, and sent to U.S. Army Pacific to assist the commands in understanding existing disposition instructions; to provide on-the-spot disposition; and to effect the necessary communication between the sub-commands, Department of the Army, and the appropriate Continental U.S. agencies to obtain rapid disposition instructions (note the relationship with CLEAN). Later the teams turned their efforts to rendering management assistance to U.S. Army Pacific in such areas as interpretation of Department of the Army, Army Materiel Command, and Defense Supply Agency regulations, policies and/or disposition priorities and instructions and effecting communication and co-ordination with U.S. Army Pacific, Department of the Army and/or other appropriate Continental U.S. agencies. Also, they provided U.S. Army Pacific with guidance and on-the-spot disposition instructions for categories of excess matériel not otherwise covered by instructions.

The teams were headed by a representative from Deputy Chief of Staff for Logistics with members provided by Defense Supply Agency, U.S. Army Pacific, and U.S. Army Materiel Command. In-country U.S. Army Materiel Command technical assistance personnel were also utilized. Rotation of personnel was at the discretion of the agency concerned. The teams operated under the overall direction of the Deputy Chief of Staff for Logistics and under the control of U.S. Army Pacific. They were deployed to Vietnam and Okinawa in February 1970 and terminated their operations on 15 June 1970. During this period, one team was also sent to Europe.

KEYSTONE was the name given to the program for the withdrawal of the U.S. Forces from South Vietnam. In mid-June 1969, the President of the United States announced the first incremental withdrawal of U.S. Forces. This initial redeployment phase was given the project name KEYSTONE EAGLE.

KEYSTONE EAGLE began on 19 June 1969, and was initially planned as a unit redeployment, with 9th Infantry Division (less one brigade and provisional supporting elements) scheduled to redeploy to Hawaii to reconstitute the Pacific Command reserve. The redeployment was scheduled to be completed on 27 August 1969 to meet the Presidential commitment of having the initial troop withdrawal of 25,000 personnel completed by 1 September 1969. Department of the Army published a Letter of Instruction for the redeployment of United States Army Forces from South Vietnam on 21 June 1969, providing general logistics and personnel policies governing the redeployment. The redeploying units were authorized to redeploy with all Modified Tables of Organization and Equipment equipment, less selected U.S. Army Vietnam designated "critical" items (such as radars and M16 rifles), which were to be retained in-country to satisfy existing shortages within U.S. Army Vietnam units.

The 1st Logistical Command was tasked by Lieutenant General Frank T. Mildren, Deputy Commanding General, U.S. Army Vietnam to provide assistance to the Commanding General 9th Infantry Division and the mission was assigned to the Saigon Support Command. This mission was ultimately expanded to include the provision of complete logistics support of the division during the final 30 days of the redeployment phase. This entire support operation was unique in that it represented the first time in U.S. Army history a unit, actively engaged in combat, was disengaged from its mission, withdrawn to a base camp and required to prepare itself for redeployment. The logistic support of this unit redeployment was extremely complex because of the need to continue to support other units still engaged in combat operations while simultaneously inspecting, preparing, packing and shipping the redeploying unit's Table of Organization and Equipment equipment.

The problem was compounded by the fact that the majority of the personnel turning in the division's equipment were not redeploying with their parent unit, but would be reassigned in-country for completion of their twelve month tour. This personnel policy alone taxed the command and control element to the maximum.

Finally, the complexity of this initial redeployment was further compounded by the lack of procedures and matériel to process Table of Organization and Equipment equipment for overseas redeployment to meet the strict U.S. Public Health Service and U.S. Department of Agriculture sanitation and entomological requirements. To assist U.S. Army Vietnam in overcoming these problems, the Commanding General U.S. Army Materiel Command assembled a team of forty civilian personnel and deployed them to South Vietnam in early 1969. Additionally, a Composite Service Maintenance Company (604th Composite Service Company) and a Transportation Detachment (402d Transportation Corps Detachment) were organized in the Continental U.S. and deployed to South Vietnam to assist in unit redeployment. The 604th Composite Service Company was specifically organized to assist in inspection, packaging and preparing equipment for redeployment and the Transportation Detachment was organized to assist with required documentation.

Because KEYSTONE EAGLE was planned primarily as a unit redeployment, the Department of the Army logistics guidance was minimal. This situation changed drastically on 8 August 1969 when Department of the Army directed that the redeploying units of the 9th Infantry Division would be deactivated in South Vietnam. The logistics impact of this decision, almost two-thirds of the way through the redeployment was traumatic. Approximately one-third of the redeploying units' equipment was already enroute to Hawaii. Another one-third was at the Port of Newport awaiting out-loading, while the remaining one-third was being staged for movement to the port. Property accountability could not be maintained because the Property Book Officers were already in Hawaii with the advance party, and two-thirds of their equipment was frustrated in South Vietnam.

The combat situation at the former division base camp (Dong Tam), as well as the scheduled transfer of this facility to South Vietnam dictated that the equipment be moved, and the equipment was diverted to a holding area at Long Binh Depot, north of Saigon. Port clearance at Newport dictated that the matériel awaiting outloading be moved, and it also was moved to the Long Binh area. Because of the lack of documentation, this matériel was ultimately capitalized in the depot account and redistributed to in-country requirements. The KEYSTONE EAGLE incremental phase–down was completed on 28 August, although redistribution of all the matériel was not completed until mid-October. The KEYSTONE EAGLE project provided an indication of what was to come, and it was recognized at Department of the Army that Department of the Army level control over the redistribution of assets generated from these phase–downs was essential.

In late September 1969 the second KEYSTONE withdrawal was announced. This was KEYSTONE CARDINAL, which was a troop space reduction of 40,500 personnel. The principal large Army unit involved was the 3rd Brigade of the 82d Airborne Division. Units involved in this withdrawal were to be brought to zero strength in South Vietnam by 15 December 1969. None were to be redeployed intact to the Continental U.S.

To provide control over the redistribution of the assets generated from these unit inactivations, Department of the Army provided logistics guidance in the form of an Annex to the Department of the Army Letter of Instruction for redeployment of U.S. Forces from South Vietnam published on 1 October 1969. This logistics guidance included instructions on property accountability, canceling of requisitions, processing of matériel, inspection and maintenance standards and, perhaps most important, it established a reporting procedure for both obtaining and tracking disposition of matériel turned in during KEYSTONE CARDINAL. This reporting procedure involved the establishment of a telephone conversation between U.S. Army Vietnam, U.S. Army Pacific, and Department of the Army on a daily basis. The intent of this telephone conversation was to provide to U.S. Army Vietnam, on a twenty-four hour basis, the disposition for selected items of equipment turned in (Department of the Army Distribution and Allocation Committee and Department of the Army High Interest Items). This telephone conversation system also provided Department of the Army with visibility of assets redistributed in and outside of South Vietnam. Although this system did provide the desired controls it was not responsive to U.S. Army Vietnam requirements.

The 24-hour turn-around of disposition requests at Department of the Army equated to 8–10 days delay at the turn-in location and caused matériel to stack up with attendant storage and accountability problems.

During KEYSTONE CARDINAL, a new maintenance inspection procedure was implemented to expedite processing of matériel. This procedure, referred to as SCRAM (Special Criteria-Retrograde of Army Materiel), included a much simplified inspection procedure which permitted classification of equipment into one of four categories. It also included maintenance expenditure and transportation cost data which could be utilized to determine ultimate disposition of matériel. This new SCRAM procedure was extensively tested during KEYSTONE CARDINAL and adopted for future KEYSTONE operations. KEYSTONE CARDINAL was completed on 17 December 1969 and the logistics support procedures developed in KEYSTONE EAGLE were polished and refined in KEYSTONE CARDINAL, providing for publication of a U.S. Army Vietnam redeployment guide for logistics support. By the end of KEYSTONE CARDINAL, however, the requirement for complete predisposition instructions for matériel being turned in was recognized as essential for future withdrawals.

In early January 1970 KEYSTONE BLUEJAY, the third KEYSTONE withdrawal was announced. This was the largest increment to date—50,000 personnel. The principal units involved were the 1st Infantry Division and one brigade of the 4th Infantry Division. This increment was scheduled for the period 20 February through 15 April 1970. Logistic guidance was again published in a logistics annex to a Department of the Army Letter of Instruction. The predominant theme of these instructions was to retain all matériel required by U.S. Army Vietnam in-country to preclude Continental U.S. shipment. The predisposition instruction problem had not been completely resolved at the beginning of the increment so the telephone conversation procedure continued to be employed. In early March 1970, however, Department of the Army did develop and publish predisposition instructions for equipment forecasted to become available during the third increment. This list included all Department of the Army Distribution and Allocations Committee items and additional selected items referred to as Department of the Army High Interest Items.

Because of the size of this increment, and the extremely short time frame, another critical problem surfaced—the cleanliness standards required for equipment retrograde. This problem had been anticipated and washing facilities had been constructed to accommodate the expected workload. It soon became apparent, however, that the pacing operation in unit stand-down and equipment turn-in was cleaning the equipment to meet U.S. Public Health Service and U.S. Department of Agriculture standards for retrograde. Special equipment providing extremely high water pressure jets were procured in the Continental U.S. under ENSURE provisions and the special wash areas were operated around the clock to keep abreast of the work load.

The massive size of this third increment also had a dramatic effect on depot operations throughout U.S. Army Vietnam. At the same time that force reductions were reducing the size of the supported forces, the evacuation of matériel back to depots posed an awesome workload. Recoup operations had to be significantly expanded to accommodate this matériel being returned while at the same time the depots were in a massive retrograde operation of their own, purging stocks of identified excesses. The Commanding General 1st Logistical Command initiated an intensive, command wide, retrograde program not only to identify and move excesses but to do it with correct packing, preservation and true identification. The entire logistics effort of U.S. Army Vietnam was now focused on both responsive combat service support to the combat elements and on retrograde of both serviceable and unserviceable matériel from the combat zone.

Three times as much effort is required to process matériel for retrograde as to receive incoming matériel and accomplish issue; nevertheless, this task was accomplished by a logistic force reduced in size in equal proportions to the combat elements.

KEYSTONE BLUEJAY was the beginning of an intensive effort to satisfy Army of the Republic of Vietnam requirements from assets being generated by U.S. unit inactivations in-country. To assist in this effort, the Commanding General 1st Logistical Command established the 79th Maintenance Battalion as a KEYSTONE Battalion. This unit was assigned the mission of receiving matériel from KEYSTONE designated units, repairing it to meet Army of the Republic of Vietnam transfer standards, and accomplishing the issue to Army of the Republic of Vietnam. KEYSTONE BLUEJAY concluded on 15 April 1970 and the ultimate disposition of the generated matériel was completed in mid-June 1970.

The fourth increment, KEYSTONE ROBIN, was announced on 1 July 1970. This title was designated to encompass all troop withdrawal increments scheduled in fiscal year 1971. The first phase, ALPHA, extended from 1 July 1970 through 15 October 1970 with a total projected troop strength reduction of 50,000 personnel.

With the experience gained in the three preceding KEYSTONE increments, the preparations and preliminary planning for KEYSTONE ROBIN were well documented in the Department of the Army Letter of Instruction, U.S. Army Pacific, and U.S. Army Vietnam implementing instructions. The two most significant improvements made in logistics planning were:

1. Predisposition instructions for Department of the Army Distribution and Allocation Committee and Department of the Army High Interest Items were provided in early August covering the entire ALPHA phase of KEYSTONE ROBIN.

2. U.S. Army Vietnam developed a computer based accounting system for establishing an audit trail on all transactions generated from KEYSTONE actions. The ALPHA phase of KEYSTONE ROBIN terminated on 15 October 1970 and the BRAVO phase began immediately.

Because KEYSTONE ROBIN phases were scheduled to occur almost back-to-back, it was decided at Department of the Army to develop equipment and predisposition instructions for the two remaining KEYSTONE ROBIN phases and publish them in one document. Additionally, it was decided to expand the coverage of these predisposition instructions to include all Procurement of Equipment and Missiles for the Army principal items forecasted to be generated during the remainder of the fiscal year 1971 KEYSTONE redeployment and inactivations. The document was published late in October 1970 and forwarded to U.S. Army Pacific in early November. KEYSTONE ROBIN BRAVO concluded on 31 December 1970.

Petroleum Support

The supply of and the policies relating to bulk petroleum are under the purview of the Department of Defense and the Unified Commanders. Headquarters Military Assistance Command, Vietnam, received consumption data and demand forecasts for the four major products (motor gasoline, diesel fuel, jet fuel, and aviation gasoline) from the three component commands and forwarded it through the Joint Petroleum Office at Headquarters Commander in Chief Pacific to the Defense Fuel Supply Center for procurement and shipping action. The Army in Vietnam was responsible for receiving, storing, distributing and accounting for all bulk petroleum in II, III, and IV Corps. The Navy was responsible in the I Corps area with Headquarters Military Assistance Command, Vietnam, coordinating tanker arrivals between the two commands. When U.S. Army Vietnam took over logistical responsibility from the Navy in I Corps in June 1970 it also took over petroleum operations.

A big petroleum storage construction effort was necessary to support the supply of petroleum. The Army and Navy constructed approximately 1.6 million barrels of fixed storage facilities; the bulk of these were in port areas such as Cam Ranh Bay, Qui Nhon and Da Nang. The Air Force had about 350,000 barrels of storage at air bases, and there was also slightly less than one million barrels of commercial storage (Shell, Esso, Caltex). About 90 percent of the commercial storage was located at Nha Be, not far from Saigon, and was the sole source of petroleum supply for the III and IV Corps areas. Military storage facilities in these areas were filled from products that had first been delivered to one of the three commercial facilities.

TABLE 3—COUNTRYWIDE PETROLEUM CONSUMPTION
(IN THOUSANDS OF BARRELS)

Date	Quantity	Date	Quantity
1964	2,700	1968	43,650
1965	6,785	1969	41,725
1966	21,850	1970	36,450
1967	36,280		

Table 3 shows the consumption of petroleum in thousands of barrels. When related to consumption, the in-country storage capacity shows that after 1966, the maximum possible number of days of supply on hand at any one time was 30. However, this does not take into consideration the fact that storage facilities are rarely full due to the need for flexibility in distribution and receiving times. After considering this factor, it is more accurate to conclude that 20 days of supply was the normal maximum quantity on hand. In order to deliver 100 gallons to a troop unit, more than 100 gallons had to be delivered by tanker to care for normal handling and evaporation losses, enemy caused losses, and pilferage. These losses probably were as high as 3 percent of the quantity actually consumed (or 5.7 million barrels).

Prior to 1965, requirements were small and although there were no refineries in Vietnam, three international oil companies (Shell, Esso, Caltex) had adequate storage and delivery capabilities for Military Assistance Command, Vietnam, demands. These capabilities were sufficient until early 1965 when the petroleum supply and distribution system in Vietnam was supplemented by military equipment in III and IV Corps areas, and a predominantly military system was established in other areas of the country.

Even though procedures had been developed for a military supply system, it was decided in 1965 to augment the existing commercial storage and distribution network with military facilities thereby reducing the number of facilities required.

Contracts with the in-country firms prior to 1965 provided for delivery, as required, of the products specified into designated locations in Vietnam. The military used only 2,700,000 barrels in 1964. In 1965, however, consumption jumped to 6,785,000 barrels. As a result of the increased tempo and shifting combat operations, monthly requirements changed frequently. Requests for purchases were submitted to Defense Fuel Supply Center on a piecemeal basis for deliveries at new locations as dictated by the need. Sometimes the requirement was received after the product had been ordered, accepted, and used. The Defense Fuel Supply Center contracting officer ratified such agreements by contract amendments.

Often quantities purchased for delivery to certain locations were not called forward because shifts in the fighting to other locations had eliminated the specific requirement. As the requirements increased and locations became more numerous, frequent small-emergency procurements and contract changes were necessary. As the delivery capabilities of the oil companies became extended, contracting in the normal manner became difficult. Effective competition had disappeared, and often one contractor had to be called upon to make delivery to locations covered under another contractor's contract. Moreover, price analysis became next to impossible, and the urgency of the situation did not allow adequate time for negotiation.

Assigned to Headquarters Military Assistance Command, Vietnam, the Sub-Area Petroleum Officer, Vietnam, sent each change in requirements by message through Commander in Chief Pacific to Defense Fuel Supply Center and to the appropriate Service inventory control points. Defense Fuel Supply Center was not authorized to take contractual action until furnished the authenticating Military Interdepartmental Procurement Request by the Service Inventory Control Point. Notwithstanding these conditions, no contract administrator was assigned to Vietnam, and direct-communication between Headquarters Military Assistance Command, Vietnam, and the contracting officer was not authorized.

The problems associated with contract administration included duplicate billing, improper pricing guides and inadequate controls. These and other problems were evident in such areas as: government-owned product in custody of contractors, commercial delivery procedures, and uncalibrated tanks and barges. As late as June

1968, the contractors' operations and records were not reviewed on a continuing and systematic basis. There were instances in which the contractor billed twice for the same product, and/or had borrow and loan transactions involving commercial and U. S. fuel outstanding as long as six months beyond the contract period. Control over the requests for delivery of petroleum, oils, and lubricants from commercial sources to authorized users was not established. Requests were often placed directly on commercial oil companies by various individual users throughout Vietnam, and as a result, the full quantity of petroleum products ordered from and delivered by the contractors was not known at one centralized location.

It was apparent that in this environment, drastic changes were needed in the kind of contracts used and in the contracting procedure employed. It was also apparent that contracts had to be more flexible to be manageable, and some better means was necessary to analyze the overall pricing structure to obtain for the Government a fair and equitable price.

Defense Fuel Supply Center took steps beginning in early 1965 to initiate the innovations that were needed. Some of the steps that were taken are as follows:

Estimated requirements of each product to be supplied through in-country contractor terminals at each ocean terminal for one year, by six month periods, were obtained.

The quantity of each product to be supplied or services to be performed by each contractor during a given period were covered by a single contract.

Locations to which ultimate delivery was to be made were covered in more than one contract. No contract limitations were placed on amounts to be supplied from each terminal or to each destination, though the total contract quantity was not to be exceeded.

Deliveries to unspecified locations or deliveries by circuitous routes to specified locations (due to enemy interdiction) were covered by pricing on the basis of mileage traveled.

Specific provisions were developed to cover vessel delays or diversions.

Prices were broken down by price components showing components for product Free On Board refinery, transportation to Singapore area, handling in Singapore area, transportation to Vietnam, handling in-country, transportation in-country, drumming services, and into-plane delivery. Contracts provided for delivery Free on Board refinery to avoid Saudi-Arabian taxes.

In-country war risk charges and charges for tie-up of contractor's inventory were eliminated.

The coastal vessels to be provided and the conditions governing their use were specifically set forth in contracts.

Defense Fuel Supply Center furnished guidance, in the form of product allocations, to Commander in Chief Pacific as to the volumes of each product to be supplied by each in-country contractor and Military Sea Transportation Service at each terminal, on the basis of proposed contract awards.

Defense Fuel Supply Center included provisions requiring the contractors to handle Government-owned products delivered by Military Sea Transportation Service at contractors' terminals north of Nha Be. Nha Be, the main terminal, was not included, because the contractors declined to permit Military Sea Transportation Service to make delivery into their facilities there. Apparently they feared enemy attacks on military ships might result, and effectively close out the terminals. However, the enemy did not attack commercial shipping to any degree.

The extent to which we depended on the three in-country commercial distributors for resupply and distribution is illustrated by the percentages of fuel supplied by them versus that supplied by the Military Sea Transportation Service. *(Table 4)*

TABLE 4—PERCENTAGE OF FUEL DISTRIBUTED BY COMMERCIAL
AND MSTS

Date	Commercial	MSTS
1965	100	0
1966	87	13
1967	61	39
1968	57	43
1969	69	31
1970	43	57

Facilities in Vietnam were vulnerable to enemy action. The large commercial contractors Shell, Esso and Caltex had contiguous petroleum, oils, and lubricants facilities at Nha Be which were particularly vulnerable to mortar attack and other hostile acts. In addition, access to the facilities by tankers would have been in jeopardy if one or more vessels had been sunk at a strategic point in the channel leading to Nha Be. Since 1965, there have been a number of attacks on commercial facilities at Nha Be, Tan Son Nhut, Qui Nhon and Lien Chieu. The most significant losses were at the Shell Nha Be Terminal in 1967 which amounted to approximately $3.5 million.

No single in-country contractor had adequate facilities and equipment to handle the entire military requirement. It was necessary to award concurrent contracts to all three companies (Esso, Shell and Caltex). Moreover, because of the large and rapid increase in demand after 1965, all three suppliers together were unable to furnish the additional product that was required.

Insufficient quantities of tank trucks both commercial and military and the Army's ability to install military Victualic pipelines (constructed by joining 20 foot lengths of 6″ steel pipe with bolted couplings) resulted in the decision to install these pipelines wherever they were most needed and they could be protected. Map 2 shows the locations of these pipelines throughout Vietnam. The Army was successful in effectively operating all of these lines with the exception of II Corps—primarily the Qui Nhon area where losses ran as high as 2.5 million gallons per month due mostly to enemy action. The important lesson to be learned here is that if assets are not available to protect and secure the pipeline (although it can easily be repaired), it is more efficient to resupply fuel by truck, rail, and barge.

The large volume, the long supply lines, and the uncertainties in schedules resulted in significant disruption in the worldwide tanker schedules of the three in-country contractors. Consequently they were unwilling to commit more tankers than were absolutely necessary to support the military requirements. While we never ran out, there were times when the tankage at Nha Be was uncomfortably low.

To overcome the lack of storage ashore, the expensive expedient of using tankers as floating storage to supplement the onshore storage was implemented. In addition, tankers making deliveries often incurred substantial amounts of demurrage and made extensive backhauls from Vietnam to Singapore or other Pacific military discharge areas (Korea, Japan, Thailand). Initially most of the floating storage tankers and tankers delivering petroleum, oils, and lubricants to Vietnam were provided by the in-country commercial suppliers. In February and March of 1968 these were supplemented or replaced by Military Sea Transport Service tankers.

The complexity of the commercial and military distribution system and the difficulties affecting accounting and reimbursement are indicated in the following paragraphs by examples in the Saigon area in 1968.

In the Nha Be commercial storage site, Esso and Caltex received US Government-owned product as well as their own. Shell

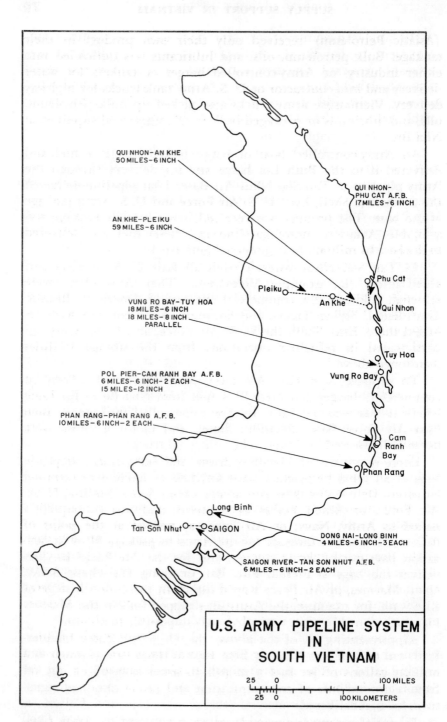

QUI NHON–AN KHE
50 MILES–6 INCH

QUI NHON–
PHU CAT A.F.B.
17 MILES–6 INCH

AN KHE–PLEIKU
59 MILES–6 INCH

Phu Cat

Pleiku

An Khe   Qui Nhon

VUNG RO BAY–TUY HOA
18 MILES–6 INCH
18 MILES–8 INCH
PARALLEL

Tuy Hoa

POL PIER–CAM RANH BAY A.F.B.
6 MILES–6 INCH–2 EACH
15 MILES–12 INCH

Vung Ro Bay

PHAN RANG–PHAN RANG A.F.B.
10 MILES–6 INCH–2 EACH

Cam
Ranh
Bay

Phan Rang

Long Binh

Tan Son Nhut   SAIGON

DONG NAI–LONG BINH
4 MILES–6 INCH–3 EACH

SAIGON RIVER–TAN SON NHUT A.F.B.
6 MILES–6 INCH–2 EACH

U.S. ARMY PIPELINE SYSTEM
IN
SOUTH VIETNAM

25   0   100 MILES

25   0   100 KILOMETERS

MAP 2

(Asiatic Petroleum) received only their own product in their tankage. Bulk petroleum, oils, and lubricants was outloaded into either industry- or Army-controlled barges or tankers for water delivery and into contractor or U. S. Army tank trucks for highway delivery. Vietnamese army trucks also picked up bulk petroleum, oils, and lubricants or packaged bulk from commercial suppliers at Nha Be.

An Army-controlled boat or barge picked up JP–4 fuel and delivered it to the Binh Loi barge site for delivery through the Army pipeline to Tan Son Nhut Air Base. That pipeline delivered the product to Shell, Esso, U. S. Air Force and U. S. Army tankage at the base. The product was received into whatever tankage was available. Aviation, motor gasoline and diesel fuel was delivered to the base by military or commercial tank trucks.

At Tan Son Nhut, aircraft from all four U. S. Services and allied forces (for example, Vietnamese, Thai, Australian) were refueled. Additionally, commercial charters of American, Braniff, Continental, Flying Tigers, and Southern Air Transport were refueled there. Esso, Shell, the U. S. Air Force, and U. S. Army, all participated in refueling operations from the storage facilities mentioned above.

To support Bien Hoa Air Base, Army-controlled (Army or commercial) barges delivered JP–4 fuel from Nha Be to Bu Long where it was pumped into Air Force-controlled tankage at Bien Hoa Air Force Base. Aviation, diesel, and motor gasoline were normally delivered by Army and commercial trucks.

Large quantities of 55-gallon drums and 500-gallon collapsible bags of all types of product were airlifted to upcountry terminal locations. Delivery of these containers was to Army, Marine, Navy, Air Force, or Allied Forces as required, and was subsequently issued to Army, Navy, or Air Force as needed at the point of delivery. It was not unusual for the Army to package JP–4 in 500-gallon bags out of Army storage, and for the Air Force to then deliver the bags to Pleiku, Phu Bai, or Dong Ha where Army, Navy, Marines, or Air Force would use it. In the 3-month siege of Khe Sanh, for example, the Army air-dropped fuel to the Marines for which signed receipts were obviously impossible to obtain.

Supplementing all of the above, the U. S. Air Force bladder-birds out of Tan Son Nhut or Bien Hoa at times flew as much as a million gallons of jet fuel a month to areas isolated or cut off from a ground line of communication and rarely obtained signatures for fuel delivered.

Financial accounting procedures were not used by Army Class

III supply points because of the decision not to extend the stock fund into Vietnam. Signed receipts were many times impossible to obtain from consignees because of the following reasons:

1. Tank trucks loaded with product enroute to Forward Support Areas were destroyed or damaged by enemy action.

2. Deliveries by air were air-dropped if aircraft were unable to land because of enemy fire.

3. All shipment to Forward Support Areas were consigned to Army activities although the Air Force could have been the predominant user of the product.

4. At supply points within Forward Support Areas product was stored and dispensed from rubber bladders and 500-gallon drums with no means to measure quantities delivered to consumers.

5. Self-service supply points were set up and no issue documentation was made at these points even when the consumer was a reimbursable customer.

6. It was impossible to get all reimbursement issue documents collected and forwarded to a central accounting office because of communication difficulties.

A number of steps were taken to reduce the reimbursement accounting problems. The most-far reaching of these is the Memorandum of Understanding between the three Services, wherein the Services were billed and reimbursed for bulk petroleum, oils, and lubricants issues in Vietnam on the basis of the Military Assistance Command, Vietnam, Monthly Bulk Fuels Report, modified to include documented base-level issues and prorated handling losses. All Army agencies have indicated satisfaction with this system. However, the Army Accounting System differs from that of the Navy and Air Force in that financial accountability was not extended by the Army into Vietnam. The Department of the Army had granted a deviation from accounting in accordance with Army Regulation 735–5:

The accounting problems that were encountered in POL support in Vietnam were primarily the result of a requirement for detailed financial accounting for reimbursement procedures based on the bulk fuels report. However, many of the problems of a combat area will be solved only with the assignment of a qualified Contracting Officer's Representative in-country.

The Vietnam experience clearly demonstrated that, in an unstable area, the extent of financial accounting and the method of reimbursement should be decided early in the operation, preferably prior to deployment of forces.

A joint field assistance team would have been of great value in

Vietnam in lessening problems in accounting as well as in assisting in the area of contractor relations and contract administrations.

The relationships and responsibilities of the Defense Supply Agency/ Defense Fuel Supply Center and other Department of Defense (DOD) activities were not clearly defined as to their respective roles in contract administration for POL overseas in DOD Dirctive 4140.25, *Management of Petroleum Products,* January 6, 1965, and the implementing instructions thereto.

Much of the joint Service participation in POL policy making was lost with the inactivation of the Directorate, Petroleum Logistics Policy, Office of the Assistant Secretary of Defense (Installations and Logistics), in 1966. A high-level Joint Petroleum Committee with representation from the Services. Defense Supply Agency, and Joint Chiefs of Staff would fill the void left by the inactivation of the Directorate in 1966 and would enhance overall POL logistics.

Pilferage was a problem. About 5.7 million barrels of fuel was "lost" through pilferage, evaporation and enemy actions. At 15 cents per gallon that is about $36 million. On the Vietnamese economy, it might be three times that amount. The drivers of commercial trucks were generally poor men and carrying 3,000 gallons or more of fuel in a truck was a temptation. Many methods were devised to divert fuel illegally and sell it on the economy. Truck drivers installed false bottoms on tanks, had separate hidden compartments constructed, tampered with seals, forged documents, and took other devious measures to pilfer quantities of fuel from every delivery. A great deal of effort and educating of U.S. military personnel was required to eliminate such practices.

The above ground cross country steel bolted pipelines could be easily uncoupled with a wrench or pliers allowing fuel to be carried away in cans and buckets as it leaked from the line. This usually occurred in areas where villages were close to the pipeline. Some of the fuel taken from pipelines was used for cooking. Several large fires which caused considerable damage were started by such actions.

To assure that the U. S. Government received the full measure of its assets in the custody of commercial suppliers as well as accurate receipts of commercial products from in-country procurements, the following steps were taken in II, III, and IV Corps. A file of authorized customer signature cards was established at each call-forward office. All customers were required to forward one copy of each delivery ticket to the call-forward office. Special imprinting devices were issued to all major customers for imprinting delivery tickets with a coded impression. Contractors were required to log all truck shipments to each customer, each month, in numerical sequence. Contractors were required to submit delivery summaries with supporting delivery tickets to the appropriate call-forward office for verification of deliveries prior to submission of Form DD 250 for billing purposes. Meters were installed at receiving activities. Standard Operating Procedures with check lists were made available to customers for use in receiving contractor deliveries. Training classes for personnel involved with receiving contractor deliveries were conducted. Similar procedures were established by the Navy in I Corps.

Despite the shortcoming the dual distribution system (military and civilian) may have had, it did provide the required support. Without the cooperation and dedication of personnel employed by the commercial contractors, petroleum resupply to U. S. Forces in Vietnam could have been degraded in such a manner as to limit and drastically curtail military operations.

Common Supply Support

The situation facing Army, Navy, and Air Force logisticians in Vietnam during the early days of the build-up was such that no one Service was particularly anxious to support another. Nonetheless, it was recognized as far back as 1962 that overall economies could be realized through Common Supply Support.

Common Supply Support in Vietnam began with the introduction of the U. S. Military Assistance Advisory Group and the assignment of responsibilities to the Navy in 1962 as the designated administrative agency to provide logistic support to the Military Assistance Advisory Group. As advisory forces grew, the support tasks soon grew well beyond that of an administrative agency. Common supply items were issued directly to Army, Air Force, and Marine Corps units, the U.S. Military Assistance Advisory Group staff and to the senior logistics advisers in the four corps tactical zones for further distribution to advisers in the field. Included were subsistence, clothing, and general supplies totaling 3,500 items that were primarily for housekeeping, maintenance, and administration. This system was barely sufficient for the limited initial U. S. involvement.

Primary logistics functions in the northernmost corps tactical zone in Vietnam were assigned to the Navy in October 1965, and to the Army (1st Logistical Command) in the other three corps tactical zone in April 1966. This system continued through the build-up and into the post build-up period.

The biggest drawback of Common Supply Support throughout the Vietnam era was the lack of a definitive list of items for this support. Where common use was a criterion, none of the lists developed for common item support constituted more than a relatively small portion of the total line items stocked by the Military Services in Vietnam. They were, however, in many cases, high-volume demand items.

Efforts by the Department of Defense, Joint Chiefs of Staff, and the Services during these periods to establish a single common supply system in Vietnam were singular in their lack of accomplishment. In November 1965, the Department of Defense had approved a Joint Chiefs of Staff study that recommended a single supply system and tasked the Army with establishment and operation of the proposed system. The Army plan called for implementation in four phases over a twelve month period. The final impact of this plan would have made the Army the sole source of common supply items in the entire theater. While General Westmoreland felt that a single system would be the most economical for responsive long-term support, the peculiar situation in I Corps (predominately Navy-Marine forces ashore and uneasiness of the tactical situation) dictated that the existing system be continued as being least disruptive and most responsive for the short-term support.

As a result of Commander in Chief Pacific recommendations and General Westmoreland's comments, the Department of Defense disapproved the plan in December 1966 and concluded that required procedures for operating integrated depots in South Vietnam were not sufficiently advanced to accommodate a large expansion in common supply at that time. Until further planning could be accomplished and the I Corps assignment could be shifted to the Army, the Navy was to continue to provide I Corps support. Again, in March 1968, a modified expansion plan was submitted for implementation but again disapproved citing the disruptive effect of such an expansion, the reported poor response experienced by the Air Force for common supply items in II, III, and IV Corps, and the continued low demand satisfaction provided by the 1st Logistical Command depots.

Thus, common supply, as it existed in Vietnam throughout the post buildup period, amounted to a continuation of the interim arrangements set up in 1966 among the Services for the support of common items.

The Army implementation in II, III and IV Corps of Common Supply Support was limited initially to the 1965 Navy list of 3,500 items. Late in the post buildup period, Army depots at Long Binh, Cam Ranh Bay, and Qui Nhon were stocking between 2,550 and 2,650 of these items. The system required that Navy and Air Force requests for common supply items in the II, III and IV Corps be submitted to one of the three Army Depots. If stock was not available at the depot receiving the requisition, it was passed via the Inventory Control Center to whichever other in-country depot had stock available. The Services did not have a list of common supply items which showed acceptable substitutes.

When stock was not available, in-country requisitions were normally forwarded to the Continental U.S. via 2d Logistical Command, Okinawa. Due to an early poor record of fill, the Navy and Air Force elected to requisition from the Army on a fill or kill basis. When requisitions were killed by the Army source, the Air Force and the Navy then would re-requisition through their particular service supply system. This situation continued until mid-1969, when both the Navy and Air Force either stopped or substantially reduced the use of fill or kill procedures, indicating that the Army-run common supply system was effective.

Upon the transfer of the logistical support mission from the Naval support activity in Da Nang to the U.S. Army, the 1st Logistical Command directed rescreening of all items declared surplus and excess prior to final disposal action. Over $6 million worth of property was physically moved to the U. S. Army property disposal activity at Da Nang from the Naval support activity. It took twelve months to complete the screening and redistribution of the majority of the items. The bulk of the items were transferred to the Vietnamese Army based on valid requisitions they had outstanding and a U.S. advisor validation of the requirements prior to transfer.

The U. S. Army supported other elements besides the military services. Many of the contractors performing services for the Army were supported by the Army supply system. Many repair parts items used by contractors were either available or could be made available through the Army supply system. U. S. Government contractors in South Vietnam, however, experienced a great deal of difficulty in obtaining support from the U. S. Army supply system. Whether this is a result of the contractors not effectively meshing with the supply system or the supply system's failure to anticipate the nature and extent of contractors' requirements is not completely clear. Nonetheless, there are several factors which are readily apparent.

Contractors were used in Vietnam because construction and service requirements were beyond the capabilities of the assigned military units. Ordinarily a contractor procures his own supplies, but this was not feasible in Vietnam. Therefore, contractors were added to the supply system as a "using unit." In theory this works well, but from a practical viewpoint, it did not work satisfactorily.

The contractor, because of his large scale operation, should not be classified as a normal "using unit." Experience revealed that the direct support unit was unable to handle the multitudinous flow of needed support for the contractor, therefore the attempt to do so resulted in delay and inefficient support to the contractor. To prevent this happening in the future, all large contractors should receive support for their requests directly from the depot.

Contractor operations were different from normal military operations and usually required non-standard supplies. An example was the generator problem. The Vinnell Corporation and Pacific Architects and Engineers operated a number of 1500 kilowatt generators, which supplied electrical power to facilities in South Vietnam. Parts for these generators were incorporated into the supply system as non-standard repair parts and given Federal Stock Numbers. Unfortunately these parts did not move through the depot system fast enough to satisfy the contractors' needs. Since the items often were not available through the Army supply system, the more responsive (and more expensive) contractor procurement sources were frequently used.

Financial Controls

In order to get supplies to Vietnam during the buildup and to stop them once the drawdown began, an appreciation of the funding, in-country procurement activity, and management techniques that were employed in Vietnam and in the United States is necessary.

The Planning, Programing, and Budgeting System was the basic financial management vehicle used by the Army during the early phase of the war in Vietnam to support operations.

The Operations and Maintenance, Army appropriation financed that portion of the logistics system devoted to the procurement, supply management, storage, handling, and second destination transportation of matériel. It also provided the framework for budgeting for consumer funds which were utilized for purchasing operating supplies and equipment to support the deployed forces in Vietnam. The Army decided not to extend the stock fund to Vietnam feeling that the management constraints were too burdensome in a combat environment.

In fiscal year 1966, Operation and Maintenance, Army funds received by U.S. Army Pacific for support of U.S. Army Vietnam were issued to General Accounting Office 86 in U.S. Army Ryukyu

Islands. This was due to a shortage of qualified accounting personnel and adequate automatic data processing capability in Vietnam and further it was an attempt to relieve the U.S. Army Vietnam Commander of the added burden of financial reporting.

By mid fiscal year 1967 the Army approved establishment of the Centralized Financial Management Agency in Hawaii. This agency was given the responsibility for maintaining control over all funds extended to U.S. Army Pacific in support of Vietnam except those allotted in-country and funds allocated to U.S. Army Ryukyu Islands for Okinawa support activities. Table 5 shows Operation and Maintenance, Army, direct fund comparisons.

Establishment of the Centralized Financial Management Agency centralized control and accounting of funds for support of U.S. Army Vietnam out-of-country requirements. The system provided for centralized obligation of funds upon receipt of billing from the supplier. The basic concept of the system was that fund reservations were to be established at Centralized Financial Management Agency based upon receipt of an image copy of all out-of-country requisitions. Essentially there was a policy of free flow of requisitions from U.S. Army Vietnam with dollar accounting and control established at Centralized Financial Management Agency. The weakness of the system was that Centralized Financial Management Agency was not in the requisition channel and consequently was bypassed on numerous requisitions. As a result, bills were received for material without fund reservations having been established at Centralized Financial Management Agency. It was difficult to determine at a given point in time the status of funds

TABLE 5—DIRECT FUND COMPARISONS FOR OPERATION AND
MAINTENANCE, ARMY DURING THE BUILD-UP PERIOD
(IN THOUSANDS OF DOLLARS)

Funds	FY 1965	FY 1966	FY 1967	FY 1968	FY 1969
Appropriated	3,482,910	4,594,200	7,148,477	6,995,132	7,986,310
Basic	3,439,000	3,483,600	5,122,427	6,942,375	7,805,000
Pay Supplemental	43,910	33,400	93,000	52,757	+85,000
Southeast Asia Supplemental	—	1,077,200	1,933,050	—	96,310
Appropriation Transfers & Reprogramming	+63,042	+258,899	+142,571	+1,134,904	−1,835
Southeast Asia	+65,700	+139,600	+45,135	+1,255,234	—
Other	−2,658	+119,299	+97,436	−120,330	−1,835
Total Non-obligated Appropriations Available	3,545,952	4,853,099	7,291,048	8,130,036	7,984,475
Total Obligated	3,545,952	4,853,099	7,290,438	8,129,992	7,984,475
Unobligated	—	—	610	44	—

and fund requirements. To alleviate this situation, Centralized Financial Management Agency proposed that a central control point be established through which all Military Standard Requisitioning and Issue Procedures transaction documents would flow for supply and fund management purpose. The Inventory Control Center, Vietnam, the Aviation Materiel Management Center, and 32d Medical Depot were to play active parts. The 3S (Standard Supply System), which U.S. Army Pacific installed, mechanized supply and financial information for Vietnam and assisted in resolving this problem.

Centralized Financial Management Agency was the proponent of a monthly report (RCS CSCAB–254) which served as the primary source of financial information. However, this occurred at the end of the buildup phase (31 October 1967). During the early years (1965–1967) only limited information was available. If the total financial picture was desired, information had to be requested from U.S. Army Vietnam, U.S. Army Pacific, Army Materiel Command, U.S. Army Ryukyu Islands, Logistics Control Office, Pacific and the Comptroller of the Army.

Centralized Financial Management Agency used tapes for transaction report information or requisition copy images but found that by using this method, reconciliation of supply and fiscal records was virtually impossible. In the first reconciliation, 49,608 requisitions were outstanding.

Since U.S. Army Vietnam had no capability to determine or project funding requirements for procurement of either consumption or stockage items, U.S. Army Pacific provided budget estimates based on the best available records and assumptions. Using historical data to produce costs per man year supported and flying hour costs, U.S. Army Pacific projected matériel costs based on the force structure as provided by Department of the Army.

Budgets for Operation and Maintenance, Army supply operations were based on a combination of U.S. Army Pacific forecasts of matériel requirements, historical costs of supporting military man years in country, and approved changes in the force structure.

It can be seen that a solid financial management plan was not implemented until after the buildup phase in Vietnam. In fact, the Army did not elect to financially account for in-country inventories until 1969 when a system for financial inventory accounting was established for depots. Until that time all formal appropriation accounting for the initial buildup requirements was done at a location outside of Vietnam.

Experience gained in Vietnam proved that financial management must receive concurrent attention and priority with logistics management. When this occurs, effective and efficient matériel management can follow.

Procurement

Early in the buildup, it became apparent that to conserve resources and to meet demanding deadlines it would be necessary to contract for much of the support traditionally provided by military organizations. Thus, the United States Army Procurement Agency, Vietnam was born. During the peak fiscal year 1968—fiscal year 1969 time frame, this Agency awarded and administered contracts valued at approximately one-half billion dollars. Performing these contracts required contractors to employ over 52,000 people.

The first Army procurement organization was established in Vietnam during February 1962. This was the Purchasing and Contracting Office which was assigned to the U.S. Army Support Group, Vietnam. On 1 April 1965, this office was redesignated as the Purchasing and Contracting Division of the 1st Logistical Command. As a result of the build-up of forces, the procurement effort was expanded and on 10 May 1966 the activity was again reorganized and designated as the U.S. Army Procurement Agency, Vietnam and was assigned to the 1st Logistical Command. The commanding officer of U.S. Army Procurement Agency, Vietnam also served on the 1st Logistical Command Staff as the Director of Procurement. The mission of the U.S. Army Procurement Agency, Vietnam was to:

1. Provide responsive procurement support to the combat and combat support elements of the United States Military Assistance Command, Vietnam, the United States Army Vietnam, Free World Military Assistance Forces, and elements of other military or civilian services as directed.

2. Assist the Civil Operations and Revolutionary Development, support the Agency for International Development, and support the U.S. Embassy in the survey and development of industrial, service, and agricultural sources and capabilities to provide increased production in the Republic of Vietnam.

In performance of this mission, the U.S. Army Procurement Agency, Vietnam executed and administered a variety of contracts for supplies, subsistence, and services such as repair and utilities services, electrical power generation and distribution, stevedoring, transportation, equipment maintenance as well as laundry and

miscellaneous services. The following table depicts the dollar value
of these procurements:

PROCUREMENT PROGRAMS BY FISCAL YEAR
(MILLIONS OF DOLLARS)

	1967	1968	1969	1970	1971
Supplies	$ 6.9	$ 11.2	$ 6.7	$ 6.9	$ 2.3
Subsistence	12.0	13.6	22.2	19.8	23.0
Services	156.4	234.3	207.1	210.8	163.7
Totals	$175.3	$259.1	$236.0	$237.5	$189.0

Although these contracts were solicited, negotiated, executed, and
administered in a combat zone, all of the procurement actions
taken were in accordance with the Armed Services Procurement
Regulation and pertinent Army procedures and instructions.
There were no unusual authorities or deviations granted the U.S.
Army Procurement Agency, Vietnam. Their contracts, organization, and operations were reviewed and audited in the same manner
as procurement activities in other overseas areas and in the
continental U.S.

The largest contract, measured in the number of contractor
personnel and dollar value, was the contract for Repair and
Utilities services. The concept of tactical operations in Vietnam
called for the construction of base camps throughout the country
from which tactical operations were conducted. Each base camp consisted of temporary and semipermanent structures which provided
living areas, supply areas, and a base of operations. These base
camps were similar to posts, camps, and stations throughout the
world and required similar Post Engineer services. In addition to
providing Repair and Utilities services, the contractor was also
responsible for the backup maintenance and supply functions to
support the Repair and Utilities mission.

The Repair and Utilities contractor also provided field maintenance and repair parts support for installed equipment such as generators, air conditioners, refrigerators, and pumps, as well as
operating the Class IV supply yards for construction materials. Obtaining Repair and Utilities services by contract was not a new
undertaking. This technique has been utilized in Korea, under
peacetime conditions, for a number of years. The scope and rapid
growth of the Vietnam requirement resulted in situations which
had not previously occurred. The lack of skilled labor in Vietnam,
for example, resulted in the contractor hiring large numbers of
U.S. and Third Country Nationals to maintain the desired level of
performance.

In addition to organizing for performance of the Repair and Utilities mission, the contractor had to perform several functions not usually allied with normal Repair and Utilities activities. In supporting the growth of the Repair and Utilities requirement, available military transportation was insufficient to move the contractor's supplies and materials. The contractor and subcontractor had to use their own resources. In addition, communications throughout Vietnam posed a significant control problem; therefore a separate radio network was established and operated. It was therefore necessary for the contractor to establish a procurement organization to supplement government resources. In each of these instances, the magnitude of the requirement was not envisioned sufficiently in advance to allow in-depth planning that would result in efficient utilization of resources.

The power requirements for military operations in Vietnam were unique compared to previous military operations. In Vietnam, practically all areas were illuminated by floodlights at night for security reasons. The hot, humid climate required a heavy usage of electrical refrigeration and cooling equipment to protect food, medical supplies, and other weather-sensitive materials. Further, the Army's sophisticated communication, transportation, and weapons systems also require increased quantities of electrical power.

During the summer and fall of 1965, the U.S. Forces in Vietnam began to experience a critical shortage of utility type electric power generating equipment. Due to the long lead time in procurement of large generators and the immediate need for electrical power generation, a plan was conceived to send standard size (T–2) petroleum tankers from the mothball fleet to Vietnam and convert them into electrical power generating barges when moored on site. In March 1966, a contract was executed to provide for rehabilitating, manning, and provisioning the ships, then sailing them to Vietnam and mooring them on the planned sites. The turbo-electric generators of the vessels were connected to a transmission cable which led to a transmitter station on shore for further distribution to land line systems. Subsequent contracts were executed to provide for land based power generating facilities to replace these power barges.

The procurement of supplies and equipment in Vietnam was limited, with certain exceptions, to combat emergency requirements. There were two basic reasons for this policy; it acted as a control against inflation by limiting the flow of dollars into the economy and was a supporting factor in the U. S. Balance of Payments Program. Further, the poor quality of Vietnamese manufactured end items compatible with U. S. military requirements made it impractical to consider the local purchase of most equipment.

The variety and magnitude of the services provided U. S. and Free World Forces by contract augmented the logistic system very effectively. The successful techniques and procedures developed by U.S. Army Procurement Agency, Vietnam in providing these procurement services, in the combat zone, will be the basis for contract logistical support in future conflicts.

VIETNAMESE FARMER OPERATES ROTO-TILLER ALONGSIDE PLOW PULLED
BY WATER BUFFALO

GUN TRUCK—5-TON M54A2 "HARDENED" VEHICLE, ABOVE; GUN TRUCK—
5-TON M54A2 MOUNTED WITH STRIPPED DOWN HULL OF ARMORED
PERSONNEL CARRIER, BELOW.

FIELD DEPOT THU DUC STORAGE AREA 5 MILES NORTH OF SAIGON, ABOVE;
FIELD DEPOT THU DUC STORAGE AREA AFTER IMPROVEMENTS, BELOW.

UNLOADING OF 2½-TON TRUCK AT SAIGON PORT.

FISH MARKET AREA IN SAIGON AFTER IMPROVEMENTS, ABOVE; QUI NHON
LOGISTICAL DEPOT, BELOW.

AERIAL VIEW OF NEWPORT

AIR DROP OF SUPPLIES IN OPERATION JUNCTION CITY

ARMORED PERSONNEL CARRIER GIVES 5,000-GALLON TANKER PUSH UP MUDDY HILL TO FIRE SUPPORT BASE, ABOVE; AERIAL VIEW OF VUNG TAU, SHOWING POL JETTY, TANK FARM, AND AIR FIELD, BELOW.

POL STORAGE FARM AT TAY NINH USING BLADDERS FOR STORAGE, ABOVE;
LOADING OF CLASS I SUPPLIES FROM DEPOT AT CHOLON, BELOW.

REFRIGERATION CONTAINERS AND STORAGE AREA AT CHOLON, ABOVE;
2½-TON TRUCK POL CONVOY AT PLEIKU, BELOW.

AMMUNITION SUPPLY POINT UNDER CONSTRUCTION NEAR A FIRE BASE IN KONTUM PROVINCE, CENTRAL HIGHLANDS, ABOVE; CRANE LOADING AMMUNITION ON TO TRANSPORTER FOR SHIPMENT TO AMMUNITION DEPOT, BELOW.

FORK LIFT WITH 175MM SHELLS TO MOVE TO THE STOCK PILE AREA,
VUNG RO BAY, VIETNAM, ABOVE; BERMED OPEN STORAGE COMPLEX
OF THE 542D AMMUNITION FIELD DEPOT, BIEN THU,
VIETNAM, BELOW.

AERIAL VIEW OF AN AMMUNITION STORAGE AREA, CAM RANH BAY,
VIETNAM, ABOVE; ARTILLERY AMMUNITION PREPARED FOR SLING
LOADING BY HELICOPTER, BIEN THU, VIETNAM, BELOW.

FORK LIFT UNLOADING PALLETS OF 105MM HOWITZER ROUNDS FROM A
SEA-LAND VAN, PLEIKU, VIETNAM.

CHAPTER IV

Ammunition Logistics

This chapter identifies the problems that developed in ammunition support. Ammunition is considered to be a "stovepipe" commodity in that it is requisitioned and reported on through a single channel. The high degree of ammunition support provided to the combat elements in Vietnam was the result of intensive management at Department of Defense, Department of the Army, and Theater level, and the dedicated efforts of men in ammunition units in the ammunition depots and supply points in Vietnam.

The buildup in Southeast Asia impacted on the entire spectrum of ammunition logistics: design and development, procurement and production, budgeting, distribution, transportation, storage, personnel and units, reporting procedures, command and control, security, maintenance and disposal.

The Buildup

In March of 1965, the only U.S. Army ammunition stocks in Vietnam were those belonging to the 5th Special Forces units based in Nha Trang and the armed helicopter units based at Tan Son Nhut.

The former was a mixture of modern, World War II and foreign munitions, all in limited quantities re-supplied monthly from Okinawa. The latter was essentially helicopter ammunition: 7.62= mm, 40-mm Grenade, 2.75" Rocket, and various signal flares and smoke grenades.

The stockage on hand fluctuated around 1,500 short tons at Tan Son Nhut which was stored in an old French storage site on the Airbase. Even this quantity was too much for the facility which had safe storage capacity of approximately 900 short tons under a waiver due to its proximity to fuel storage, napalm mixing sites, and the main airbase runway.

Elsewhere in the Pacific Theater, U.S. Army Pacific had ammunition reserves stored in Korea, Japan, Hawaii, Okinawa, and Thailand plus a limited supply in the Department of the Army Forward Floating Depot in the Philippines. These stocks were for the most part reserved for Commander in Chief Pacific contingency plans and were earmarked for deployment with U.S. Army Pacific units. The contingency plan for Southeast Asia stated that units would carry their basic loads and would be supported for the first 180 days by Push Packages of ammunition shipped from Continental U.S. depots.

Based on the decision at the 9–11 April 1965 Hawaii Conference to deploy combat units to Vietnam, several ammunition related actions were implemented: ammunition depot and supply point locations were selected, real estate was acquired, ammunition units were included in force requirements plans, and a stockage objective of 60 days in-country was planned in conjunction with a 30-day off-shore reserve to be established on Okinawa. The 60-day in-country stockage objective was to consist of 45 days at Qui Nhon, Cam Ranh Bay and the Saigon area, and 15 days in Ammunition Supply Points.

Concurrent with this planning and, perhaps a portent of things to come, the 1st Logistical Command requisitioned from the 2d Logistical Command on Okinawa a 15-day supply of ammunition to support the 173d Airborne Brigade which was earmarked for early deployment to Vietnam. However, this requisition was canceled by the 2d Logistical Command as the Push Packages from Continental U.S. would sustain the deploying units until normal pipeline operations could be established. Things didn't work quite that well. The 173d Airborne Brigade deployed rapidly and immediately commenced combat operations and the Push Packages, delivered in 30-day increments were far short of the quantity being consumed and also contained obsolete ammunition such as anti-tank mines, 3.5" rockets, and anti-tank munitions for 90-mm tank guns and 100-mm recoilless rifles. As a consequence, the 1st Logistical Command requisition was purified and initiated anew. This time ammunition, approximately 225 tons, was immediately airlifted from Okinawa to Tan Son Nhut. This action tied up all the available transport aircraft in the theater for a 7-day period and also dangerously overloaded the ammunition storage site at Tan Son Nhut, as this input coupled with the Push Packages totaled more than 4,000 short tons.

From April through June, the ammunition picture was chaotic at best. Push Packages arrived before units, units were diverted from their scheduled debarkation points where their ammunition was offloaded, and ammunition piled up on the beach at Cam Ranh Bay and aboard leased sampans and barges on the Saigon River. The problem was compounded by the delayed arrival of transportation terminal units and Ammunition Companies to clear the port and manage the receipt, storage, issue, and requisitioning of ammunition.

With the establishment of Headquarters U.S. Army Vietnam in July 1965, some order began to appear in the ammunition logistics picture. The arrival of the 182d Ammunition Stock Control Detachment along with one ammunition company and several detachments also helped although difficulties were still experienced in the next six months. These centered around the lack of ammunition command and control units, the lack of senior ammunition officers and staffs at Headquarters U.S. Army Vietnam and the 1st Logistical Command, and the malassignment of the 182d Stock Control Detachment to the Saigon Area Support Command. The 182d, through co-ordination with the few ammunition units that had by then arrived in Vietnam (one company and two detachments) began the task of establishing an ammunition support system. Based on estimates of the ammunition on the ground and on unofficial counts of weapons densities, stockage objectives were computed and requisitions were initiated to maintain the 60-day stockage objective in-country.

With the buildup proceeding, the 182d Stock Control Detachment, without direct access to the 1st Logistical Command Ammunition Staff Office, continued to manage the ammunition support program. Requisitions were developed and passed to the 2d Logistical Command who in turn either filled the requisitions from stocks on hand or passed them to Headquarters U.S. Army Pacific. If Headquarters U.S. Army Pacific was unable to fill the requisitions from other theater assets, the requisitions were passed on to the Ammunition Procurement and Supply Agency. It didn't take long—three months—to exhaust available U.S. Army Pacific assets. By then it was clear something else had to be done. Consumption rates were higher than planning had foreseen and weapons density calculations were inaccurate.

Improvements were made, some almost immediately, others later. Some of the delays in the requisitioning system were eliminated when, in July 1965, Okinawa was by-passed. Requisitions then flowed directly to Ammunition Procurement and Supply Agency with information to Headquarters U.S. Army Pacific's Inventory Control Point, who filled requisitions to the extent possible and notified Ammunition Procurement and Supply Agency of those requisitions on which U.S. Army Pacific had taken action. Even so, improvement in reporting was warranted to the extent that the Secretary of the Army dispatched a team of ammunition experts to Vietnam to examine the problems incident to the validity and timeliness of the U.S. Army Vietnam "U.S. Army Worldwide Ammunition Reporting System (WARS), RCS CSGLD-1322" feeder report.

The findings and recommendations of this team represented a critical upturn in ammunition logistics and are synopsized as follows:

1. Immediately implement the doctrine for Ammunition Service in the Theater of Operations (FM 9–6) throughout the theater.

2. Organize an Ammunition Staff headed by a full colonel, reporting to the G–4, U.S. Army Vietnam.

3. Establish an Ammunition Group as quickly as possible to provide operational control and management over ammunition and ammunition units.

4. Reassign the 182d Stock Control Detachment to G–4, U.S. Army Vietnam.

5. Assign all ammunition units to include the 182d Stock Control Detachment to the Ammunition Group upon its establishment.

While these recommendations were never fully implemented, the extent to which they were resulted in an overwhelming improvement for ammunition logistics. An operational staff headed by a full colonel was activated at Headquarters U.S. Army Vietnam. The 52d Ammunition Group Headquarters and Headquarters Company was activated, sent to Vietnam in February 1966, and used as the nucleus of the Directorate of Ammunition at 1st Logistical Command. The 182d Stock Control Detachment was assigned to the Ammunition Directorate at 1st Logistical Command. Command and Control of Ammunition Units was obtained through the expedited arrival of Battalion Headquarters and Headquarters Companies and the establishment of Directors of Ammunition at each of the Area Logistics Commands. Of equal importance, a system was developed whereby the G–3, U.S. Army Vietnam provided valid weapons densities to the 182d Stock Control Detachment.

Ammunition Supply Rates

The overriding issue during the time frame January—June 1966, (more important than the port thru-put of ammunition which will be addressed later) was that of determining valid supply rates. The supply rates had far-reaching implications in that they impact on the length of time D to P stocks would last. (D to P stocks are those war reserves of ammunition which are stocked in peace time to provide the necessary reservoir of ammunition to sustain combat operations until such time that the planned production base can be activated and producing at a rate which equals consumption. The designation "D" signifies deployment date or the date that hostilities commence and "P" signifies production day, hence D-P stocks.) Supply rates are also a factor in determining when, in what quantities, and at what rate production of ammunition should be established. For these reasons, it was virtually necessary that realistic supply rates be determined and approved, so that necessary funds could be provided in the revised fiscal year 1966, 1967, and 1968 budgets.

Prior to the onset of the buildup in Vietnam, the authorized ammunition expenditure rates (supply rates) were published in Supply Bulletin 38–26. These rates had been derived from historical data generated from World War II and the Korean conflict and modified by subsequent studies and war gaming exercises. The alarming scale at which most of these consumption rates were being exceeded in Vietnam, due to the unique environmental conditions and operational concepts, resulted in a dramatic drawdown of reserve ammunition stocks.

Headquarters U.S. Army Pacific in coordination with Headquarters U.S. Army Vietnam and Department of the Army concurrence, issued U.S. Army Pacific Regulation 710–15 on 9 June 1966, titled Theater Required Supply Rates for Ammunition—SEA. Essentially, this regulation provided for two rates; one being the Theater Stockage Objective Rate which provided the basis for determining U.S. Army Vietnam's Stockage Objective; and the other rate being the Required Supply Rate for the authorized expenditure rate which was the basis for requisitioning replacement of combat consumption. Provisions were made for necessary rate changes and the regulation was updated semiannually. These rates, in rounds per weapon per day or rounds per unit per day, when multiplied by the applicable weapons or unit density determined a day of supply. This day of supply for each line item was utilized in computing stockage objectives and requisitioning objectives.

At the October 1967 Munitions Conference at Headquarters U.S. Army Pacific, the dual rate was discontinued and a single Required Supply Rate based on the highest six months consumption period was substituted to bring rates in line with the latest consumption experience data. Subsequent semi-annual ammunition conferences were held at Headquarters U.S. Army Pacific for purposes of revising rates to insure their validity and to resolve ammunition maintenance problems. In the 1968 fall conference, the rates were again revised to reflect two rates, an Intense Combat Rate and a Theater Sustaining Rate. These changes were the outcome of the consumption experienced in the 1968 *Tet* offensive and resulted in a significant tonnage reduction in the U.S. Army Vietnam Stockage Objective and in the Offshore Reserve. The 60-day in-country stockage objective was based on 30 days at the Intense Combat Rate and 30 days at the Theater Sustaining Rate whereas the offshore reserve was based on 30 days at the Intense Combat Rate. During fiscal year 1969 three ammunition conferences were held at Headquarters U.S. Army Pacific wherein joint Department of the Army-U.S. Army Pacific revisions to the Required Supply Rates were hammered out. The fact that flexibility was allowed contributed significantly to the success of the overall ammunition support in the Vietnam conflict.

Subsequent to the initiation of expenditure rates for U.S. and Free World Forces in Vietnam, similar rates were approved by Commander in Chief Pacific for Vietnamese Forces which were integrated into the separate ammunition supply system in support of the South Vietnamese Army. This system, known as the Vietnam Ammunition Procedures, had been established in 1964. Essentially, it began as a "push" system, but later in conjunction with rate integration became a "pull" system. The system was managed by Ammunition Procurement and Supply Agency who received from J-4, Military Assistance Command, Vietnam, a forecast of the ensuing 120 days consumption. The effectiveness of this system is attributed to its small scope and intensive management efforts by both Military Assistance Command, Vietnam, and Ammunition Procurement and Supply Agency as the increase in the tempo of the South Vietnamese Army combat effort increased.

Ammunition Reporting

Ammunition stock status reporting also played a significant role. The ammunition logistics system demands a comprehensive and timely report, but such a report did not exist at the onset of the buildup in Vietnam. However, the necessity for such a report was soon evident, and a program was initiated to establish a meaningful report.

The ammunition reporting systems in effect on 1 January 1965 were peacetime oriented and were adequate for that environment. Within the Pacific Theater two reports existed. For management of munitions within the U.S. Army Pacific Theater, an *Asset Balance Report* was prepared and furnished monthly to the U.S. Army

Pacific Inventory Control Point by each subordinate command to include U.S. Army Support Command Vietnam. The report was prepared manually or by computer, dependent on the capability of each subordinate command. It contained the data pertinent to peacetime management and was adequate for a peacetime environment. The second report was the *Ordnance Ammunition Stock Status Report*. This was called the ORD 26 report due to its unique reports control symbol—ORD 26 R1 and was used by the Munitions Command for worldwide management of ammunition. This report, submitted on a quarterly basis, was consolidated at major command levels except in the U.S. Army Pacific theater where each subordinate command submitted individual reports direct to the National Inventory Control Point at Ammunition Procurement and Supply Agency (Ammunition Procurement and Supply Agency was established as an ammunition procurement supply agency under the munitions command). The exception was based on the fact that all ammunition assets stored in the theater were not theater-owned assets but included stocks in Department of the Army ownership accounts over which the theater had no control. These assets were primarily in the Department of the Army Forward Depot and Department of the Army Forward Floating Depot ownership accounts. The excessive manual effort and time required to prepare this report limited its usefulness to a historical record. It consisted of data for each line item typed on 12 by 18 inch preprinted forms and, depending on the subordinate command, consisted of up to 300 pages with as many as 60 pages of clarifying notes. The preparation efforts resulted in a submission date of about 60 days subsequent to the cutoff date. The content of this report, coupled with its frequency and age of data at submission, negated its value as a wartime management tool (although it did provide the National Inventory Control Point with the necessary munitions data for asset and distribution planning and determination of procurement objectives in peacetime).

Prior to the onset of the buildup, the ORD 26 report posed an almost impossible task for the limited resources of the small ammunition detachment of the US Army Support Command. With the establishment of U.S. Army Vietnam and the advent of the buildup, the task of preparing this report was a nearly impossible one for the 182nd Stock Control Detachment, and the report failed to provide necessary and timely information to the National Inventory Control Point. Relief from the requirement for U.S. Army Vietnam was sought by Headquarters U.S. Army Pacific in mid-1965 and was reluctantly granted in July 1965. Meanwhile, Department of the Army was involved in a program to develop a replacement report for the ORD 26 report. In July 1965, the efforts of this program resulted in the *Worldwide Ammunition Reporting System,* the 1322 report due to a new reports control symbol (RCSGLD 1322 (R1)). The intial implications of establishing this report were that there would be relief for the preparing elements in that it was desired on a semi-monthly frequency and required 98 elements of data for each line item.

Based on recommendations from Commander in Chief U.S. Army Pacific to Department of the Army and prior to the initiation of the 1st report in September 1965, the report was revised to the extent that the frequency was changed to monthly, the cutoff date was changed from the last day of the month to the 26th of the month, and the due date in Ammunition Procurement and Supply Agency for the theater rollup was moved back from the 5th of the following month to the 15th.

The Inventory Control Point at U.S. Army Pacific responsible for rolling up the sub-command feeder reports into a single theater report was faced with a dilemma in that the Theater Asset Balance Report did not contain all the necessary input for the 1322 report. Alternatively, the input data for the 1322 report did not provide all the necessary information required for management of theater assets.

Confining the comments to U.S. Army Vietnam, the problem was overcome by a complex but workable system. The report data was assembled each month and a member of the 182d Stock Control Detachment hand carried it to the Inventory Control Point at U.S. Army Pacific. There the courier provided the necessary interpretation for the theater rollup, then accompanied an Inventory Control Point courier to Ammunition Procurement and Supply Agency to assist that agency in further interpreting the data.

The necessity for a courier continued as the buildup progressed and the reporting system went through a period of purification. With the establishment of the Directorate of Ammunition in the 1st Logistical Command in late 1965 and the organizational relocation of the 182d Stock Control Detachment as an integral part of that office, the situation improved. Physically, the Detachment moved from a warehouse in downtown Saigon to take up residence in two pyramidal tents on the front lawn of the 1st Logistical Headquarters. While this move served to improve the communications between the Directorate and the Stock Control Detachment, the environment subjected stock records files to constant ruination by humidity, rain, mud, and dust. This situation continued until late in 1966 when the total Directorate Office moved into newly erected Quonset huts adjacent to the 1st Logistical Headquarters.

Crucial not only to the management of ammunition logistics in Vietnam, but to the reporting system as well was the amount of ammunition in-transit to and within Vietnam. Obtaining visibility of this ammunition was slowly but effectively overcome through the improvement in the communications system and by the then formalized structure of the Directorates of Ammunition in each of the Area Support Commands.

The situation was further improved in 1st Logistical Command by the arrival of two Department of the Army civilian management and reporting experts dispatched by the Munitions Command at U.S. Army Vietnam's request. These two civilian personnel made a significant contribution during their six-month stay. By the time they departed, just prior to mid-1966, the 1st Logistical Command was capable of not only managing ammunition assets in a professional manner, but were also producing an acceptable 1322 report. By mid-1966, the volume of the report and its related preparation had reached unforeseen proportions. The U.S. Army Pacific Inventory Control Point, newly reorganized and titled the Materiel Management Agency, was hard put to roll up such a voluminous report for the theater.

The problem was magnified at the National Inventory Control Point not only by the turbulence in ammunition stock status in the Pacific Theater but also by the reverberations experienced in all other major commands as the result of significant shifts and activity in their stock status which occurred from their contribution of ammunition to Vietnam.

As a consequence, the Munitions Command initiated a program to automate the preparation of the 1322 Report. In essence each major command was to input by card or tape the information that heretofore had been typed on blank formats for the 1322 report. A Munitions Command team visited Headquarters U.S. Army Pacific in late 1966 to present the program and discuss input requirements. As the requirement unfolded, it was apparent that the conversion of the theater rollup to cards would entail a greater effort than the manual production of the reports. U.S. Army Pacific non-concurred in this program at the time. However, in early 1967, in recognition of the need for improving and automating ammunition management within the theater, Headquarters U.S. Army Pacific established a team to accomplish this objective. The objective was two-fold: develop a computer program that would provide the optimum in ammunition management and that would also provide theater input directly to the National Inventory Control Point for the 1322 report. The concept was developed and implemented within six months.

Included in the system design were the necessary programs for each subordinate command (Korea, Japan, Hawaii, and Vietnam), taking into consideration the peculiarities of operations and available computer equipment. Teams were dispatched to each subordinate command to implement the system. The team dispatched to U.S. Army Vietnam carried completely developed programs for application to the UNIVAC 1004/1005. The implementation progressed smoothly and within two weeks time the system was installed and operating on shared time with a locally adjacent Machine Record Unit across the street from the 1st Logistical Command.

However, this was only an interim measure and subsequently the system was reprogrammed for application to the IBM 360/50 equipment at the 14th Inventory Control Center. The initial report was key-punched and airmailed to the U.S. Army Pacific Inventory Control Point in September 1967. Once the installation of the autodin transceiver system was completed in 1967, the cards were dispatched via autodin direct from the terminal drop in U.S. Army Vietnam to U.S. Army Pacific. The team had developed and was prepared to implement automation of depot stock control which would not only further improve the management of ammunition at the depot level, but would also provide directly daily input of management information and monthly 1322 input data to the 182d Stock Control Detachment. However, other overriding priorities for available computer time, coupled with the pressure of day to day commitments at the Ammunition Supply Depots precluded the application of automation to the management of depot operations. As a consequence the total automated management information system was not accomplished.

Ammunition Shortages

Almost from the onset ammunition shortages developed. Some shortages initially evolved from port thru-put problems and in-country distribution problems. The effects of these shortages were blunted to a degree in some instances by application of Available Supply Rates and by airlift of ammunition from the offshore reserve on Okinawa. These shortages were generally short lived and correctable within the capability of the system. However long term shortages also developed which were not easily overcome.

On the one hand were those long term shortages which prevailed from the onset. On the other hand were those shortages which developed in late 1966 which were attributed to the unforeseen high consumption rates and the inability of the Continental U.S. production base to expand at a pace consistent with the buildup of forces in Vietnam.

In the former category were shortages related to ammunition items which were: developed for, or highly applicable to, Southeast Asia, were either still in the research and development or product improvement phase, or so newly into production that required production schedules had not been attained. Examples of items in this category were the 40-mm ammunition for the M75 helicopter armament system, M557 Fuze for 81-mm Mortar, the new family of antipersonnel artillery ammunition, the 2.75" rocket, and the M564/M565 family of Mechanical Time, Superquick and Mechanical Time artillery fuzes. Most of these shortages were ultimately resolved through adherence to controlled expenditures or Available Supply Rates, and temporary use of substitute items.

In the latter category, an entirely different situation existed. Certain ammunition items were being expended at such a high rate that D to P stocks, as well as all other available assets, would be consumed to the extent that the situation would culminate in a zero balance in-country before production could catch up to expenditures (P-day). A reevaluation was made to encourage a reduction in the Required Supply Rate and application of stringent Available Supply Rates where necessary to preclude additional leadtime for production expansion. Commander U.S. Military Assistance Command, Vietnam, immediately conducted a detailed analysis of the worldwide asset status contained in the 1322 report and notified Commander in Chief Pacific on 7 September 1966 that eight ammunition items would reach zero balance in the near future and the situation would not be alleviated even with immediate increases in production due to order and shiptime limitations. Concurrently, Commander in Chief U.S. Army Pacific's analysis revealed that 21 additional items would also reach zero balance in forthcoming months.

At an ammunition conference at Commander in Chief Pacific in October 1966, the correlation of data and a review of the facts emphasized the gravity of the situation. Immediate action was initiated at the highest levels of the Department of Defense and the Department of the Army to bring the situation under control. At the Deputy Chief of Staff for Logistics level, the Office of Special Assistant for Munitions, headed up by Brigadier General Henry A.

Rasmussen was informally established on 14 November 1966 and formally chartered on 15 December 1966 for the express purpose of putting the necessary resources together to provide intensive overall management of forty combat critical high dollar value ammunition items. A corollary action involved the establishment of the Department of the Army Allocation Committee Ammunition in September 1966. This committee, under the control of Deputy Chief of Staff for Logistics, was concerned with the allocation, distribution and redistribution of all allocable ground ammunition. Ammunition was designated as allocable when actual or potential demand was determined to be greater than supply availability. The number of allocable items increased steadily from the initial eight items to ninty-seven by late 1969. Initially, the Department of the Army Allocation Committee Ammunition met almost daily. However, the frequency soon stabilized to a monthly schedule and by February of 1970, the Committee was meeting bi-monthly. The task undertaken by these two agencies was successful in alleviating the gravity of the envisioned shortages to the extent that no combat operations failed or were unduly influenced in their outcome by lack of adequate ammunition.

It soon became apparent that multi-service implications for certain ammunition items indicated a need for resolution at the joint Service level. In recognition of this problem, the Deputy Chief of Staff for Logistics on 27 January 1967 forwarded a Memorandum of Understanding to the Logistics Chief of each of the other Services, recommending the establishment of the Military Services Ammunition Allocation Board. On 20 April 1967, with the concurrences of the Chiefs of Staff of the Army and the Air Force, the Chief of Naval Operations, and the Commandant of the Marine Corps, this Board was formally approved. The Military Services Ammunition Allocation Board charter provided for the allocation and control of the distribution and redistribution on a worldwide basis of selected items of ground ammunition common to two or more services. The Office, Special Assistant for Munitions, was reorganized into the Directorate of Ammunition, Office of the Deputy Chief of Staff for Logistics, in early 1968 (with expanded mission to cover all ammunition items) and continues in existence at this writing. Three examples of short supply ammunition and actions taken to resolve the shortages follow:

The first item is the 2.75 inch Rocket. This rocket was originally designed as an air to air weapon, however circumstances in Vietnam led to the weapon being used primarily in an air to ground role. The increased number of aircraft employed using the 2.75 inch rocket increased the demand to a degree that production capability and production capacity was not available to meet the demand. The Army was designated as the service manager for the 2.75 inch rocket procurement. The Army accordingly established a project manager for the rocket in December 1965. The initial task for the project manager was to find commercial contractors with the capability and capacity to produce quality components and deliver the quantities desired by the Services. Contracts were terminated with producers who could not meet delivery schedules and incentive awards were offered for production above scheduled quantities. These measures were successful in obtaining the required stock of rockets and cost reductions from $88 to approximately $39 per rocket. Since 1965, over 27 million 2.75 inch rockets have been produced. In addition, rocket reliability was improved from 80 percent to over 99 percent, a 17 pound High Explosive warhead with increased lethality and cost effectiveness has been produced, a proximity fuze and flechette warhead have been produced and fielded, and safety devices have been developed.

The second item, the 4.2 inch high explosive cartridge saw production lagging behind usage till February 1968. This was due to poor forecasting. After improving this fault, production rates actually equaled or exceeded the usage rates.

The third item, the 105-mm cartridge, both the high explosion and illuminating types, was in critical status through April of 1967. This situation was primarily caused by the continuing deployment of troop units not included in support programs and the lead time required for the production base to accelerate to meet these increased requirements.

Munitions Procurement

Of the many facets of ammunition logistics, the role of design, development, and product improvement were especially significant. The adverse weather and terrain, new combat concepts, and triple canopied jungle growth seriously influenced the storage and explosive effects of ammunition. The situation also dictated the hurried design and development of special purpose munitions such as the tunnel destruction kit or extensive product improvement as in the case of the 2.75 inch rocket. In the latter example, the size of the warhead more than doubled, the types of warheads expanded, the fuzes were completely redesigned, and the overall reliability increased from 80 percent to 97 percent.

To further compound the overall situation, Department of the Army had estimated ammunition expenditures for fiscal year 1966 to be the sustaining rate, 54 percent of the U.S. Army Pacific rates set forth in SB 38–26, and the fiscal year 1966 budget was constrained initially by this factor. This constraint was removed by supplemental budget action, but valuable leadtime had been lost.

To support the ammunition consumption and stockage requirements during 1965–1970, the munitions procurement programs increased as shown in Table 6.

TABLE 6—MUNITIONS PROGRAMS, FISCAL YEARS 1965–1970
(IN MILLIONS OF DOLLARS)

Fiscal Year	Army Total	Army Southeast Asia
1965	338	303
1966	1313	853
1967	1329	1007
1968	2328	2266
1969	2913	2719
1970	1731	1456

These programs provided for support of U.S. Army Vietnam and South Vietnamese Army forces as well as other Free World Forces which were supported from U.S. Army assets. The requirements on which the programs were based included ammunition consumed, on hand, in off-shore reserves, and in the pipeline, and provided for the building of U.S. combat divisions to a peak strength in fiscal year 1969.

With the buildup in Southeast Asia, munitions requirements increased significantly. This placed considerable strain on procurement agencies of the military departments since they were operating at peacetime personnel levels and under peacetime constraints. Required resources were not mobilized, as they were in previous wars, to support the increased munitions procurement activity. Although sufficient flexibility was provided in the Armed Services Procurement Regulations to allow timely contract placement through negotiation, there was a tendency to tighten rather than relax pre-contract administrative controls. This anomaly was heightened by the emphasis at the highest levels of government on obtaining maximum competition through the means of formal advertisement; or alternatively, if negotiated procurements were utilized, competition was required. This tightening of controls, coupled with the emphasis on competition, created a serious obstacle to the timely execution of contracts. Contracting for ammunition was further inhibited by a lack of interest by private enterprise, shortages in trained procurement personnel, dependency on foreign sources for certain munitions components, time required for processing Secretarial determinations and findings, cancellation of administrative leadtime, fluctuating requirements, and limited capability of the production base. A few of these factors are discussed in the following paragraphs.

Considering the impact of large expenditures of munitions on the national economy and to ensure that the procurement actions were properly executed with maximum competition, Secretary McNamara promulgated a directive in July 1965 requiring certain approvals for all contracts awarded in support of Southeast Asia operations, when the basis of procurement was shifted from competitive to noncompetitive. This directive required "before the fact" Service Secretarial approval for awards over one million dollars and Assistant Secretary of Defense (Installations and Logistics) approval of awards in excess of ten million dollars. If the exigency was such that extraordinary procurement actions were utilized to ensure continuity of production, then an after-the-fact review and notation was required. In 1969, in recognition of the fact that the buildup had been accomplished and that the above control had been established during a period of increasing procurement activity and was based on a concern that the exigencies of this activity tended unnecessarily to cause a shift from competitive procurement, this control was rescinded. This recision highlighted the need for continued maximum emphasis on competitive procurement.

The established mobilization plans included the provision of production of munition metal parts by planned mobilization producers in private industry. In response to the munitions requirements generated from the buildup in Southeast Asia, the necessity for rapid acceleration of munitions production developed almost overnight. In the absence of full mobilization of national resources, these planned producers did not feel a strong obligation to respond to the needs of the Department of Defense.

Historically, the decisions pertinent to the production of munition metal parts have culminated in situations whereby contract delivery schedules ran out in February of a given year. To maintain continuity of production, thus avoiding shut-down and start-up cost, follow-on procurement needed to be placed in the preceding July-August time frame. However, since funds were not normally available until the July–August time frame, the munitions program could not be released as a total package at that time. Therefore, munitions items were required to be broken out by component for procurement. The time available precluded the letting of all the necessary contracts in a manner designed to ensure the best interest of the government. Experience indicated that a minimum of six months administrative leadtime was required to accomplish quality procurement and a minimum of three months was essential for reorder leadtime. To circumvent this lack of adequate leadtime, shortcuts were taken in the form of letter contracts, utilization of option clauses, and non-competitive procurements; or alternatively, production schedules were extended to retain continuity of production and bridge the delay. These shortcuts and alternatives were costly to the Army.

Ammunition Units and Personnel

Just as contingency plans depended on mobilization of private enterprise to augment in-house ammunition production capability, so too, did they envision mobilization of reserve forces. Since the number of ammunition support units required in time of war greatly exceed the number required in peacetime, these contingency plans provided for the selective activation of ammunition support units to accompany large scale deployments of combat units. Mobilization of reserve units did not take place and the peacetime ammunition support structure was grossly inadequate for the task. A Continental U.S. training base for military personnel was almost non-existent as Continental U.S. depots and post, camp, and station storage areas were largely civilianized. This same condition prevailed at the National Inventory Control Point. In short, the Army's ammunition qualified military personnel and organic units were fully committed to peacetime support operations. Additional necessary support existed only in reserve units and they were essentially inaccessible for the conflict at hand. This shortage delayed the activation and deployment of ammunition units to Vietnam and resulted in a shortage of ammunition management skilled officers, warrant officer, and enlisted men to staff the various headquarters and operating units. For example a detachment, deployed in late 1965, was formed at Fort Devens with the detachment commander being a master sergeant with no ammunition experience whatsoever, being instead a transportation Non Commissioned Officer with a truckmaster's Military Occupation Specialty. None of his personnel were experienced in ammunition renovation either. Although all were ammunition handlers, MOS 55B, less than 10 percent were school trained. The detachment had a renovation capability in name only and required civilian augmentation to provide on-site training.

At the beginning of the Vietnam buildup, the Army was in the process of converting the logistics support system to the Combat

Support To The Theater Army concept. Under this concept, ammunition support is accomplished as an Army-wide service with the command and operational control of ammunition and other commodity oriented systems vested in a Group or Brigade Headquarters as appropriate. Since the total conversion was incomplete and untried in combat a decision was made to remain with the Logistical Command concept in Vietnam as opposed to assigning all ammunition units to the command and control of the 52d Ammunition Group. Ammunition battalions, once they arrived in-country were, for control purposes, assigned to a General Support Group or Field Depot Command or direct to Army Support Commands as separate battalions. Hence, the ammunition channel of communication was from an Ammunition Battalion to a Group or Depot Command to the Director of Ammunition at the appropriate Area Logistics Command to the Director of Ammunition at 1st Logistical Command.

The buildup of ammunition support units continued to lag behind the increase in combat and combat support units to the extent that a balanced ratio of ammunition support units to units supported was not achieved until 1967. The initial ammunition supply units to deploy to Vietnam were two ammunition supply detachments which arrived in May 1965. By Tables of Organization and Equipment, these units had little or no equipment and were designed to be attached to a conventional Tables of Organization and Equipment 9–17 ammunition company where they could augment the handling capability of the company by 150 short tons per day. By August 1965, the number of ammunition units had increased to four supply detachments, one ammunition company, and one stock control detachment. In September, three additional ammunition companies had arrived while the supported force had increased to two and two-thirds division equivalents. The first ammunition battalion Headquarters and Headquarters Company 3d Ordnance Battalion, arrived in November 1965 and assumed command of the subordinate units and became the 3d Ordnance Battalion (Ammo). The battalion immediately moved to Long Binh to assume operational control of the Long Binh Ammunition Supply Depot and the two companies and detachments already on hand. The second battalion to arrive, the 191st, moved to Cam Ranh Bay, was assigned to the 504th Field Depot, and assumed the operational control of the Cam Ranh Bay Ammunition Supply Depot and command of the two companies and two detachments on hand. Subsequently, the 3d and last ammunition Battalion Headquarters to arrive, the 184th, moved to Qui

Nhon, and was assigned directly to the Qui Nhon Area Logistics Support Command as a separate battalion. The Battalion assumed the operational responsibility of operating a U.S. depot within a South Vietnamese depot until late 1966 when a wholly owned U.S. depot was developed at a separate location. The Da Nang Area Logistics Command in the I Corps area did not receive an Ammunition Battalion Headquarters and Headquarters Company at first. The three ammunition companies and one detachment in the Da Nang Area were among a number of reports units assigned directly to the 80th General Service Group until the 336th Ordnance Battalion (Ammo) Headquarters and Headquarters Company, a National Guard unit, was activated and deployed to Vietnam in July 1968 as an aftermath of the 1968 *Tet* offensive. This battalion was deactivated and redeployed in July 1969. At that time the 528th Ammunition Battalion (Provisional) was formed and remained as the command and control element for ammunition units in support of I Corps. In September 1970 the 528th Headquarters and Headquarters Company was redeployed and the ammunition units split up among the 26th and 80th General Support Units where they were assigned to various types of battalions for command and control. In early 1971 when the command and control of ammunition for the Laotian incursion indicated a need for these units to be assigned to an ammunition battalion another provisional battalion Headquarters and Headquarters Company was formed and all ammunition units assigned to it.

While this overall organization provided for the systematic and orderly processing of ammunition matters, there was room for improvement. The capabilities of the battalion staff were never fully exercised and the delays incident to processing actions through these unrelated supply channels comprised of staffs and commanders unfamiliar with ammunition logistics resulted in unwarranted time-consuming delays. This observation is borne out by the operations of the 3rd Ordnance Battalion during the incursion into Cambodia in early 1970 unencumbered by a unique organizational relationship as a separate battalion reporting directly to the Saigon Support Command with free access to the Director of Ammunition at G–4, U.S. Army Vietnam. (1st Logistical Command was de-activated in early 1970). The successes achieved in this operation were instrumental in de-activating the Saigon Support Command (Directorate of Ammunition) shortly after the successful completion of this operation.

The revision of the 9–17 Table of Organization and Equipment to change the ammunition company magazine platoon leaders from commissioned officers, MOS 4514, to Warrant Officers, MOS 411A, resulted in a significant drawdown on the skilled senior non-commissioned officer corps as this was the source from which this sudden demand was filled. The majority of the ammunition personnel who were instrumental in developing and operating the ammunition logistics system completed their one year tours and redeployed. Not only were there few if any qualified personnel to replace them, but the turnover was so complete over such a short time span that many lessons learned through experience had to be learned again. While the impact of each subsequent cycle was lessened, the initial cycle re-emphasized the need for a continuing Continental U.S. training base.

Transportation of Ammunition

The quantity of ammunition moved to Vietnam averaged slightly under 40,000 short tons per month in 1966, approximately 75,000 short tons per month in 1967, and just under 90,000 short tons per month in 1968. In February and March of 1968, receipts exceeded 100,000 short tons per month.

The problems in Continental U.S. ports encompassed an initial lack of adequate ship bottoms, the glutting of ports with ammunition cargo, and an inadequate number of berthing facilities. The resolution of these difficulties was relatively easy when compared to those faced in Vietnam.

The lack of adequate ports and port facilities in Vietnam required initially that all ammunition had to be offloaded onto barges and lighters for transport to shore. From the shore it was moved by truck.

Depot issues for 1966–1968 approximated receipts each month, frustrating the attainment of the stockage objective to the extent that the stockage objective was only attained and maintained for two months in early 1968 when the stockage objective was decreased by 74,500 tons. Had the capability existed to routinely offload each ammunition ship as it arrived, the stockage objective could have been maintained to the extent of availability of assets from Continental U.S. almost from the beginning. The situation was compounded by the Army's responsibility for offloading Air Force munitions at Cam Ranh and Saigon. In 1965 Air Force tonnage alone increased from 2,576 short tons in January to 23,000 Short tons in December 1965. Air Force munitions requirements also increased each year.

There were three major ports for offloading ammunition; Da

Nang, Cam Ranh Bay, and Saigon. Other ports that played a lesser role in ammunition offloading were Qui Nhon and Vung Tau.

At Da Nang, the amount of ammunition offloaded for the Army by the Navy was relatively small when compared to that of the Air Force and the Marine Corps. The total stockage objective was slightly under 20,000 tons. With the redeployment of the 3rd Marine Division in late 1969 the situation changed to the extent that the Army became the largest user and the stockage objective increased to approximately 45,000 short tons. The ammunition was largely distributed among 7 Ammunition Supply Points. Initially all ships were offloaded in the outer harbor, although an isolated LST ramp was constructed and used for redistribution up and down the coast.

At Qui Nhon all ammunition ships were offloaded off-shore as sand bars at the river mouth precluded bringing oceangoing ships even into the outer harbor until 1967. In adverse weather with high seas running ammunition ships could not discharge and had to put to sea for safety. (This same condition existed in Da Nang until a breakwater was constructed in 1968). An LST ramp was also available inside the harbor for coastal movement.

At Cam Ranh Bay, a natural harbor, ammunition ships were offloaded in the outer reaches of the harbor, and the ammunition was barged or lightered ashore just as at Da Nang and Qui Nhon. A DeLong pier was implaced specifically for ammunition in late 1966. Here too LST ramps were available for coastal movements of ammunition. Only at Cam Ranh Bay was an optimum operational arrangement established. However, the logistical remoteness of this location to the supported units and the need for transhipment of ammunition to more active ammunition depots precluded more effective utilization.

At Vung Tau, ammunition for the Delta region was offloaded. A pier was available, however the depth of the water precluded fully loaded vessels from offloading ammunition and the facility saw little use. Ammunition was largely discharged into barges for direct movement to the delta while the overflow to those needs was stored in a large Ammunition Supply Point at Vung Tau.

Saigon was the most active of all the ammunition ports. This is attributed to the stockage objective at Saigon Support Command being almost double that of any other support command, all South Vietnamese Army ammunition initially being offloaded there, and the Air Force requirement there exceeding that of all other locations. Ammunition was discharged in mid-stream at Cat Lai, barged to a river port at Cogido, and then trucked to the depot.

All of the major and most of the minor ports were operated by mixed military and civilian contractor contingents. In some instances the contractor discharged the ship, barged the ammunition ashore, moved the ammunition over-land, and even offloaded it in the depots. At Saigon the contractor was restricted to discharging and barging to shore. From the shore the ammunition was transported overland by Army Transportation Units and offloaded by depot personnel.

Until mid-1966, the discharging of ammunition ships was constrained by the fact that ammunition was removed from pallets at Continental U.S. outloading ports and loaded aboard ship by individual boxes and projectiles. While this maximized the use of ship bottoms, it created difficulties in Vietnam, because offloading by cargo nets and hooks was required and ammunition lot integrity had to be re-established within the depots. (Management of ammunition dictates that ammunition be stored and accounted for by lot number).

At the request of the Commanding General 1st Logistical Command this practice was halted and all ammunition shipped to Vietnam was palletized. Lot integrity was maintained by ships' holds to the maximum extent practicable. This decision improved the discharge rate of ammunition ships almost 100 percent, allowing discharge offloading time to be decreased from seven days to four days.

Prior to this improvement in December 1965 52 ammunition ships with an estimated 165,000 short tons aboard were awaiting discharge. This predicament was an outgrowth of the effort to build up to the stockage objective while concurrently supporting the demands of combat units. A further factor was the necessity for selective discharge of certain ammunition items that were in a short supply status in the depots. This situation required manifests and stowage plans to be reviewed so that certain ships could be moved on berth for partial discharge. The ships would then be returned to a holding area while other ships were called in for selective discharge. Steps were taken to relieve the backlog in December 1965 by redistributing the ships to Da Nang, Qui Nhon, and Cam Ranh Bay.

This situation added impetus for the installation of the De-Long Pier at Cam Ranh Bay and general improvements in over-the-shore offloading at other ports. However, ammunition ships continued to have to await discharge and the number of days spent waiting for an empty berth remained serious until a general downward trend began in January 1968. For example, 12 ammunition ships were offloaded in December 1967, but eleven of them had spent some time in a hold category. The total number of days for all eleven ships totaled 71. January 1968 was the turning point and improvement continued thereafter.

During the period October-December 1968, management techniques were applied to ammunition movements which made possible the reduction of ammunition stockage on-the-ground in Southeast Asia. This new management technique identified as *Inventory in Motion* made possible a significant reduction from approximately 285,000 S/tons of ammunition to approximately one-half that amount. This was achieved without reduction in unit readiness by providing the theater with total visibility of ammunition on-the-ground, ammunition in-transit-to-theater, and in-transit-in-theater, that is, a transparent pipeline. With this visibility, the stockage objectives were reduced from 113 percent in October 1968 to only 81 percent of the total United States Army Vietnam and the South Vietnamese Army objective being on the ground in Southeast Asia in February 1971.

In order to establish the *Inventory in Motion* concept it was necessary to study order and ship time and regulate issuance of requisitions to ensure prompt shipment of the needed items. Unnecessary delays had to be precluded at all points in the shipment. Management controls involved a teletype forecast of heavy tonnage items being received in Vietnam on the first of each month so that scheduling could be accomplished. This was followed by a transmittal of requisitions for the balance of ammunition items to arrive at Joliet, Illinois on the 10th of each month. These actions permitted planning for ships to be placed on berth over an entire 30-day span. This permitted direct shipments from a place of production to the eventual destinations within a 30-day period and provided for an even workload at the discharge point.

Inventory in Motion was originally applied to U.S. Army Vietnam forces and was broadened to include South Vietnamese Army ammunition as well.

Storage and Handling of Ammunition

The criteria for selection of an ammunition storage site are subordinated to the overriding factor of ensuring that surrounding facilities are a safe distance from the storage site. The determination of this safe distance is a general function of the quantity of net explosive weight and the allowable safe distance to adjacent facilities. Another constraint is that of hazard class which determines what ammunition items can be stored together or adjacent to each other. Any deviation from these criteria requires a waiver of safety requirements. Once the stockage objective for each line item has been determined, its hazard class established, and net explosive weight computed then the unwaivered size of the storage site can be determined. If ammunition is stored strictly in accordance with this criteria, the probability of an explosion on a single storage pad causing explosions on other storage pads is remote.

Even though available expertise and time would have permitted calculating storage area sizes, the results would have been negated as the size of the buildup and the magnitude of the stockage objectives were not envisioned at the time real estate was acquired. Gross estimating techniques were utilized and, based on the envisioned deployment strength in 1965, real estate was acquired to provide unwaivered storage capacity for approximately 85,000 short tons of ammunition. However by the end of 1966, the stockage objective had climbed to 231,000 short tons and by the end of 1967 had reached a peak of 284,500 short tons.

The expansion of ammunition depots stabilized in about mid-1968 with a capacity of approximately 238,000 short tons. The capacity above this figure was vested in Ammunition Supply Points. The number of Ammunition Supply Points fluctuated with the tactical situation; in mid-1968, there were eight Ammunition Supply Points with a capacity in excess of 50,000 short tons.

At Da Nang, there was no major Army Ammunition Supply Depot. Army stocks were essentially maintained in three Ammunition Supply Points at Da Nang, Dong Ha, and Chu Lai, and co-located with U.S. Marine Corps storage in Da Nang. The number of Ammunition Supply Points increased with the redeployment of the 3d Marine Division in late 1969. These Ammunition Supply Points were under adverse waivers as they were, for security reasons, inside secure cantonment areas. They, like most of the Ammunition Supply Points, literally developed in their locations because that was where the ammunition was offloaded by units on hand. While the risk associated with these heavily waivered Ammunition Supply Points was known and accepted, the trade off for security of the Ammunition Supply Point against enemy infiltration was necessary.

At Qui Nhon, the Ammunition Supply Depot was initially co-located with a South Vietnamese Army Ammunition Supply Point. However, the demand for additional capacity dictated the development of a new U.S. Army Ammunition Supply Depot which was established at Phu Tai in early 1966 and was operated by the 184th Ordnance Battalion. From the standpoint of safety, the site and the layout of the depot were excellent. It was located in a bowl-shaped valley surrounded on three sides by high ridges. The open side provided entrance to the main highway between Qui Nhon and Pleiku. It had minimum waivers, but had two serious drawbacks: Ammunition offloaded from ships had to be trucked through the city, and the security of the depot was not good. Enemy attacks on the depot could be easily mounted by merely directing recoilless rifle, rocket, and mortar fire from the surrounding high ridges. The terrain lent itself to an easy approach for enemy sapper teams. As a result of this Phu Tai suffered more enemy attacks than any other depot. The two Ammunition Supply Points at Pleiku and An Khe supported by this depot were relatively good and reasonably secure. However, they were subject to the same waivers as those in the Da Nang Support Command because of their being within heavily populated cantonment areas.

The Ammunition Supply Depot established at Cam Ranh Bay in early 1965, operated by the 191st Ordnance Battalion, was initially well located and required limited waivers for its location. However, subsequent location of petroleum storage facilities on the high ground behind the Ammunition Supply Depot and the adjacent location of the Air Force ammunition storage site eventually resulted in having to obtain waivers for its operation. The most adverse aspect of this depot was posed by the sandy terrain. It was not uncommon for a storage pad to be inundated overnight by constantly shifting dunes. Also, the soft sand all but prohibited the orderly movement of vehicle traffic. Ultimately, approximately two-thirds of the depot underwent a major upgrading consisting of concrete storage pads with berms stabilized by the application of peni-prime, a petroleum based product that formed a hardened crust over the sand to preclude its movement by wind action. Road networks were also stabilized to a degree by application of latterite, a clay-gravel combination that was locally available. The battalion's inherent capability for maintaining berms and road nets, two bulldozers in each ammunition company, was unequal to the task of properly maintaining this Ammunition Supply Depot.

The largest field Ammunition Supply Depot in Vietnam was at Long Binh. While the site was well located at first, it suffered the same encroachment as other Ammunition Supply Depots in that it was ultimately surrounded on three sides by other activities and units within the Long Binh cantonment area. However, by the time the encroachment had subsided, the Ammunition Supply Depots had expanded from an initial capacity of approximately 35,000 short tons to 100,000 short tons in early 1968.

At the peak of combat operations, it was not uncommon for receipts and issues within a 24-hour period at an Ammunition Supply Depot to exceed 5,000 short tons. The workload associated with this effort can be appreciated by the fact that for every ton of ammunition received an average of three tons of ammunition must be re-warehoused—moved from the rear of the pad to the front so that oldest stocks could be issued first. Further, lot integrity had to be maintained.

Security of Ammunition Depots

In the initial months of the buildup, security of Ammunition Supply Depots was of minor importance in that stocks of ammunition were relatively small and were stored in secure areas. However, as permanent sites were developed and occupied in late 1965, security became significant. The first attack on an ammunition depot occurred at Qui Nhon in April 1966. This attack established the extreme vulnerability of the ammunition depots and over the ensuing four-year period no less than 31 incidents at Ammunition Supply Depots were recorded.

The greatest danger was the threat posed by enemy sapper teams. This threat was a constant one and required aggressive defensive measures twenty-four hours a day. The other threat was from enemy rocket and mortar attacks with the only defense against this being recurring tactical sweeps of the outer perimeters conducted by combat security forces.

Prior to enemy sapper attacks vegetation had been cleared out from the storage sites to a distance of approximately 100 meters, a single row of coiled barbed wire installed, and anti-personnel mines, in some instances, implanted. Guard posts were established along with roving patrols. The increasing tempo of enemy probing actions culminating in three closely spaced attacks against Long Binh in late 1966 emphasized the necessity for more stringent security measures.

At the Qui Nhon Ammunition Supply Depot, extra land clearing was initiated, coiled barbed wire interlaced with trip flares was installed, perimeter lighting and guard towers were constructed, and the number of guards was increased. However, due to the terrain surrounding the Qui Nhon Ammunition Supply Depot, it still remained a vulnerable target for enemy attacks.

At Cam Ranh Bay, the Ammunition Supply Depot was afforded

much security by its location on the peninsular arm of land encircling the bay and its security was further assured by land clearing and minimal fencing.

Long Binh Ammunition Supply Depot, by far the largest storage depot, was probably the most lucrative target. During the period 1966 through 1971, Long Binh Ammunition Supply Depot suffered seven successful enemy attacks; three in 1966, one in 1967, two in 1968, and the last one in 1969. After the initial attacks, it was evident that the single row of coiled barbed wire backed up by anti-personnel mines was inadequate. A crash program was undertaken to clear the jungle vegetation 300 meters out from the perimeter and the perimeter fencing was increased from a single row of coiled barbed wire to three rows triple stacked. All three rows were interlaced at 10 meter intervals with trip flares. The necessity for keeping the vegegation cleared out of, as well as between the rows of wire required the removal of the mines. Observation towers, 44 in all, were built, with fighting bunkers at their bases, and perimeter lighting installed. By 1968 the increase in sapper attacks against all Ammunition Supply Depots resulted in a plan for installing sensing systems. However, this was delayed until 1969. The only available sensing devices were pressure sensitive and they were largely ineffective. During the 1968 time frame, the Long Binh Post perimeter was expanded to the extent that the eastern border of the Ammunition Supply Depot was no longer the post perimeter but was now approximately two miles inside the overall perimeter. No successful attacks were carried out against the Long Binh Ammunition Supply Depot subsequent to March 1969. The use of ammunition personnel as security guards for Ammunition Supply Depots proved to be ineffective for two reasons: (1) it detracted from their efficiency in ammunition operations and (2) the security of such critical installations required a professionally trained and operated security force to include sentry dogs and the best available electronic sensing equipment.

Maintenance and Disposal

Maintenance of ammunition in a combat zone is normally a routine function. In past conflicts, trained military renovation personnel were available to perform this function. However in the Vietnam conflict, the largely civilianized operation of ammunition facilities had precluded the availability of adequately trained military personnel or units skilled in maintenance of ammunition. The degradation of ammunition stocks due to the environmental conditions in Vietnam established the maintenance problem as one requiring more than a routine effort.

Early in 1966, it became apparent that some maintenance capability was required and each ammunition battalion was provided with a renovation detachment. However these units, each of approximately seventy men, were not provided with the necessary Ammunition Peculiar Equipment to perform renovation, but they did have sufficient tools to perform preservation and packaging. Munitions packaging deficiencies were the first major problem as wooden boxes, pallets, and containers deteriorated rapidly in the South Vietnam climate. Each Ammunition Supply Depot established a local "box shop," augmented with local labor, to produce these items. By early 1967, each battalion had an improvised renovation line where repackaging and some very limited renovation was performed.

Unit returns and long term stockage items kept all detachments busy inspecting, repainting, and remarking where possible, and condemning where required. Typical missions assigned these detachments were: inspecting all 40-mm (duster) munitions for fuze tightness; inspecting the 81-mm High Explosive plastic containers for moisture damage to the rounds, derusting projectiles, mines, and rockets; repainting and restenciling as required; and continual repackaging. Some mortar fuze and ignition cartridge replacements were also performed. However, lack of components restricted any large scale renovation by U.S. depots in South Vietnam.

The disposal of condemned ammunition has been a special problem in every conflict. For this reason, highly skilled, thoroughly trained Explosive Ordnance Disposal teams were available from a well organized peacetime training base. These teams in Vietnam worked under the command and control of a detachment assigned to the Director of Ammunition at 1st Logistical Command and subsequently to Headquarters U.S. Army Vietnam. They were equipped to respond almost immediately to any situation and provided support in the following areas:

1. Destroying deteriorated ammunition.

2. Destroying enemy damaged ammunition in storage. Explosive Ordnance Disposal personnel were also responsible for return of storage locations to operational use as soon as possible.

3. Assisting in the recovery of downed gunships and other aircraft, clearing booby-traps, and rendering safe the ordnance aboard these aircraft.

4. Clearing of heavily booby-trapped and mined facilities and

areas, disposing of discovered caches, and rendering U.S. sites unusable prior to abandonment.

5. Clearing of dud munitions and time delay munitions in operational and support areas.

6. Training combat troops on the enemy booby-traps and mines.

All depots and forward support activities had personnel assigned or attached to destroy ammunition. Normally disposal was by detonation or burning at an approved disposal site. Care had to be taken in disposal shot site selection to prevent damage to nearby friendly real estate. Disposal shot size was determined by real estate and surroundings, but calculations were not always perfect; for example, one shot at Long Binh, during a low cloud ceiling, jarred buildings severely and broke several windows. Prior to any in-country disposal actions, efforts were made to return the munitions to Okinawa or Continental U.S. for renovation or demilitarization. At the Ammunition Supply Depots, condemned munitions were disposed of by the battalion Explosive Ordnance Disposal sections. In the forward areas, Explosive Ordnance Disposal personnel from area assigned Explosive Ordnance Disposal detachments disposed of hazardous munitions on an as required basis.

In an effort to assure Class V support to the combat arms, each Ordnance ammunition battalion provided Technical Assistance Contact Teams to advise and assist on maintenance, storage, and safety in the Forward Support Areas and Fire Base areas. The 184th Ordnance Battalion (Ammo) at Qui Nhon was a leader in this effort and its assistance program was copied by the other units of the 1st Logistical Command. This technical assistance program was extended in mid-1969 to the South Vietnamese Army and to Republic of Korea Forces Vietnam through the 1st Logistical Command's Project BUDDY. Major assistance was given South Vietnamese Army units in and around Nha Trang by the 191st Ordnance Battalion (Ammo).

CHAPTER V

Aviation Logistics

Growth of the Aviation Fleet

Since 1965, the Army Aviation Program has experienced an unprecedented and unprogrammed acceleration of aircraft production, deployments, and utilization. During this time, it was frequently necessary to support the program with inventories of repair parts, components, and engines that in pre-Vietnam war years would have been thought completely inadequate. At the same time aviation operating and support units in the field reached and maintained levels of operational readiness and flying hour rates that many believed were beyond reach with the "state-of-the-art" helicopters deployed to Southeast Asia. In order to meet operating requirements, it was necessary to improvise, innovate and in some cases revolutionize logistic support systems. As so often happens with emergency improvisations, when they work they become part of the system and yesterday's emergency often becomes tomorrow's norm.

From a relatively evenly balanced inventory of fixed wing and rotary wing aircraft in fiscal year 1960 (totaling some 5,528 aircraft) the Army has progressed to over 12,000 aircraft in 1970, most being rotary wing. The acquisition value of the inventory, which in fiscal year 1960 totaled $600 million, increased five times during this period. (*Chart 4*) The dollar value of secondary items required to support the aircraft fleet increased from $261.4 million to $2.2 billion, or eight times, as compared to the fivefold increase for the end item inventory. (*Chart 5*)

Chart 6 outlines fiscal year 1961–1970 Army aviation funded programs. The Procurement of Equipment and Missiles progression was significant during the 1966–1968 time frame. During this period the Army was procuring and deploying large numbers of aircraft and Procurement of Equipment and Missiles secondary items for support of increased inventories and flying hours. The latter were essentially "Life of Type Subsystems." After the initial procurement, requirements were met from overhaul programs.

Repair parts for Army aviation have been provided for in the Army Stock Fund since 1963. However, prior to that time air-

CHART 4—ARMY AIRCRAFT INVENTORY AND VALUE
FISCAL YEAR 1960–1970

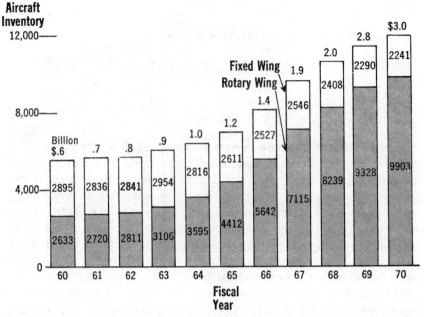

CHART 5—SECONDARY ITEM INVENTORY REQUIRED TO SUPPORT THE
AIRCRAFT FLEET

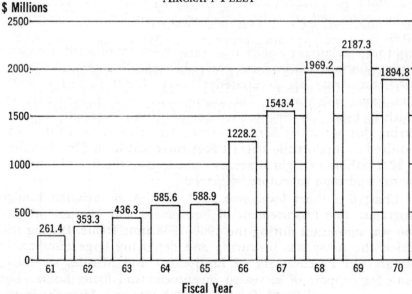

craft repair parts were purchased with Operation Maintenance
Army funds. Since the inclusion of aircraft repair parts in the
Army Stock Fund, the Operation Maintenance Army account has

CHART 6—AVIATION FUNDING PROGRAMS

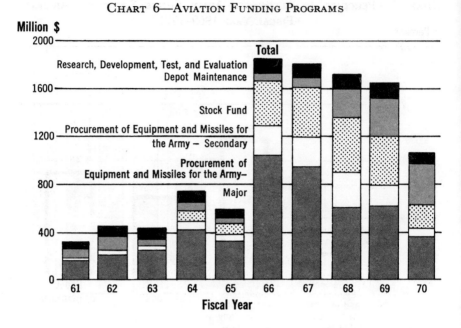

provided only those dollars required to overhaul aircraft engines, components, and associated equipment (avionics, armament systems, and so forth) at depot level. The amount funded for Research, Development, Test, and Evaluation remained relatively stable. The total funding program for Army aviation reached a high of $1.8 billion in fiscal year 1966.

Chart 7 shows the percent of total Army funds spent on aircraft during the period 1969–1971. A major problem was caused by rapidly changing requirements for particular aircraft, both increases and decreases. Table 7 shows the monthly UH–1 production

TABLE 7—UH–1 PRODUCTION SCHEDULE

Month	1965	1966	1967	1968	1969	1970
Jan	57	74	150	85	73	100
Feb	58	81	150	82	82	100
Mar	58	87	155	80	89	94
Apr	60	93	152	85	100	74
May	63	99	150	80	100	73
Jun	66	100	143	66	44	74
Jul	68	102	139	65	100	71
Aug	67	114	120	65	101	67
Sep	70	109	110	65	101	67
Oct	71	125	106	65	101	64
Nov	74	133	98	65	101	66
Dec	75	142	85	53	101	67

CHART 7—PERCENT OF ALLOCATED ARMY FUNDS SPENT ON AIRCRAFT
FISCAL YEAR 1969–1971

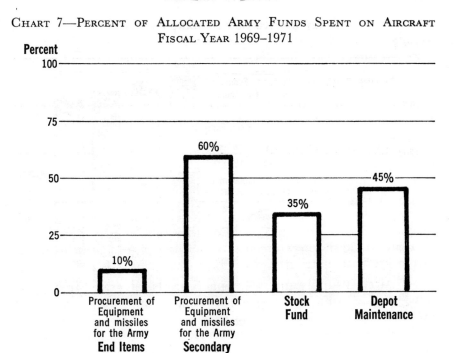

schedule since 1965, which is illustrative of the general turbulence that was experienced.

Airframes have a relatively easily identifiable basis of issue, and requirements and assets can readily be computed. A major difficulty, and one which resulted in problems and shortages throughout the period was the determination of requirements for ancillary equipment such as avionics, armament and ammunition, tools, and test equipment.

Growth of Aviation Logistic Support in South Vietnam

From an austere beginning when two helicopter companies arrived in Vietnam on 11 December 1961, the total number of U.S. Army aircraft increased to 510 by 1 January 1965 and then further increased to a peak of 4,228 by September 1969. When the buildup commenced in 1965, the U.S. Army Support Command Vietnam had one aircraft maintenance and supply battalion (765th Transportation Battalion) to provide backup direct and general support for all Army aircraft in-country. This battalion was located at Vung Tau and consisted of direct support companies and one general support company. The three direct support companies were located at Vung Tau, Saigon, and Nha Trang. They provided backup support for separate aviation companies having their own organic or attached direct support and they provided direct support for small aviation detachments that lacked this capability.

The one general support company was located with the battalion headquarters at Vung Tau. An aviation supply point in Saigon, operated by the aviation detachment of U.S. Army Support Command Vietnam, provided aviation-peculiar supplies for all Army aircraft in Vietnam.

In 1965 the Commanding General, U.S. Army Support Command Vietnam established a committee to devise a plan to support a large influx of Army aircraft. Basic criteria for the plan were that it should provide for one-stop supply and maintenance service, and provide for an expansion of this service commensurate with increases in aircraft densities. Consideration of the operational structure to be supported led to the development of plans for three prime alternative organizations. These were as follows:

1. Aircraft supply and maintenance units integrated in an aviation brigade, which was planned as a control element for all non-divisional aviation activities.

2. Aircraft supply and maintenance units integrated in the 1st Logistical Command, which had been recently activated.

3. A separate headquarters commanding all non-divisional aircraft supply and maintenance units, assigned to the Aviation Brigade, assigned to the 1st Logistical Command, or a separate command under U.S. Army Vietnam.

The decision reached was to establish a separate headquarters under the direct command of U.S. Army Vietnam. This basic organizational structure has operated throughout the Vietnam Era with only one minor variation. Originally, the command was under the staff supervision of the U.S. Army Vietnam G-4. In October 1967, staff supervision was changed to the U.S. Army Vietnam Aviation Officer.

Following the September 1965 decision to establish a separate command, the next two months were spent in developing an organizational structure and preparing the necessary authorization documents. In November 1965, a group headquarters was established on a provisional basis and finally, on 17 January 1966, a U.S. Army Pacific General Order was published activating the 34th General Support Group.

As previously stated, the total Army aircraft density increased to a high of 4,228 in September 1969. The deployed aircraft were assigned to a total of 142 company-sized units plus a number of miscellaneous smaller detachments. Of the 142 companies, 63 were organic to division, brigades, or squadrons and had their own organic direct support supply and maintenance capability. The remaining company-sized units were supported by cellular direct support detachments. The 34th General Support Group provided backup support to these company sized units as well as direct support and general support for all aviation activities in U.S. Army Vietnam.

The 34th General Support Group as displayed in Map 3, ultimately had 2 depot companies, 5 general support companies, 11 direct support companies, 4 aviation electronics companies, and the Aviation Materiel Management Center with which to accomplish its mission.

Aircraft Maintenance Personnel

Qualitative personnel problems in supply and maintenance were particularly critical for aircraft because of the nature of the matériel maintained. Civilian contractors were used to augment the military capability in critical skill areas, particularly in the areas of sheet metal and structural repairs. Table 8 shows strength authorizations by fiscal year for contractor personnel.

TABLE 8—CONTRACT MAINTENANCE MANNING LEVEL

Company	FY 65	FY 66	FY 67	FY 68	FY 69	FY 70
Lockheed	—	—	—	100	232	287
Lear Siegler	—	—	457	624	832	733
Dynalectron	34	239	550	847	1056	872
TOTAL	34	239	1007	1571	2120	1892

The Aviation Systems Command provided either Department of the Army civilians or manufacturer's field service representatives to advise and assist in problem areas arising from the operation of complex and sophisticated equipment in the field. In the summer of 1969, 151 field service representatives were authorized. These field service representatives were in addition to the new equipment training teams sent into Vietnam upon introduction of a new equipment item. Project COUNTER team, discussed in another section, were also provided to the 34th General Support Group.

This augmentation with contract labor and the employment of field service representatives and other teams to provide instruction was necessitated, to a large degree, by the fact that there was not an adequate military rotational base in Continental U.S. from which to draw upon for such critical skills as sheet metal and structural repair workers. Because of Vietnam priorities, nearly

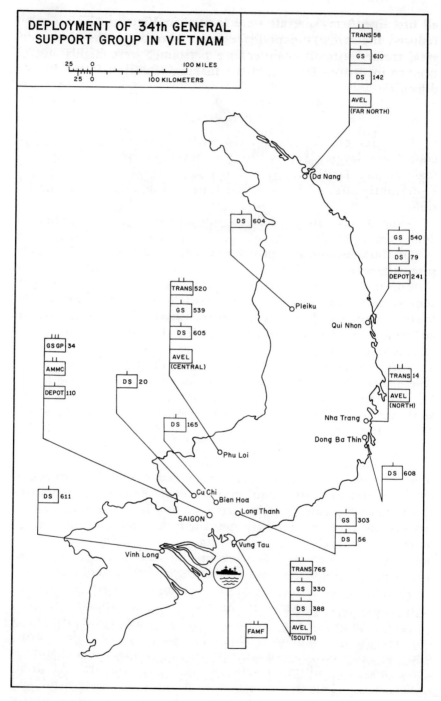

DEPLOYMENT OF 34th GENERAL SUPPORT GROUP IN VIETNAM

MAP 3

all first line Army aircraft were located in Vietnam. This further reduced the military experience base. Also, as in the electronics area, trained aircraft maintenance personnel were highly susceptible to incursions from industry, making retention in the Service difficult.

Facilities

Facilities problems associated with the support of Army aircraft were largely related to the development of storage and maintenance facilities. Overall operation of the system was not significantly affected by port and Line of Communications limitations.

Some deterioration of packaging and damage to supplies occurred as a result of delays in expanding storage facilities at Saigon, but the impact was not comparable to that in the general supply depots.

Construction of aircraft maintenance facilities presented more serious problems because of the sensitivity of aircraft components to the elements. Maintenance tents provided as organizational equipment were not only shortlived in the tropical climate and expensive to replace, but generally were too small for the volume of work, resulting in a significant loss of valuable man-hours. These man-hours were consumed in moving aircraft in and out. In addition, shop vans proved too small to handle sheet metal work on bulky cowling and also for balancing blades. Construction of permanent facilities to offset these problems proved time consuming. For example, the 604th Direct Support Company moved into Pleiku in March 1966, and an adequate hangar facility for them was not completed until the summer of 1969. Although available statistics are inadequate to allow precise measurement, the weight of evidence indicated that a lack of adequate maintenance facilities appreciably degraded the efficiency of maintenance operations.

Weapons Systems Requisitions Techniques

During 1965, aircraft repair parts were provided by the aircraft supply point at Tan Son Nhut. This supply point was operated by personnel of the U.S. Army Support Command, Vietnam Aviation Detachment and augmented by the supply platoon of the 330th General Support Company and about 70 local national employees. All requisitions from operating units, general and direct support companies, other Services, and free world forces were submitted directly to the supply point which provided a retail service. Items not available within the 8,000 item Authorized Stockage List were requisitioned from Okinawa. At Okinawa the requisitions were filled if the items were available. However, if they were not available the requisitions were passed through U.S. Army Pacific to the appropriate Continental U.S. National Inventory Control Point. Chart 8 shows this requisition and supply flow.

CHART 8—REQUISITION AND SUPPLY FLOW, 1965

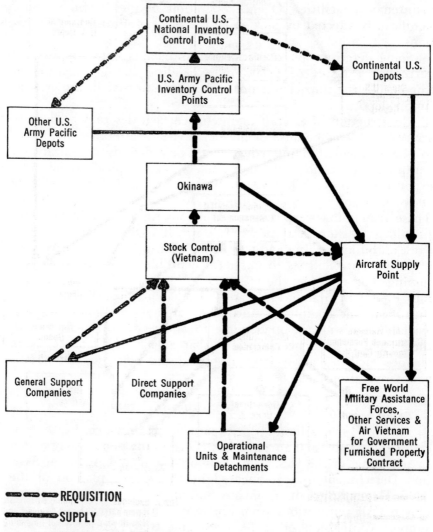

●━━ ●━━ ●━━ REQUISITION

●━━━━━━●SUPPLY

●━●━●━●━● MATERIEL RELEASE ORDER

Following activation of the 34th General Support Group, several changes were made in the basic supply system. Chart 9 shows the requisition and supply flow beginning in April 1966. Major changes included the following:

CHART 9—REQUISITION AND SUPPLY FLOW, APRIL 1966 TO APRIL 1968

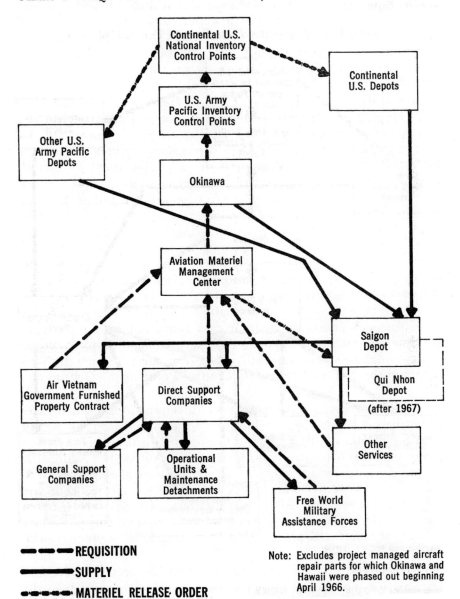

REQUISITION
SUPPLY
MATERIEL RELEASE ORDER

Note: Excludes project managed aircraft repair parts for which Okinawa and Hawaii were phased out beginning April 1966.

Establishment of the Aviation Materiel Management Center using resources of the 58th Transportation Battalion. Resources of this battalion continued to be used for this purpose until February 1968 when an Aviation Materiel Management Center Table of Distribution was approved and the 58th was assigned to I Corps. The Aviation Materiel Management Center served as an inventory control center for all aviation matériel and provided centralized accountability for all depot stocks. Inventory control was converted from a manual operation to the use of an IBM 407 Electronic Accounting Machine in early 1966, to a UNIVAC 1005 at the end of 1966, to an IBM 1460 in March 1968, and to an IBM 360/50 in mid-1969.

In April 1966, the Saigon Aviation Depot was removed from retail operations. After this, all requisitions passed through direct support companies except those for the U. S. Air Force and Air Vietnam. Beginning in late 1966 direct support companies were equipped with NCR 500 equipment to enable them to furnish data and interface with Aviation Materiel Management Center.

An increased density of aircraft supported, together with increasing delays in obtaining supplies through the Okinawa U.S. Army Pacific route, resulted in the third major change in the supply system. (*Chart 10*) Beginning in July 1966, Okinawa and Hawaii were bypassed for all aircraft parts. This introduced the stovepipe system whereby Aviation Materiel Management Center passed all requisitions directly to the Aviation Systems Command in St. Louis, with only an information copy to U.S. Army Pacific for billing purposes. In addition to a reduction in a high-dollar pipeline, this stovepipe system (Weapons System Requisitioning) greatly improved communications between the consumer in Vietnam and the National Inventory Control Point in the Continental U.S.

In September 1969, weapons systems requisitioning procedures were further modified. Techniques were introduced to permit Aviation Materiel Management Center requisitions for aviation items to be routed through the Defense Automatic Addressing System with an image copy of all transactions being passed to the Aviation Systems Command. A weapons system project code and the Aviation Systems Command distribution code were used to identify aviation item traffic. With minor variation, this procedure is being standardized for use by all Army weapons systems worldwide.

Overall, the aviation repair parts system has been effective and responsive as was indicated by the low percentage of aircraft in the not operationally ready supply category (a 5.2 percent rate as of 31 December 1970 compared with a standard of 7 percent) and a demand satisfaction rate consistently around 65 percent. From an authorized stockage list of 8,000 lines in 1965, stockage increased to a high of 46,000 lines late in 1968.

CHART 10—REQUISITION AND SUPPLY FLOW, APRIL 1968 TO SEPTEMBER 1969

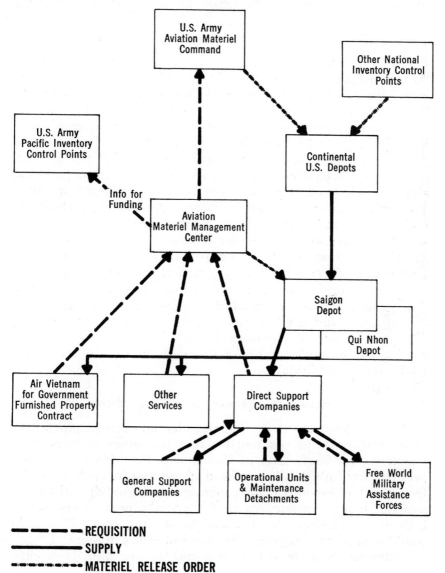

In line with the objectives of the Logistics Offensive, they were subsequently reduced to 25,495 lines by December 1970 without adverse effect on supply effectiveness.

There was some item duplication in stockage lists of the Aviation Materiel Management Center and the 1st Logistical Command. The items were primarily industrial bulk matériel items used in repair operations and certain items of common hardware. The value of providing aviation units with a single point for obtaining aircraft repair parts outweighed the cost of multiple stockage.

Floating Aircraft Maintenance Facility

In April 1966, the Army deployed a Floating Aircraft Maintenance Facility to Vietnam. This was the USNS *Corpus Christi Bay*. This ship had been converted from a seaplane tender at the Navy yard in Charleston, S.C. in 1965. The Floating Aircraft Maintenance Facility was designed for use in contingency operations, initially for backup direct support and general support and provided a limited depot capability for the repair of aircraft components. It was equipped to manufacture small machine parts and also to repair items requiring extensive test equipment operating in a sterile environment such as avionics, instruments, carburetors, fuel controls, and hydraulic pumps. The mobility offered by the ship also contributed to the effectiveness of aircraft support since it could move from one deep water port to another as the density of aircraft units shifted with changing tactical situations.

Through the return of components to a serviceable condition, the issuance of parts from its shop stock in direct response to user requests, and the fabrication of hard-to-get repair parts, the Floating Aircraft Maintenance Facility was responsible for removing a substantial number of aircraft from a not operationally ready supply condition.

Intensive Management of Critical Assets

Prior to Vietnam, it was believed that an overseas pipeline of 13 months would be required for aircraft engines (8 months for engines at wholesale level in Continental U.S. depot stocks and overhaul facilities plus 5 months in transit and in stock overseas). One month of pipeline is the equivalent of the number of unserviceable engines generated in 30 days. At the peak of operations, each day of pipeline was worth $1.16 million, while 13 months would require spare engines in the value of $452.4 million.

Through intensive management and the use of air transportation, actions were taken to reduce the pipeline time first to 9½ months, then 8 months, 7 months, and by December 1970 to 6½ months. Some of the methods and techniques used to keep the aviation inventory in motion included better asset visibility and control, weapons system management, closed loop/direct exchange, and retrograde control.

Early in 1967, a reporting system was established to account for worldwide assets of the T53 and T55 gas turbine engines. This system, known as the Aircraft Component Intensive Management System, provided a postcard report to the Aviation Systems Command for each engine by serial number and gave every change in condition, location, or status, whether the engine was installed or was a spare. The reporting system later was broadened to cover 45 Aviation items including both engines and components representing a value of $1.3 billion.

For critical and high-value items required for Vietnam, Aviation Systems Command established a system known as Aircraft Intensively Managed Items. This system, which in March 1971 included 227 items and extended worldwide, required that a forecast of monthly requirements be submitted to Aviation Systems Command each quarter. The customers and Aviation Systems Command met and "negotiated" monthly levels. Levels were based upon forecasts of consumption (replacement) with minimal safety levels to preclude running out of stock. The customer requisitioned once a month, and Aviation Systems Command shipped the items by air to arrive in-country 15 days in advance of the month in which required.

By May 1968 partly as a result of the *Tet* Offensive the requirement for T53 engines for Huey and Cobra helicopters and T55 engines for the Chinook helicopter (CH–47) increased greatly. Since production and overhaul programs were behind schedule, a major problem developed. The only way to meet this problem was to reduce the pipeline further. Elements in the pipeline with the potential for providing an early response were the intransit time, and the in-country unserviceable engines. Accordingly, a combined ground and air transportation system was established. All new or overhauled T53 and T55 engines were accumulated at the Army Aeronautical Depot Maintenance Center, Corpus Christi, Texas, for direct air shipment to the Republic of Vietnam three times a week by special mission aircraft. At the same time, unserviceable engines authorized for repair in Vietnam were reduced to those that could be repaired in 15 days; the remaining unserviceable engines were returned for repair to the Continental U.S.

by the special mission aircraft. This system flushed out large quantities of unserviceable engines, reduced transportation costs, and provided a closed loop/direct exchange program with U.S. Army Vietnam. This program was so effective that since early June 1968 there were no not operationally ready supply problems for these engines in spite of the reduced pipeline.

Closed Loop Support for Aviation

The first Aviation Closed Loop Support Conference was held at Headquarters U.S. Army Pacific in March 1967. Through 1970, nine Aviation Closed Loop Conferences were held. Initially Closed Loop Support was limited to U.S. Army Vietnam, but as aircraft became available for other commands the program was expanded worldwide. In addition to providing a means of controlling the distribution of assets and providing visibility of equipment returning to Continental U.S. for overhaul, the Closed Loop Support program provided a forum for presenting and resolving problems in aviation logistics operations worldwide.

From September 1969 to June 1970, the Army was confronted with a large backlog of unserviceable first line aircraft consisting principally of the UH–1, AH–1G, CH–47 and OH–6. This situation not only denied aircraft to army units in the field, but also placed the Army in the position of needing to buy new aircraft while having a backlog of unserviceable aircraft on hand. A critical analysis was made of the mandatory time between overhauls for aircraft; and based on Vietnam experience during the previous year (when 85 percent of all hightime Hueys returned to Continental U.S. averaged 2,140 hours), it was agreed by Closed Loop Support conferees that the Huey (UH–1) Time Between Overhauls could be increased from 2200 hours to 3300 hours. Appropriate increases in Time Between Overhauls were also made for other aircraft. In this manner, aircraft utilization was increased by delaying returns to Continental U.S. for overhaul. Transportation and depot maintenance requirements were reduced, increasing the number of serviceable aircraft in the inventory at the least cost. This life extension program was carefully monitored to preclude any adverse impact on safety-of-flight or matériel readiness.

Also during the September 1969 Closed Loop Support Conference, attendees evaluated the requirement for modifying the CH–47C helicopters (equipped with the T55–1–7C engine) to a full "C" configuration with the –11 engine. This requirement included 27 separate modifications and required approximately 3,500 manhours to accomplish. During the Closed Loop Support conference, it was determined that the work could be done by Air Vietnam at less cost and in less time than if the helicopters were returned to the U.S. In January 1970, the modification effort began with Air Vietnam performing the work. This program required approximately two years at a cost of about $2.6 million versus an estimated $10.2 million, if the aircraft had been returned to the Continental U.S. Also the aircraft were out of action for only 90 days rather than the 150 days that would have been required, if the work had been done in the Continental U.S.

Prior to the March 1970 Closed Loop Support conference, it had been planned to deploy 23 CH–54B's, the modified "Flying Crane," to U.S. Army Vietnam. However, after consultation with the U.S. Army Vietnam representative, and recognizing the potential phaseout of "Flying Cranes" in the next 18 months, it was agreed that such a transfer would be costly and was unnecessary since the CH–54A's in U.S. Army Vietnam were accomplishing the required mission in a satisfactory manner. Accordingly, the CH–54A's were retained in U.S. Army Vietnam, except for those hightime and crash-damaged aircraft that had to be returned. The CH–54B's were assigned elsewhere in the Army. This program reduced both transportation and depot maintenance overhaul costs that would have been incurred, if the CH–54A's had been returned to the Continental U.S.

For aviation it was found practicable and in many cases more economical to ship by air nearly all aircraft support including the aircraft as well as the supporting repair parts, components and engines.

Direct Support Maintenance Concepts

Three separate concepts of direct support aircraft maintenance were employed in Vietnam. The infantry divisions centralized the aircraft direct support capability in the aircraft maintenance company of the maintenance battalion; the airmobile divisions centralized the capability in the transportation aircraft maintenance battalion; and the 1st Aviation Brigade company-sized units were authorized an attached direct support aircraft maintenance detachment.

Through the extensive operational experience in Vietnam it was found that conventional organizational maintenance organizations supported by centralized direct support units did not provide the desired level of availability to meet tactical requirements. As a result various methods of maintenance support were tried in an attempt to increase readiness. The concept employed by the 1st Aviation Brigade was found to provide 10 percent higher readiness with 12 percent higher utilization when compared with units not having a direct support capability. In February 1968, as a result of an analysis made by Deputy Chief of Staff for Logistics the Chief of Staff approved the concept of integrating the direct support detachments into the aviation companies of the 1st Aviation Brigade. U.S. Army Vietnam was also requested to apply the concept to the infantry and airmobile division.

Within the 1st Cavalry Division and the 101st Airborne Division a combined total of nineteen detachments were organized, utilizing the resources of two of the divisions' four direct support aircraft maintenance companies. The detachments were initially attached to the aviation units with an objective of integrating them at a later date if the concept proved to be practicable.

A test was conducted in the 9th Infantry Division to determine the feasibility of adopting the decentralized direct support concept to all infantry divisions. Although this was highly successful in improving aircraft operational readiness rates, agreement could not be reached on additional personnel requirements for the decentralized organizations.

The major aspect of the integrated system was that both organizational and direct support maintenance became the responsibility of a single commander. This responsibility permitted the commander to accomplish all functions associated with scheduled maintenance to include component replacement and minor battle damage repair. The increased organic maintenance capability for aviation units permitted the units to schedule maintenance according to their operational requirements, without an unacceptable degradation of tactical deployment capability. Backup direct support maintenance units were still required to take care of extensive crash damage repairs; operational readiness float support; and repair parts storage, receipt and issue requirements.

The Aircraft Readiness, Utilization, and Loss Reporting Systems

The reporting system and techniques employed to monitor aircraft readiness, utilization, and losses have undergone several major revisions since 1960. Changes were made to improve the accuracy, timeliness, and scope of information collected in order to have greater visibility over aviation inventories and to promptly highlight logistic support problems.

Initially the Army's reporting system included three major categories. These were (1) aircraft inventory, (2) flying hours, and (3) days in commission. It provided for the monthly reporting of worldwide army aircraft by serial number, unit assignment, flying hours accomplished during the month, and the operational readiness rate (which was variously known as aircraft in commission or aircraft available). Readiness data were compiled on the basis of the total number of days in commission and out of commission during the month reported and the reasons (that is supply, maintenance, other) for being out of commission. The number of days in commission for four plus hours was counted as being operationally ready for the 24-hour period. Conversely, aircraft out of commission for more than four hours were reported as being not operationally ready during the entire day and the downtime was charged to supply, maintenance, or other. Reporting criteria allowed a wide range of interpretation and there were no aircraft readiness standards showing the degree of readiness to be maintained.

In 1962 a supply bulletin, "Army Aircraft Maintenance Manhour Factors and Availability Norms," was published. It provided the factors and formulas needed to compute aircraft maintenance manpower requirements. It also gave guides to be used as a yardstick in measuring aircraft availability rates. This supply bulletin was not directive in nature but was widely used as containing the best data available. Readiness standards placed little demand on the commands, permitting down times for supply in excess of 10 percent and an average maintenance down time for the fleet as high as 26 percent. Because of the low standards, there was little emphasis in the field or in the logistics system for improving aircraft readiness.

In early 1963 Department of the Army Project 35, "Availability and Downtime Rates for Army Aircraft," was established. Project 35 had as its objectives to establish and maintain realistic worldwide aircraft availability standards; to assure that aircraft readiness was compatible with mission requirements and priority of assignment; and to provide to the Department of the Army information on the maximum potential use of its aircraft consistent with manning, matériel and money. All major commands and Department of the Army staff agencies were represented. Separate standards were set for aircraft with significant differences in mission requirements and logistic support capabilities; for example, the UH–1A in the training base versus UH–1 elsewhere. While Project 35 was getting underway, the Office of the Secretary of Defense had established a working group to develop a uniform equipment readiness reporting system. This resulted in Department of Defense Instruction 7700.5, which became effective in January 1964.

This Instruction prescribed standard readiness definitions: operational ready, not operational ready-supply, and not operational ready-maintenance. The services were directed to establish standards and to report aircraft readiness and down time to the nearest hour in a 24-hour day. Department of the Army Project 35 was well on the way to accomplishing all these things, and in January 1964 a new army regulation (AR 710–12) was published implementing the Department of Defense Instruction.

The Army's application of the Office of the Secretary of Defense system retained reporting aircraft utilization (flying hours). Later changes added reporting of the time accumulated on installed gas turbine engines by serial number. This information has proved extremely valuable in forecasting engine replacement requirements. Loss reporting is also included in the Army's reporting system.

Chart 11 shows helicopter readiness rates of U.S. Army Vietnam for the period fiscal year 1965 until the 1st half of fiscal year 1971. A sharp decline in fiscal year 1965 was attributed to buildup activities. Inventories of helicopters in U.S. Army Vietnam increased more than ten times during the period and a readiness rate in excess of 70 percent was maintained despite the fact that these aircraft had to fly in excess of the programmed hours. In May 1970, following a Project 35 Committee review, U.S. Army Vietnam standards were adjusted upward because

CHART 11—OPERATIONAL READINESS OF U.S. ARMY VIETNAM ROTARY WING AIRCRAFT

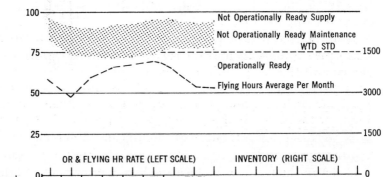

Dec 65 STD	May 70 STD		FY 65	FY 66	FY 67	FY 68	FY 69	FY 70	FY 71 10	FY 71 20	FY 71 Jan
7	5	NORS	4.6	9.2	9.4	7.6	7.0	4.8	5.0	5.3	4.3
21	20	NORM	12.8	18.8	20.3	22.1	21.2	21.3	19.0	18.8	19.6
72	75	OR	82.6	72.0	70.3	70.3	71.8	73.9	76.0	75.9	76.1
PROG	65.5	FHAM	56.1	48.0	58.5	65.7	67.3	69.2	64.6	53.9	53.5

experience showed that logistic support operations permitted the attainment of higher goals. The new goals decreased Not Operational Ready—Supply from 7 percent to 5 percent and Not Operational Ready—Maintenance from 21 percent to 20 percent. Despite the aging of the fleet and the high utilization rates, these new standards were met.

Use of Helicopters in Logistic Support

Significant to operations in Vietnam was the use of helicopters in the logistic support role. Their use freed the Army from a complete dependence on surface transportation. The helicopter became an indispensible link in the forward area of operation because of its ability to operate in virtually any weather condition, day or night, with little or no preparation of landing sites.

The majority of the logistic missions were carried out by UH-1, CH-47, and CH-54 aircraft. The UH-1's and CH-47s were primarily to support the forward areas and delivered such diverse types of cargo as hot food, medical supplies, ammunition, consumable supplies, and repair parts.

The UH-1's operated forward to the platoon level, while the CH-47's transported heavier and more bulky loads to battalions and companies. The CH-54's were primarily employed to lift larger items of equipment to otherwise inaccessible locations and for evacuation of heavy lifts from the combat area to the support area. Extensive use was made of the external sling load concept. This required only the time to fasten the load to a cargo hook suspended beneath the aircraft. By employing the sling load technique, it was not uncommon for the CH-47 to airlift 100 tons of supplies a day within a 10 mile radius. The significance of the helicopter role in combat support is further substantiated by data shown in Table 9.

In addition to the daily combat service support and resupply missions, the larger helicopters, the CH-47 and CH-54, developed a major capability in the recovery of other aircraft, vehicles and equipment requiring removal to the rear. Through extensive experience, procedures were developed whereby aircraft and other equipment and matériel could be rigged for pick-up by helicopters in a matter of minutes, even in enemy territory under fire. To date, helicopters have accounted for the recovery of over 10,000 aircraft, belonging to all of the services, valued in excess of $2.5 billion.

TABLE 9—INTRA-VIETNAM CARGO MOVEMENT BY AIR, 1967–1969

Month	1967		1968		1969		Monthly Total	
	Common Service Airlift System	Helicopters	Common Service Airlift System	Helicopters	Common Service Airlift System	Helicopters	Common Service Airlift System	Helicopters
Jan.	59,000	40,000	78,721	82,602	78,250	98,968	215,971	221,570
Feb.	55,000	41,000	75,012	77,362	70,727	95,356	200,789	213,718
Mar.	65,000	50,000	92,483	80,750	73,086	120,697	230,569	251,447
Apr.	65,400	55,000	88,948	94,387	69,382	110,353	223,730	259,740
May	64,700	66,000	85,374	98,181	69,209	111,822	219,283	276,003
June	64,800	60,500	83,967	108,176	58,620	114,407	207,387	283,083
July	64,700	65,000	82,937	110,800	57,026	103,479	204,663	279,288
Aug.	65,000	81,000	80,945	97,546	61,311	111,342	207,256	289,888
Sep.	64,700	81,500	81,703	91,421	61,686	110,564	208,089	288,485
Oct.	74,800	106,000	81,723	87,322	62,923	102,559	219,446	295,881
Nov.	64,900	68,500	83,182	89,929	62,023	98,116	210,105	256,545
Dec.	72,000	113,500	82,179	104,547	67,442	99,460	221,021	317,507
Total	780,000	828,000	997,174	1,123,032	791,685	1,277,123	2,568,859	3,228,155

Note: Helicopter tonnages are for Army and Marine Corps rotary wing aircraft. Army tonnages include air assault and tactical operations passenger and cargo movements. Marine tonnages do not include tactical operations tonnages. Common Service Airlift System includes C–7A dedicated movements.

Aerial Resupply

To test the feasibility and effectiveness of an intensive aerial resupply campaign, Operation Task Force Remagen was formed and a test of aerial resupply was conducted during the period 16 March through 29 April 1969. Task Force Remagen was conducted by troops from the 1st Infantry Brigade, 5th Infantry Division (Mechanized).

The Task Force was composed of an armored battalion and a mechanized infantry battalion cross-reinforced, with the mission to prove or disprove that an armored and mechanized force could operate effectively over extended distances without a ground line of communication. For 47 days Task Force Remagen operated at a distance of between 40–60 kilometers from its base at the U.S. Marine Corps Vandergrift Combat Base, and relied entirely on helicopters for resupply.

Requests for supplies and repair parts were forwarded to the Forward Support Element, who in turn forwarded the requests to the 75th Support Battalion Logistic Operations Center at Quang Tri. The requested supplies were assembled overnight and either flown or sent by convoy the next morning to the Forward Support Element for further delivery to the task force by air.

Both battalions involved in the task force maintained combat trains consisting of tracked maintenance and resupply vehicles. All replacement parts were flown to the units in their field locations, exchanged for the defective part and installed on the spot. Defective parts were then returned to the support element for repair. Over 1000 tons of cargo were moved by helicopters from the forward element supply base at Vandergrift Combat Base during the course of the operation.

During this operation the task force received an average of thirteen helicopter sorties per day. It was estimated that with an average of thirty minutes per round trip, four helicopters could have met Task Force Remagen's average daily resupply requirements.

Looking to the future, a project known as Log Lift has been established to incorporate current and future helicopters into the logistic system in order to help in carrying out the aims of the *Inventory In Motion* and *Maintenance Support Positive* programs. Under Project Log Lift, the Army will analyze experience gained in Vietnam in order to develop future policy, practices and procedures. Log Lift will also evaluate the use of existing helicopters and will project into the future when the Army plans to have a heavy lift helicopter with a payload of at least twice that of the currently available Chinooks and Cranes. This greater lift capability will reduce requirements for stocking of supplies and equipment in the forward area of the combat zone and will further assist in retrograding equipment and matériel requiring heavy maintenance and returning them to the user in minimal time; permit ship-to-shore operations any place in the world; and enhance the overall mobility of the Army by providing a logistic support system as mobile as the combat arms being supported.

CHAPTER VI

Service Support in Vietnam:
Transportation and Maintenance

Service support described in the next three chapters include the transportation, maintenance, construction, facilities engineering, real estate, communications and aviation elements logistics. Also service support includes food service, graves registration, laundry, bath and property disposal activities. There is also a brief discussion of other support missions unique to the Vietnam war.

Staggering amounts of supplies of all types (construction, maintenance, communication, aviation, transportation, and personal items for the soldier) traveled along extensive sea and air routes across the Pacific to Vietnam ports, into depots and storage areas, finally down primitive roads and an almost non-existent rail network to supply points where they were finally delivered to the individual soldier or unit.

Service support followed the same trail and to meet the challenge service support units also had to institute special management techniques.

Transportation

Between 1965 and 1969 over 22 million short tons of dry cargo and over 14 million short tons of bulk petroleum were transported to Vietnam. In addition to the cargo there was also the requirement for transporting personnel. Approximately 2.2 million people were transported to Vietnam and approximately 1.7 million were returned to the U.S. during this period. All the petroleum and more than 95 percent of the dry cargo were transported by ship. The remainder of the dry cargo and 90 percent of the passengers travelled by air.

Because of the similarities in military and commercial transportation operations, the transportation corps had a good base of professional knowledge to draw upon. For the most part, transportation personnel sent to Vietnam, both officers and enlisted personnel, had been in the business before.

Transportation Buildup—1965–1966

This period was characterized by a rapid increase in combat troop strength and the tremendous influx of supplies and equipment for their support. The transportation units that arrived during the May to August 1965 period were company and detachment sized-units which were stationed along the coast.

They were occupied primarily with their mission performance, their daily existence, security, and improvement of their cantonment areas. The 11th Transportation Battalion (terminal) arrived in Saigon on 5 August 1965 to assume control of the Saigon military port from the U.S. Navy. Two days later, the 394th Transportation Battalion (terminal) arrived at Qui Nhon to assume command of transportation units in that area and plan for the September arrival of the 1st Cavalry Division at An Khe. On 23 September, the 10th Transportation Battalion (terminal) arrived at Cam Ranh Bay to assume responsibility for the Cam Ranh Bay terminal.

The 4th Transportation Command (terminal Command) was the first senior transportation command and control unit to arrive in Vietnam. It arrived on 12 August 1965 and was given technical and operational control of all land and water transportation units assigned to the 1st Logistical Command. Included in this mission were the operation of the Saigon port, the water terminals at Cam Ranh Bay, Qui Nhon, Phan Rang, Nha Trang and Vung Tau, and operation of the Army Air Terminal at Tan Son Nhut.

Transportation Expansion—1966–1969

By early 1966, the Saigon, Qui Nhon, and Cam Ranh Bay Support Commands were established. Each was given responsibility for complete logistic support within its area of operation. This included the control and operation of all common user land transportation and port and beach facilities within the area. The Saigon area was an exception with the 4th Transportation Command retaining responsibility for port operations under the operational control of the Commanding General, 1st Logistical Command. The 4th Transportation Command was thereby relieved of its South Vietnam-wide transportation command mission, and concentrated on the Saigon Port proper. Although the 4th was not organized or manned to perform a theater level transportation command mission, the Command had done the job well. To assist the support commands in managing port operations, the 5th Transportation Command (terminal A) was assigned to Qui Nhon

Support Command, and the 124th Transportation Terminal Command (terminal A) was assigned to Cam Ranh Bay in August 1966.

Movement Control Within South Vietnam

Until September 1965 no co-ordinated movement control agency existed in South Vietnam. Air transportation was managed at the local level by individual Air Traffic Coordinating Offices located at the various aerial ports. Water transport requirements were sent directly to the Military Sea Transport Service, Far East. Highway transport needs were met by local support elements. As a result of such localized, decentralized traffic management, transport resources were either wasted or ineffectually employed and management data were not exchanged. There was no overall knowledge of the capability of country-wide transportation facilities.

In September 1965, Commander U.S. Military Assistance Command, Vietnam, established a jointly staffed Traffic Management Agency under his operational control and the staff supervision of the J–4. The agency became fully operational in early 1966 and was assigned the mission to: 1. direct, control and supervise all functions incident to the efficient and economical use of freight and passenger transportation service required for movement of all Department of Defense sponsored personnel and cargo within the Military Assistance Command, Vietnam, area of responsibility (this was later expanded to include U.S. Agency for International Development requirements) ; 2. serve as a point of contact for all users of military highway, railway, inland waterway, intra-coastal and troop carrier and cargo airlift capability as made available by the component commander; 3. arrange for movement; 4. advise and assist shippers and receivers to insure that such transport capability is effectively utilized; 5. prepare and maintain current plans in support of contingency plans and prepare other Military Assistance Command, Vietnam, plans as directed; 6. operate Military Assistance Command, Vietnam, Traffic Coordination Offices; 7. control movement of cargo and passengers into terminals through coordination with terminal operators; 8. maintain liaison with transport agencies of the host nation, host nation military organizations and appropriate U.S. Forces required to accomplish the assigned mission; 9. and control, manage and maintain the Military Assistance Command, Vietnam, container express operation.

The mission letter established the principle of centralized direction and control of traffic management and related services

at Military Assistance Command, Vietnam, headquarters and decentralized traffic operations, services, and co-ordination at field
offices operating in support of the component commands. It
authorized the Commander, Traffic Management Agency, to communicate directly with the component commands, their units,
installations, and activities concerning requirements, traffic management, and use of military owned transportation, with responsiveness to the requirements of each of the components as
the guiding principle. Originally Traffic Management Agency was
organized with a directorate staff and three traffic regions. To meet
changing requirements, two additional traffic regions were established in 1968. The total strength of Traffic Management Agency in
July 1968 was approximately 400 personnel. The regional headquarters, with their district and field traffic offices, as well as the Air
Traffic Co-ordinating Offices were located adjacent to major shipping and receiving activities and provided a point of direct contact
for all transportation users and operators. The Traffic Management Agency command communications network operated over
dedicated circuits that connected headquarters with the regional
headquarters—and each region to its subordinate district and field
traffic offices.

Since its inception, Traffic Management Agency was authorized to coordinate directly with numerous agencies outside the
specific Military Assistance Command, Vietnam, area of responsibility. The Traffic Management Agency was collocated with the Military Sea Transportation Service Office, Saigon, and was authorized
direct communication with both Commanding Officer Military
Sea Transportation Service, and Commanding Officer Military
Sea Transportation Service, Far East. To co-ordinate and obtain
sealift capabilities to support tactical operations, which could
not be supported by available resources, Traffic Management
Agency was authorized to communicate directly with the Commander, U.S. Seventh Fleet. The Air Transportation Co-ordination Offices representing all of the Services requested inter-
theater airlift allocations from Military Airlift Command. For
intra-theater airlift beyond the capability of Military Assistance
Command, Vietnam, assets, Traffic Management Agency requested assistance through the Western Pacific Transportation
Office. Traffic Management Agency provided cargo booking guidance to Western Pacific Transportation Office for inter-Pacific
Command surface movements to Vietnam ports and also co-
ordinated with the Pacific Command Movements Priority Agency
regarding surface shipments from Continental U.S. to Vietnam.

A significant point in the concept of Traffic Management Agency operations was that it did not exercise operational control of the transportation assets made available for common-user service. Rather, Traffic Management Agency operated on the basis of managing toward the optimum use of these assets. Forecasts of requirements were received from the Military Assistance Command, Vietnam, component commands, U.S. Agency for International Development, Vietnam Regional Exchange Service, Republic of Vietnam Armed Forces, and other authorized users. These requirements were matched against available common-user transportation capability, based on priorities of movement established by the shippers. If requirements exceeded the capabilities, Traffic Management Agency inititated action to obtain the additional capability. If additional lift capability was not available, Traffic Management Agency would allocate the existing capability based on the policies, guidance, and priorities of Commander U.S. Military Assistance Command, Vietnam.

The effectiveness of Traffic Management Agency improved as the theater situation stabilized, procedures were refined, operational problems were recognized, and solutions were developed. The lack of a centralized traffic management agency in South Vietnam during the early stages of the conflict contributed to an inefficient use of transportation resources. Movement control agencies proved to be highly effective in providing support to the tactical commander after the movement control agencies were implemented. Interface problems between Traffic Management Agency and the Military Assistance Command, Vietnam, components continued to exist. Rather than invalidate the system, these problems highlighted the need for an agency like Traffic Management Agency.

Truck Transportation

During the deployment of tactical units in mid-1965 most highway transport units were located at or near the major port areas. They provided port and beach clearance and local and line haul in II and III Corps.

These services were initially provided by three truck companies at Saigon and Cam Ranh Bay and a combination of medium truck companies (two cargo and one Petroleum, Oils, and Lubricants) at Qui Nhon. These capabilities were increased through 1966 by the addition of more truck companies and command and control elements.

As force levels climbed, the requirements for highway transportation units also increased. These requirements were met by three means: 1. the arrival of a Transportation Motor Transport Group Headquarters in Saigon plus the arrival of additional military truck units; 2. the use of commercial trucking contractors; and 3. the arrival of the 1st Transportation Company (GOER) in II Corps.

The 48th Transportation Group (Motor Transport) was the first truck group to arrive in South Vietnam and was assigned to the U.S. Army Support Command, Saigon in May 1966 to assume command of five truck companies then operating in III Corps. The 8th Transportation Group (Motor Transport) arrived at Qui Nhon in October 1966 and assumed command and control of the motor transport units in U.S. Army Support Command, Qui Nhon. The last truck group to arrive was the 500th Transportation Group (Motor Transport) which was assigned to the U.S. Army Support Command, Cam Ranh Bay in late October 1966. It was assigned responsibility for motor transport operations in the southern portion of II Corps.

In the summer of 1966 large scale combat operations in the Central Highlands put a severe strain on the motor transport units providing line haul support in the Pleiku area. Convoy commanders were required to continually operate over an insecure highway system. Convoy security support was provided by U.S. and Vietnamese units when priorities permitted; often the desired degree of support was not available. It was also desirable to have armored personnel carriers integrated into the convoy, but they were not always available. For this reason truck units employed the "hardened vehicle" concept (discussed in Chapter II). Within the 8th Transportation Group during the 1967–1968 time frame, the equivalent of one light truck company's capability was lost by converting their cargo vehicles to "hardened vehicles" to provide the necessary security.

Except in port and beach clearance and for local haul within secure areas, truck units operated only during daylight hours, thus achieving less productive tonnage than stated in Tables of Organization and Equipment which envision a 20 hour, two shift work day. Productivity was complicated by the unimproved roads which were made impassable by the monsoon rains. In September 1966, the GOER vehicle was introduced into Vietnam. The 1st Transportation Company (GOER) was the only company which utilized this vehicle. Total vehicles (GOER) assigned to the 1st Transportation Company (GOER) were 19. There were three configurations of the vehicle, the 8 ton vehicle, 8 ton 2,500 gallon tanker, and the 10 ton wrecker. The GOER vehicle was a large tire, rough terrain, cargo carrying vehicle built and designed by the Caterpillar Tractor Company. The vehicles were quite versatile, having a cross country and swim capability. These vehicles were used extensively, but especially during the monsoon period. The GOERS were limited in their use, particularly on hard surface roads, and maintenance was difficult as repair parts had to come directly from Continental U.S. The service they performed was noteworthy in its effect on the transportation system.

The highway tonnages moved by a combination of military and commercial motor transport during the period December 1967—December 1968 was approximately ten million tons; and by the same means during the period January—July 1969, approximately five million tons were carried.

As the buildup continued it became apparent that the conventional military truck was not designed to handle palletized and containerized loads efficiently. The fixed sides of the cargo bodies on the 2½-ton and 5-ton cargo trucks did not permit forklifts to reach the full length of the cargo compartment, therefore the push and pull method was used in loading and unloading operations causing damage to the truck bodies.

To facilitate operations, U.S. Army Vietnam obtained eighteen drop side cargo trucks from the U.S. Marine Corps to serve as test vehicles. The test proved that dropside trucks were highly desirable and effective cargo carriers and that through their use more cargo could be hauled with easier access to the entire length of the body and with little damage to the truck body. U.S. Army Vietnam requested that Department of the Army procure these trucks for use in Vietnam.

By the end of 1965, it was apparent to transportation planners that augmentation of military motor transport capability was necessary to clear the South Vietnamese port congestion. During the period March 1966—June 1966, the US Army Procurement Agency, Vietnam, awarded 10 major contracts for trucking services to augment the military capability. One of the major contractors used in Vietnam was the Vinnel Corporation which also provided stevedore support, beach and port clearance, and vessel maintenance support. The highway support offered by Vinnel included the operation of 30 Army-procured Kenworth trucks and trailers of the type and design used in the Arabian Desert. This vehicle was probably the most effective vehicle on the sand dunes of Cam Ranh Bay.

The three major trucking contractors used in the Saigon area were Equipment Inc., Philco Ford, and Do Thi Nuong. The Han Jin Company of Korea was utilized for trucking and stevedore services in the Qui Nhon area. The Alaskan Barge and Transport Company provided stevedore, trucking, and intra-coastal barge movement. Their intra-coastal operation utilized a considerable tug and barge fleet between Cam Ranh Bay and its outports. This intra-coastal barge movement included the entire South Vietnamese coast.

The use of contractor services for trucking, terminal, and marine purposes provided the extra punch needed in these operations, and provisions should be made to include in future planning consideration for use of contractors when the opportunity arises.

Rail Transportation

The Vietnam National Railway System was government owned, being operated under the supervision of the Ministry of Communications and Transportation. The Vietnam National Railway System originated at Saigon, and served the entire coastal area from Phan Thiet to Dong Ha. *(Map 4)* The overall condition of the roadbed and rolling stock was poor. The long period of intense interdiction and destruction by the Viet Cong and North Vietnamese regular units resulted in the railway system being unable to carry significant tonnages. The railroad was well engineered, however, with 413 bridges, 27 tunnels, controlling grades of less than 1½ percent, steel ties, and vertical elevations well above the waterways. In 1969, the rolling stock of the railroad consisted of 59 serviceable locomotives and over 500 serviceable freight cars. The major repair facility located in Saigon was well equipped to perform major engine and car repair. Other shop facilities along the length of the line were adequate to handle all types of minor repairs. The railroad employs approximately 3,500 personnel (operating crews, maintenance and construction forces). Overall planning for railway restoration began in June 1966 as a joint effort by the Government of Vietnam and U.S. agencies. All reconstruction efforts were coordinated through three standing committees composed of members of Military Assistance Command, Vietnam, Government of Vietnam, U.S. Agency for International Development, and the Government of Vietnam Joint General Staff with primary responsibility for railway restoration resting with the Joint Committee on railroad restoration. Actual construction was the responsibility of the Vietnam National Railway System except that rail spurs to U.S. military installations were

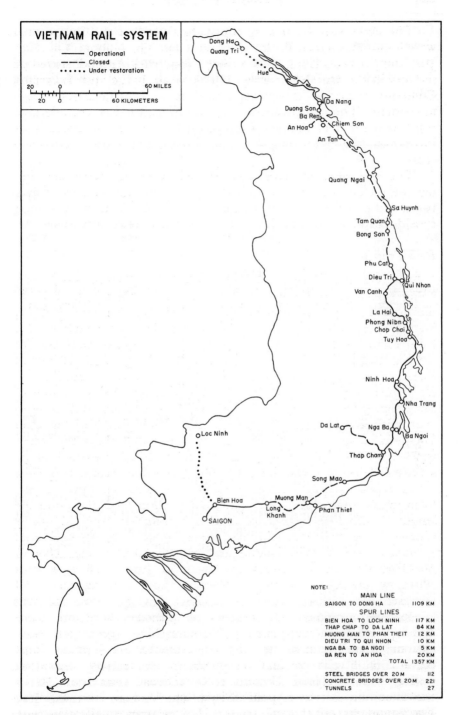

VIETNAM RAIL SYSTEM

———— Operational
– – – – Closed
•••••• Under restoration

20   0   60 MILES
20   0   60 KILOMETERS

Dong Ha
Quang Tri
Hue
Da Nang
Duong Son
Ba Ren
An Hoa
Chiem Son
An Tan
Quang Ngai
Sa Huynh
Tam Quan
Bong Son
Phu Cat
Dieu Tri
Qui Nhon
Van Canh
La Hai
Phong Nibn
Chop Chai
Tuy Hoa
Ninh Hoa
Nha Trang
Da Lat
Nga Ba
Ba Ngoi
Thap Cham
Song Mao
Loc Ninh
Bien Hoa
Muong Man
Long Khanh
Phan Thiet
SAIGON

NOTE:

MAIN LINE
SAIGON TO DONG HA   1109 KM
SPUR LINES
BIEN HOA TO LOCH NINH   117 KM
THAP CHAP TO DA LAT   84 KM
MUONG MAN TO PHAN THEIT   12 KM
DIEU TRI TO QUI NHON   10 KM
NGA BA TO BA NGOI   5 KM
BA REN TO AN HOA   20 KM
                    TOTAL   1357 KM

STEEL BRIDGES OVER 20M   112
CONCRETE BRIDGES OVER 20M   221
TUNNELS   27

MAP 4

funded and built by US forces. U.S. Agency for International Development furnished construction materials such as rail, ties, structured steel, bridge trusses, and equipment. Funds programed for railway restoration were limited as shown in the following table:

PROGRAMING FOR RAILWAY RESTORATION
($ MILLIONS)

Year	Government of Vietnam	U.S. AID	Total
1966	$ .8	---	$ .8
1967	2.3	$ 9.2	11.5
1968	2.6	3.1	5.7
1969	2.5	4.5	7.0
Totals	$ 8.2	$ 16.8	$ 25.0

The U.S. Army had considerable interest in this railroad because of the potential it offered in the bulk movement of cargo at low rates. The system was used to support the Military Assistance Command, Vietnam, construction program and transported hundreds of thousands of tons of rock and gravel to air base and highway sites. In 1967–1968, 200 U.S. procured freight cars were delivered. These cars were maintained and operated by the railroad for the U.S., and the freight rate for cargo handled on these cars was approximately 15 percent lower than normal rail rates.

Vietnamese personnel operated the engines, did their own repair work, and restored sections of track destroyed by the Viet Cong. To help the Vietnamese keep up to date, the U.S. Army assigned technical advisors to the railroad, but for the most part, the Vietnamese ran the whole operation.

Railway operations in Vietnam expanded in direct proportion to the interest and effort put forth by the U.S. and the Government of Vietnam. Besides providing low cost military transportation, railways helped the South Vietnamese in their social and economic development.

Air Transportation

Restrictions on land transportation placed added importance and reliance on intra-theater air transportation. The virtually nonexistent capability of the South Vietnamese Air Force air transport placed major reliance on U.S. air transport resources to support military operations. The main U.S. capability was provided by the Common Service Airlift System operated by the U.S. Air Force, and aircraft organic to the various military organizations.

The Common Service Airlift System was composed of fixed wing aircraft and provided tactical as well as intra-theater airlift. Organic aircraft were primarily employed by combat commanders for immediate battlefield mobility and support and were not readily available for intra-theater airlift purposes. Helicopters were not assigned to the Common Service Airlift System fleet, however they played an extensive and highly significant role which is discussed in some detail later in this chapter. The helicopter provided a highly versatile lift capability that had never been available in such great numbers in previous military operations. Use of the helicopter complemented the capability of the fixed wing aircraft and surface capability by operation from airfields and other areas to locations inaccessible to other forms of transport.

Initially the Common Service Airlift System was composed of U.S. Air Force C–123 and the C–7A aircraft of the Royal Australian Air Force and the U.S. Army. This fleet was augmented by U.S. Air Force C–130 aircraft in April 1965. The Common Service Airlift System organization further changed in January 1967 when the Chief of Staff, U.S. Army, and Chief of Staff, U.S. Air Force agreed that the C–7A aircraft assigned to the U.S. Army would be transferred to the U.S. Air Force.

Water Transportation

During the buildup phase, the few land lines of communication were in poor repair and subject to interdiction by enemy forces, and the mobility of U.S. Forces was achieved through the extensive use of water and air transportation.

To fully exploit the potential of the long South Vietnamese coastline, and to supplement improvements in South Vietnam's four major deep water ports, a series of satellite shallow-draft ports were developed. (*Map 5*) The improvements permitted intra-coastal shipping to increase tonnages between 1965–1968 from several hundred tons to over three million tons.

Ports were rapidly expanded through the use of DeLong piers. These piers were quite versatile and were fabricated in a variety of sizes and configurations ranging from 55 feet to 427 feet long and 45 feet to 90 feet wide. They were towed from their ports of origin and quickly implaced at their destination. The De-Long pier is a good concept and a good facility, and should be included in future contingency plan packages.

Although the development of the four major deep draft ports was important to the support of forces in Vietnam, the use of numerous shallow draft ports and special operations, such as

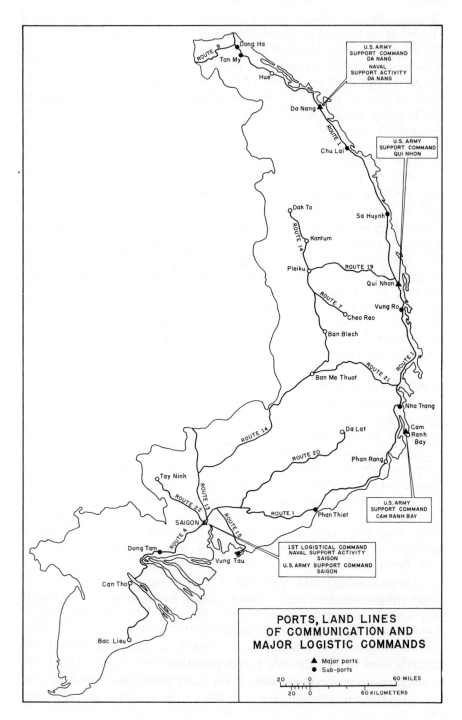

PORTS, LAND LINES
OF COMMUNICATION AND
MAJOR LOGISTIC COMMANDS

▲ Major ports
● Sub-ports

20   0   60 MILES
20   0   60 KILOMETERS

MAP 5

Wunder Beach (Than My Thuy) were vital to the support of troops in such areas as I and IV Corps. Wunder Beach (Than My Thuy) in I Corps was a Logistics-Over-The-Shore type operation which was useful during the dry season. This beach operation allowed shallow draft vessels to unload directly on the beach without the use of piers and was an effective and efficient means of discharging cargo. The support of shallow draft operations required the use and coordination of the Military Sea Transportation Service, the Seventh Fleet LSTs in the Western Pacific, and the U. S. Army watercraft resources.

The U. S. Army Beach Discharge Lighter *LTC John U. D. Page,* which was made available for use in South Vietnamese waters after repeated requests and much delay, was useful in supporting intra-coastal requirements within the Cam Ranh Bay logistics complex (Nha Trang-Cam Ranh-Phan Rang). Control of the operation of this craft was retained at the Cam Ranh Bay Support Command. Because of its shallow draft and unrestricted loading ramp area, it was more versatile and valuable than an LST on a ship-for-ship basis. Although a prototype and unique in the Army inventory since the late 1950's, this craft has justified its additional procurement for the purpose of modernizing and increasing the versatility of the shallow draft fleet. This ship moved an average of 10,000 to 15,000 short tons per month. Her propulsion system was damaged in 1967, but demand for the ship's services delayed its movement to a shipyard in Japan for overhaul until almost a year later.

Early in the Vietnam buildup Landing Craft, Mechanized (LCM) and Landing Craft, Utility (LCU), were used to perform ship-to-shore and selective discharge operations and for limited intercoastal and inland waterway operations. These craft were supported in the lighterage role by amphibians of the LARC V (5 ton) and LARC LX (60 ton) (formerly known as BARC) classes. As deep draft piers were developed, some of these craft were diverted to other missions, such as the Wunder Beach operation, where no port facilities existed.

Due to the periodic shortage of tugs in the Saigon area, LCMs were frequently used to tow ammunition barges from the in-stream deep draft discharge sites at Nha Be and later at Cat Lai, to barge discharge sites dispersed throughout the area.

In northern I Corps, LCMs were used on the Perfume and Cua Viet Rivers to shuttle dry cargo and petroleum, oils, and lubricants from coastal transfer sites to Hue and Dong Ha.

In addition to their normal lighterage use, LCMs were employed in performing a variety of harbor service functions such as resupply, maintenance, ferry service, and patrol and were also used in direct support of tactical operations.

As the capacity of deep draft piers improved, both the Army's and the Navy's LCUs were shifted to intra-coastal and inland-water ways. The use of LCUs accounted for approximately 29 percent of the total cargo moved intra-coastally during that year. Prior to the completion of the LST ramps at Tan My, Navy LCUs, with periodic Army support, were the primary media for resupply to northern I Corps. Extensive use of LCUs was also made for operations in the Saigon-Vung Tau-Delta complex. In late 1967 six SKILAKs, commercial off-the-shelf LCU/YFU type craft, were procured by the Navy to support operations in I Corps.

To help alleviate the shortage of lighterage and coastal shipping capability, Commander U. S. Military Assistance Command, Vietnam, recommended that a contract be negotiated with Alaska Barge and Transport Company. The concept of utilizing civilian contractors was approved by the Secretary of Defense in November 1965 and he directed the Military Sea Transportation Service to negotiate the contract. By 8 December the contract was signed and operations began in early 1966. This intra-coastal augmentation included a barge-tug fleet among which were two stripped down LST hulls for use as barges.

Because only one major port, Cam Ranh Bay, had a deep draft pier for the discharge of ammunition, a large number of the available barges were used to support the ammunition discharge program. The ammunition discharge in the Saigon-Cat Lai (Nha Be) complex, for example, was in effect a combination stream-discharge and inland waterway distribution system and placed a heavy requirement on the available barge assets. In each major port complex, contractor-furnished lighterage augmented the limited military capability that was available.

A new requirement was announced in 1967 to move a minimum of 85,000 short tons per month of crushed rock into the Delta to support the highway rehabilitation program. This program increased the shallow draft barge and tug requirements and necessitated expansion of the contract support provided by Alaska Barge and Transport and another company, the Luzon Stevedoring Company.

A number of LSTs were being utilized for carrying cargo from Far Eastern Pacific ports to South Vietnam. To relieve pressure on LST assets and in order to make more shallow-draft shipping available in South Vietnam, the Commanding Officer, Military Sea

Transportation Service, Far East procured small foreign flag ships and retained some of the Continental U. S.-to-South Vietnam shipping resources for intra-theater use. This additional deep-draft shipping plus the improvements in ship turn-around time in South Vietnamese ports contributed substantially to decreasing the pressure on LST resources and permitted a greater use of LSTs for deliveries to shallow-draft ports in lieu of LCM's and LCU's. Nevertheless, LST requirements continued to be sufficiently heavy to maintain pressure on the allocation and use of theater LST assets.

Transshipment of cargo from major South Vietnamese ports to areas supported by over-the-beach unloading continued on a large scale, although Commander in Chief Pacific favored the development of additional deep-water berths in various ports such as Vung Ro, Qui Nhon, and Vung Tau in order to reduce dependence on LST operations.

The maritime fleet which supported the resupply of combat operations in South Vietnam was inadequate and outdated. Although a majority of the vessels had been in moth balls, they were worn out. These ships required an extensive amount of repair to put them in service and keep them afloat. It would have been more cost effective if we had had a fleet of ships designed to meet the requirements for movement of troops and military cargo.

Containerization

Containerization was an important logistic concept used extensively in Vietnam. About 1950 the Army first developed a concept of utilizing a standard-sized container to give a semblance of automation to the movement of supplies through the pipeline from Continental U.S. stations and depots to overseas units and depots. The standard steel container called container express with a capacity of 9,000 lbs was designed to be carried on trucks and rail cars and be handled by the general purpose 5-ton capacity cargo gear on most ocean freighters.

The Army efforts in containerization originated with the port and supply problems in World War II and Korea and made use of the advances made by other services and industry in unitization and palletization of cargo. All services stressed palletization. In addition to the Army and Air Force investments in container express containers, the Marines had developed two standard-sized mount-out boxes for deploying forces; and the Air Force developed its 463–L system to handle palletized cargo in aircraft.

In early 1965 the Army and the Air Force jointly owned an inventory of almost 100,000 container express containers. Every major U. S. Army unit moving to the theater carried its accompanying spare parts and supplies in containers. For example, the U. S. 1st Cavalry deployment included about 2,500 containers, all prominently marked with the big yellow division patch. Army aviation units used containers with prebinned stockage of the myriad of small items—rivets, cotter pins, and nuts and bolts peculiar to aviation support and utilized in large volumes. As the conflict escalated, there was more and more demand for containers, and eventually the theater inventory exceeded 150,000 (of the total 200,000 units then owned by the Army and Air Force).

The 150,000 units in-theater represented about six million square feet of covered storage. This figure is impressive when compared to the fact that only about 11 million square feet of covered storage had been built in the entire theater by the middle of 1969. Few of the containers moved into the theater ever returned. They satisfied a wide variety of needs for shelter including dispensaries, command posts, PXs, and bunkers.

Containers played an integral part in a special project to make Cam Ranh Bay a major U. S. Army supply base. As in most locations in Vietnam, the construction of depot facilities did not keep pace with the influx of supplies and equipment. It was estimated in January 1966 that the Cam Ranh Bay depot would be supporting a force of 95,000 men by the end of June 1966. In an effort to overcome the lack of depot facilities, the Army Materiel Command prepared, in effect, a prepackaged container depot containing a 60-day stockage level of repair parts for all units supported by the depot at Cam Ranh Bay. When completed, the entire package of about 53,000 line items together with a library of manuals, stock records, locator cards, and other documentation, was contained in 70 military van semitrailers and 437 binned containers.

This represented container-oriented logistics in a highly sophisticated form and was also a good example of the integration of supply and transportation systems. The project packages arrived at Cam Ranh Bay on 21 May 1966 and a total of 13,538 material release orders were issued during the first 10 days of operation with only 26 warehouse denials—less than 0.2 percent.

The next step forward in utilization of intermodal containers (containers that can be shipped by rail, truck, air or ship) in support of operations in Vietnam was the introduction of container ship support by Sea-Land Services, Inc. These ships were designed to carry the more familiar Sea-Land container which is essentially a trailer van that can be set on a trailer bed and be pulled by a truck (or on a rail flat car). The container can be removed from the trailer bed and set on the container ship. Special type cranes are needed either at the port or incorporated on the ship. In 1966 Sea-Land began providing container service to the Army on Okinawa. Sea-Land container support was extended to the Navy at Subic Bay in the Philippines. In 1967 Sea-Land was introduced into Vietnam. Since that time every command concerned with the support of U.S. Forces in Vietnam expressed satisfaction with the degree of success achieved in the container ship operations moving general cargo and perishable subsistence into Vietnam.

Ammunition was also successfully handled in container ship service. During December 1969 and January 1970, a Test of Containerized Shipment of Ammunition was conducted to determine the feasibility of shipping ammunition from the United States to Vietnam by container ship service. A self-sustaining container ship was used in the test to move 226 containers of ammunition from the United States to Cam Ranh Bay. Some of the containers were unloaded in the ammunition depot at Cam Ranh Bay; others were transshipped on lighterage to Qui Nhon and on to forward supply points. The test was such a success that the 1st Logistical Command recommended the initiation of regularly scheduled ammunition resupply in container ships to reduce order and ship time and provide savings in pipeline inventory. The requirement for initial procurement of container materials handling equipment during the wind-down period in Southeast Asia and the establishment of new procedures for container movement of ammunition resulted in a decision not to use containers for routine ammunition movement.

Experiences of Southeast Asia show real advantages in the use of containers. Cargo is moved faster, there is less damage and loss of cargo and there are major savings in handling costs and packaging. The new transportation technique requires the use of large and expensive equipment and special container materials handling equipment, to include ship or shore side gantry cranes. Accounting and control procedures must also be developed to effectively operate a container system. The system approach must be followed as the size and weight of container limit improvision. If self-sustaining ships are not available, shore side equipment must be provided. All containers and their materials handling equipment must be compatible for both surface (road, rail, sea) and air movement of containers.

Experience with large intermodal containers in Vietnam clearly indicated that their full exploitation could greatly enhance the transportation, storage and handling of supplies. The following four advantages speak for themselves:

1. Container ships can be discharged 7 to 10 times faster than breakbulk ships and with fewer personnel. Drastic reductions in berthing space and in port operating personnel requirements also result.

2. The practicality of operating directly out of containers pre-binned in the United States is feasible and was demonstrated at Cam Ranh Bay.

3. All recipients of containerized cargo noted a reduction in damaged and lost cargo—particularly ammunition, perishable items, and PX supplies.

4. Because cargo is moved intact in a container from the Continental U.S. to the depot or directly to a forward unit, problems in sorting and identifying cargo are minimized.

Augmenting the container service were Roll-on—Roll-off ships. The Roll-on—Roll-off concept provided a land and water express service comprising the through put concept of cargo between continental United States depots and overseas depots; and also between inter- and intra-theater depots. Cargo is checked at the point of origin and loaded aboard a trailer type conveyance, transported to a vessel at the port of loading, rolled into the vessel, stowed, and rolled off at the port of discharge and dispatched to forward destinations.

The Roll-on—Roll-off operation combined the U.S. Army Trailer Service Agency with Military Sea Transportation Service Roll-on—Roll-off type ships to facilitate the movement of general cargo. The service was used for providing scheduled depot-to-depot delivery of combat support items, and gave a faster, more flexible response to theater logistics requirements. It reduced the intransit exposure of ship and cargo to enemy action, reduced oversea supply point requirements, and reduced shiploading and discharge times. It also lessened the requirement for permanent port and rail facilities.

The Roll-on—Roll-off service which had been operating in support of Europe was transferred to Okinawa to support operations in Southeast Asia. Beginning in March 1966, this service operated between Okinawa, Cam Ranh Bay, Saigon, Qui Nhon and Bangkok.

The Military Sea Transportation Service ships *Comet, Transglobe,* and *Taurus* plus 2,400 trailers were used in the Roll-on—Roll-off operations. A typical Roll-on—Roll-off ship had the capacity to transport Roll-on—Roll-off trailers, containers, or large or small military vehicles.

Matériel Handling Equipment was in short supply during the early build-up in Vietnam. This significantly impaired the unloading of materiel from transportation vehicles and the movement of matériel within the storage areas. This equipment was especially critical due to the palletization concept of stocking and moving supplies. Resupply and retrograde at the most forward logistic support areas were almost totally dependent on Matériel Handling Equipment. Shortages of Matériel Handling Equipment prevented the realization of the full potential of the palletization concept.

In an attempt to meet the urgent demands for Matériel Handling Equipment during the early period, 47 different makes and models were procured. However, this resulted in an almost impossible task of stocking repair parts, which in turn created a high equipment deadline rate. This rate was not lowered until a standardization program was instituted. In 1966, steps were taken to reduce the 47 models to five commercial models plus two rough terrain fork lifts. By August 1967, this has been accomplished and the Matériel Handling Equipment situation improved.

Maintenance

The U.S. maintenance capability (less aircraft) in South Vietnam in March 1965 consisted of a three-bay third echelon maintenance shop in downtown Saigon limited to vehicle and armament repair and instrument calibration, with a work force of ten personnel.

Adequate facilities in early 1965 were a problem. For example, an old rice mill located along the Saigon Canal was selected and acquired in May 1965 for the Saigon area maintenance facility. The buildings were of brick construction with dirt floors covered with two feet of rice hulls. Maintenance personnel removed and disposed of the rice hulls and cleaned out the buildings. Lacking engineer support, maintenance personnel poured their own concrete floors using a road grader to spread the concrete and installed the necessary electrical wiring in the buildings. The maintenance shops were opened one building at a time as they were made usable.

Many direct support and general support units arrived in 1965 without Authorized Stockage Lists or Prescribed Load Lists of repair parts. This problem was the result of three things. Continental U.S. activities did not know what units or types of equipment the direct support or general support units were to support;

therefore adequate parts lists could not be prepared. Requests from Continental U.S. to the 1st Logistical Command for units and equipment densities could not be satisfied because the information of units and equipment enroute to South Vietnam was not available. In addition, the very fluid tactical situation in South Vietnam in early 1965, with the resultant changes in in-country deployment of combat units, made it almost impossible to develop unit densities of equipment to be supported with any reasonable degree of accuracy. The maintenance effort started short of repair parts and it did not recover until mid-1966. The interim period was characterized by a highly skilled maintenance capability without sufficient repair parts to utilize this capability to the maximum. This period was also characterized by unusually low Operational Readiness rates for engineer equipment, Materiel Handling Equipment, trucks, water craft and generators. All of these were essential items in properly carrying out the logistical mission.

Maintenance Support Positive reevaluated the Army Maintenance System to provide for performance of tasks at the level that provides maximum readiness and cost effectiveness, achieves the best mix of modular and piece parts repair, increases the use of modular design of new equipment, expands direct exchange, improves design and application of test, measurement and diagnostic equipment, optimizes use of mobile maintenance and reduces requirements for complicated tools at the forward levels of maintenance. The maintenance structure must be flexible enough to combine selected levels of maintenance within the Army force structure to permit responsive, effective and efficient application of resources to sustain or improve the operational readiness of a complex commodity or weapon system.

The initiation of the Red Ball Express in December 1965, as a result of the Secretary of Defense's visit to South Vietnam, was a great help in improving operational readiness rates for critical items. As Authorized Stockage Lists and Prescribed Load Lists were developed and received, adequate maintenance facilities were developed, and supported units were stabilized, the Operational Readiness rates increased to the highest ever found in a combat zone. However, these rates were made possible only through the expensive replacement of entire components (engines, differentials, transmissions) at direct support levels. Table 10 shows the Operational Readiness rates for some selected items of equipment between June 1966 and June 1970.

TABLE 10—OPERATIONAL READINESS (IN PERCENT)

Items	Military Assistance Command, Vietnam Objective	Actual Operational Readiness Rates		
		June 1966	June 1967*	June 1970**
Tractors	80	80	88	82
Rough Terrain Fork Lift	80	82	87	82
M109 How (SP)	85	92	92	87
M107 Gun (SP)	85	85	86	93
Generators .... (all types)	80	85	89	87
5-Ton Trucks .... (all types)	90	88	90	88

*1968 and 1969 operational readiness rates did not differ materially from those shown for 1967.
**Slight decline shows the impact of Cambodian Operations.

Reorganization in Combat

The war in Vietnam occurred at a time of significant changes in the Army's organizational structure. At the start of the buildup, maintenance support was provided by units of the Technical Services: Chemical, Engineer, Medical, Ordnance, Quartermaster, Signal, and Transportation. Units organized and trained by the Technical Services performed support operations at the field level under doctrine and detailed procedures developed by each Technical Service. The system contained inherent disadvantages because of its fragmentation into seven virtually autonomous structures. In some instances, all seven Technical Services were involved in the support of a single end item, such as a tank. In mid-1966, a reorganization to the Combat Service to the Theater Army concept was begun in Vietnam. This was a large undertaking. It required deactivation of old units, activation of new units, realignment of functions, realignment of personnel, and redistribution of equipment. Combat Service to the Theater Army eliminated Technical Services maintenance units (except medical) and created a functional organization that was compatible with the existing force structure, the divisions and the commodity oriented Continental U.S. base. It eliminated duplication of maintenance training, skills, tools, and test equipment. It was also designed to reduce the span of control of the force commander, increase responsiveness, and provide one stop service and support. The effectiveness of maintenance, however, was impeded initially by the turbulence caused by this reorganization.

The U.S. Army Vietnam maintenance system included all categories of maintenance from the operator's level to limited depot overhaul, as well as calibration of equipment, controlled cannibalization, and repair parts supply. Chart 12 depicts the organizational relationship, and the approximate troop strengths of the major maintenance elements of U.S. Army Vietnam as of August 1969. The 1st Logistical Command provided maintenance support of ground equipment to all U.S. Army forces. The U.S. Navy provided common item maintenance support, when requested, to Free World Military Assistance Forces. Map 6 depicts the general location and nature of maintenance support units in Vietnam. All categories of maintenance support were primarily accomplished through the four Support Commands of the 1st Logistical Command. Emphasis was on direct support as far forward as practicable. General support maintenance was provided primarily from the larger logistics bases where more stabilized conditions existed. Depot level maintenance by military units was minimized by the use of contractors in-country and off-shore depot maintenance support.

Between April and September 1965, 15 maintenance companies arrived in Vietnam. By late 1968, 35 maintenance companies were operating in Vietnam. The four Support Commands directed and co-ordinated maintenance services within their areas of responsibility. The nuclei of the maintenance organizations were the general support groups which also served as the command and control headquarters for direct support and general support batta-

CHART 12—ORGANIZATION OF U.S. ARMY VIETNAM MAINTENANCE SYSTEM (AUGUST 1969)

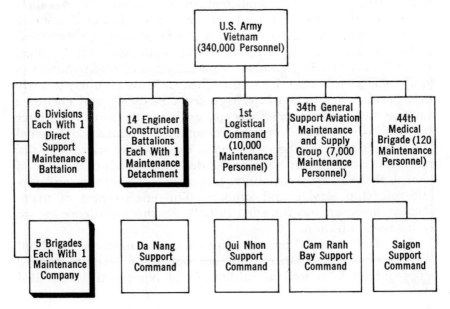

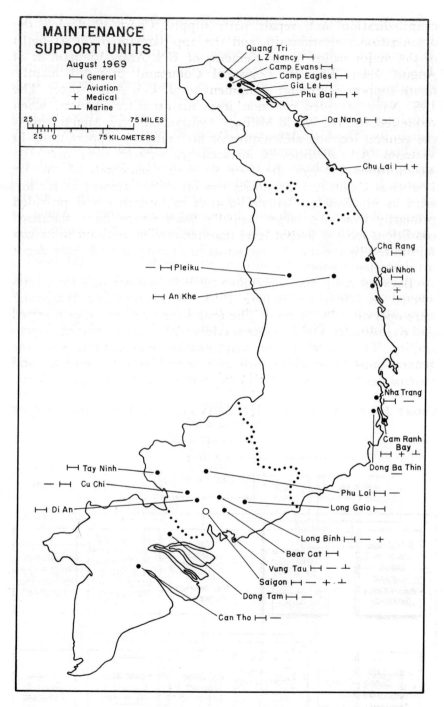

MAINTENANCE SUPPORT UNITS

August 1969

⊢⊣ General
— Aviation
+ Medical
⊥ Marine

25   0   75 MILES
25   0   75 KILOMETERS

Quang Tri
LZ Nancy ⊢⊣
Camp Evans ⊢⊣
Camp Eagles ⊢⊣
Gia Le ⊢⊣
Phu Bai ⊢⊣ +

Da Nang ⊢⊣ —

Chu Lai ⊢⊣ +

Cha Rang

Qui Nhon
⊢⊣
+

⊢⊣Pleiku

⊢⊣ An Khe

Nha Trang ⊢⊣ ⊥

Cam Ranh Bay
⊢⊣ ⊥

Dong Ba Thin

⊢⊣ Tay Ninh

— ⊢⊣ Cu Chi

⊢⊣ Di An

Phu Loi ⊢⊣ —

Long Gaio ⊢⊣

Long Binh ⊢⊣ — +

Bear Cat ⊢⊣

Vung Tau ⊢⊣ — ⊥

Saigon ⊢⊣ — + ⊥

Dong Tam ⊢⊣ —

Can Tho ⊢⊣ —

MAP 6

lions. (*Chart 13*) Composite battalions were also formed within the Support Commands, to assure service within geographical areas. For example, the 57th Transportation Battalion, located at Chu Lai, served as the composite headquarters for two maintenance companies, a transportation company, a supply and services company and several quartermaster platoons. In addition each combat division and separate brigade had its own organic direct support capability. The 11th Armored Cavalry Regiment was an exception. It obtained its maintenance support from the 1st Logistical Command on an area basis. As elements of the regiment relocated, the nearest 1st Logistical Command unit provided service. This method of support proved unsatisfactory because of the 11th Armored Cavalry Regiment's high and fluctuating maintenance demands. In the future such organizations should be assigned an organic maintenance unit.

The many isolated positions, such as fire bases and landing zones, were supported through a system of maintenance detachments and contact teams provided from the available resources of support command units. In the major base complexes such as at Long Binh, Da Nang, Pleiku, Qui Nhon and Cam Ranh Bay,

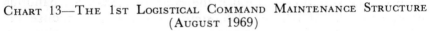

CHART 13—THE 1ST LOGISTICAL COMMAND MAINTENANCE STRUCTURE
(AUGUST 1969)

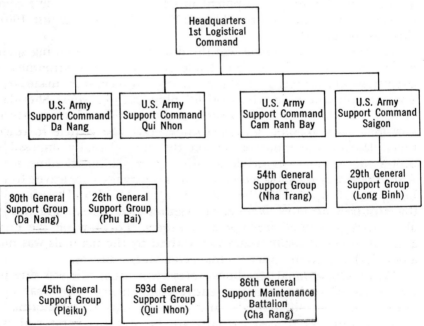

forces were concentrated enough to employ conventional battalion-sized maintenance units occupying permanent type facilities.

The in-country maintenance of medical equipment was primarily performed by base and advanced medical depots with the 32d Medical Depot providing technical assistance. However, medical units themselves, operating under the control of the 44th Medical Brigade (which was supervised by the U.S. Army Vietnam Surgeon), performed limited maintenance. Medical maintenance shops were colocated with medical supply depots. The base depot was located at Cam Ranh Bay and subordinate advanced depots were located at Phu Bai, Chu Lai, Qui Nhon, and Long Binh.

Equipment Repair Problems

Generally speaking, U.S. Army equipment in South Vietnam was the best ever fielded in combat. However, the lack of equipment standardization was a frustrating problem. For instance, initially 145 different sizes and types of commercial generators were used by the Army in Vietnam. Repair parts supply was difficult, at best, requiring extraordinary efforts for procurement, and in many cases the repair parts that were available lacked interchange-ability. The situation was much the same with material handling equipment. In March of 1966, steps were taken to reduce the 47 Materiel Handling Equipment models then in use to five commercial models plus two rough terrain fork lifts. By August 1967, this was completed.

Another major problem was the difficulty in maintaining some equipment due to its design. Under the adverse environmental conditions encountered in Vietnam, the problem was magnified. For example, the road wheel oil fill plugs on the M551 Sheridan vehicle were located on the inside of the wheels making it necessary for a crew member to crawl underneath the vehicle to reach them. During the monsoon season this was virtually impossible unless the vehicle was inside a building or shelter of some sort. Also, there was no satisfactory way to keep twigs and leaves from being sucked up against the radiator of the M551 and cutting off the required air flow. Therefore engines overheated. Practically all U.S. engines used dry-type air cleaners. To blow off the dust and wash them in soapy water as required by the manuals was not a practical operation under Vietnam combat conditions.

While Operational Readiness rates were high, this was due to the expensive replacements of entire components. The wear out rate of engines, differentials, and transmissions was abnormally high and this was at least partially attributable to operator abuse and inadequate organizational maintenance. The cost and efforts involved in transporting, overhauling, and storing the components that should not have been worn out were significant and preventable.

Though not a maintenance fault, failures of multifuel engines created the requirement for a major off-shore maintenance effort and a sizeable supply problem. In January 1967, more than 300 5-ton trucks were deadlined in Vietnam because of inoperative multifuel engines (a similar condition existed for 2½-ton trucks) due to cracked blocks, blown head gaskets, valve stems and connecting rods. A study indicated that many failures occurred between 9,000 and 10,000 miles and that the units hardest hit were the line haul transportation units whose engines were subjected to continuous use (2,000 miles per month in Vietnam). The prospect for improvement at this point was negligible because of the lack of repair parts and overhaul capacity. Multifuel engines powered both 2½- and 5-ton trucks. A similar condition also existed in Thailand. The annual engine replacement rate of 6 per 100 vehicles per year increased to a rate of one engine per vehicle per year.

By the summer of 1967, an airlift program, Red Ball Express was put into effect in an attemp to alleviate the shortage of engines and repair parts. The Red Ball Express was designed to be used in lieu of normal procedures exclusively to expedite repair parts to remove equipment from deadline status. Reserved and predictable airlift was made available for this purpose. The seriousness of the situation led to a multifuel engine conference on 28 August 1967. The conference resulted in several recommendations, the most significant of which was that three multifuel engines, LD 427, LD 465, and LDS 465, were to be placed under Closed Loop Support management because of the inability of units in the field to cope with the maintenance problem. A further recommendation was made that return to the Continental U.S. be authorized for vehicles that could not be supported with multifuel repair parts or replacement engine assemblies. Because a large percentage of the producers' production capacity was consumed in end items assembly, some repair parts and new replacement engine assemblies were not readily available. Department of the Army approved the recommendations of the conference and directed that necessary retrograde, overhaul, and shipping operations be initiated immediately.

Although the conference had focused attention on the supply aspect and premature failure of engines, significant intangibles remained unsolved, including proper operation of vehicles and user maintenance. Because of the characteristic difference of the multifuel engine from the standard internal combustion engine, periodic maintenance and specific mandatory operational procedures differed sharply from procedures used with other vehicles and required closer attention. Simply put, despite years of testing effort, the multifuel engine did not possess the ruggedness and tolerance to withstand the abuses inherent in field operations.

Marine Maintenance

With the exception of the newly developed amphibian river patrol boats and Amphibious Cargo Resupply Lighters, there was only one US Army vessel in South Vietnam less than 14 years old. This vessel, the beach discharge lighter *Page,* was the only ocean going vessel that was not of World War II design. As part of the effort to maintain the over-age fleet, a systematic overhaul of all craft began in 1967, but a shortage of repair parts caused delays. For instance, 14 tugs, or 38 percent of the tug fleet, were being overhauled in out-of-country shipyards at one time. Five of these tugs had been undergoing overhaul for more than one year. This made it necessary to lease seven commercial tugs at a cost of $1,283,000 per year to insure continuity of tug boat service. The excessive amount of man-hours and dollars spent to maintain the obsolete vessels and equipment of the marine fleet make it clear that these should be replaced by an up-to-date fleet.

The U.S. Army marine fleet consisted of amphibious and conventional lighters, landing craft, tug boats, barges and other vessels up to 2,200 long tons capacity. To support this fleet, the Marine Maintenance Activity, Vietnam was organized in 1966, with headquarters at Cam Ranh Bay. In 1967 the Marine Maintenance Activity, Vietnam consisted of a headquarters and four small detachments which were positioned in the areas with the largest concentration of marine craft. One was located at Qui Nhon, one at Cam Ranh Bay, and two under the Saigon Support Command. The Marine Maintenance Activity supported the II, III and IV Corps, while the U.S. Navy supported the I Corps. Maintenance beyond the capacity of the Marine Maintenance Activity was accomplished by in-country contractors and at off-shore facilities. Overall responsibility for the marine maintenance mission rested with U.S. Army Vietnam while operational control was the responsibility of the support commands. The Marine Maintenance Activity exercised technical supervision over the four detachments. The Marine Maintenance Activity, Vietnam organization with detachment strengths, as of August 1969, is depicted in Chart 14.

Maintenance Support of Common Items

The major area of interface between the military services and maintenance systems occurred with the support of common items. In general, common maintenance support between the U.S. military services was very limited. Similar to the area of common supply support, the objective of each service for logistical self-sufficiency dominated in the buildup period and tended to persist for the duration. Commonality of equipment too was limited, and effective common maintenance support was frequently impaired by the geographical deployment of the maintenance unit and the "customer" unit in different tactical zones. Insufficient stockage of both common and peculiar repair parts also impeded common maintenance support. An example of this was the equipment of the 3d Armored Cavalry Squadron, 5th Regiment, 9th Division, attached to the 1st Marine Division at Da Nang. Although the Marine Corps did provide Class I, II, III and V supply to the squadron it was unable to furnish maintenance support. The latter was provided by the U.S. Army Maintenance unit located at Da Nang until the Squadron was withdrawn from the zone and returned to the III Corps area. The U.S. Air Force and Navy received some maintenance support from the Army on such common items as administrative type vehicles in other tactical areas. This same type of general maintenance support was provided to medical and aviation units by the 1st Logistical Command and included some tactical vehicles. For example the Army provided maintenance support for UH–1 helicopters used by the Navy in its "Seawolf" operation and for the Air Force modernization program of 0–1 aircraft and UH–1 helicopters for transfer to allied forces. Conversely under the Army-Air Force basic support agreements the Air Force allocated some 11,000 manhours per month of its commercial contract capability for maintenance support of Army aircraft. Repair of Army owned test sets and special equipment was also accomplished by the Air Force when appropriate under these arrangements. Military Assistance Command, Vietnam, and adviser units lacking maintenance capability were also offered maintenance support. Cooperative exchange arrangements with the Navy were also conducted by the 1st Logistical Command through the Support Commands. For example, the recapping of Army tires and the re-winding of unserviceable motors was accomplished under Navy contracts. Under similar support arrangements the

CHART 14—ORGANIZATIONAL STRUCTURE, MARINE MAINTENANCE
ACTIVITY, VIETNAM (AUGUST 1969)

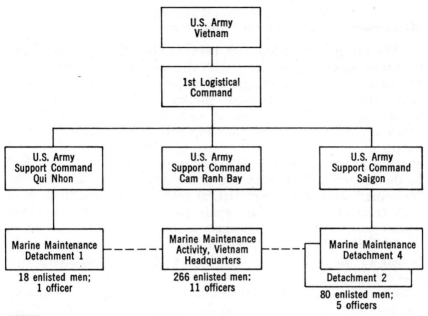

LEGEND:

— — — — Technical Supervision

Army maintained Marine Corps radar equipment to assure operational readiness. Conversely, the Marine Corps maintenance teams in the Da Nang Area assisted the Army in repairing and cleaning office machines.

The Army also provided maintenance support for common items of matériel in the hands of allied forces, beyond the capability of these forces. These services were furnished under cooperative logistics support arrangements with the allied nations involved.

Maintenance Workload

By 1966, maintenance support was characterized by the heavy over-loading of direct support maintenance units whose normal mission was to repair and return equipment to using units. General support maintenance units were forced to assume direct support missions. The Army reported to the Secretary of Defense on 29 August 1968 that 38 percent of the general support capability had been diverted to direct support level tasks. The resultant lack of general support was compensated for by the standardization of equipment, off-shore maintenance support, and the Closed Loop System. General support maintenance in-country increased from 37½ percent of total maintenance in 1966 to 49 percent in 1968.

U.S. Army Vietnam reported that the Army Equipment Records System was generally ineffective in Vietnam. While its objectives were valid, the system was too cumbersome to be used under the stress of combat. It required the collection of detailed information on all the equipment, but this required a level of skill which was not available. The Army equipment records procedures have since been revised and simplified. The new system, designated The Army Maintenance Management System, reduced the organizational reporting and recording effort at the crew and mechanic level by 80 percent and reduced automatic data processing by 50 percent.

Off-Shore Maintenance Problems

As maintenance requirements in Vietnam increased, it was essential that overhaul capabilities be established in the Pacific Theater to provide responsive support and reduce the lengthy overhaul pipeline. With the development in 1967 of Closed Loop support for armored personnel carriers in Vietnam, the Sagami depot maintenance capabilities in Japan were expanded to enable it to support the requirements of the Eighth Army, U.S. Army Vietnam and the South Vietnamese Army. Production schedules were increased after a successful effort to recruit additional personnel. A labor force of approximately 615 was employed at Sagami by the end of June 1967.

Okinawa continued the marine craft maintenance programs, with a strength of 210 personnel devoted to that mission. In 1967, as U.S. Army Vietnam overhaul requirements continued to increase, the problem with multifuel engines required the establishment of overhaul and modification programs on Okinawa. The number of maintenance personnel was increased to 1,381. These programs included maintenance of trucks, construction equipment, electronics and communication equipment, materials handling equipment, and marine craft.

During 1966 and 1967, maintenance units were deployed to Okinawa as a part of the 2d Logistical Command, which was charged with the support of island forces and offshore general support for Vietnam. The general support workload was primarily for tactical wheeled vehicles, generators, materials handling equipment, and electronic communications items, and amounted to 50 percent of the Vietnam requirement. This level of effort was maintained through 1969.

In 1965, Army overseas depot level maintenance existed on a limited basis in Germany and Japan. Depot maintenance activities were manned principally by local nationals with few spaces authorized for officers and non-commissioned officers. The only Army depot level facility in the Pacific was located at U.S. Army Depot Command, Sagami, Japan. Depot capability in Japan consisted of a work force of 504 local nationals devoted to maintenance of Military Assistance.

By 1969, overhaul in the Pacific reached a cost level of $35 million. Production of combat vehicles in Japan was increased to 100 personnel carriers and 12 tanks per month. Marine craft maintenance contracting functions were assumed from the Navy and the use of all existing commercial facilities continued. By the end of June 1970, the following offshore organic depot maintenance personnel strengths had been reached.

	Military	DA Civilian	Local Nationals	Total
Okinawa	754	141	1014	1909
Japan	56	37	1257	1350
				3259

Phasedown of Maintenance Support

Combat units in process of standing-down prior to redeployment from South Vietnam turned in large quantities of equipment. During September 1969, a Special Criteria for Retrograde of Army Matériel was instituted for Southeast Asia. This criteria provided simplified inspection and classification procedures for quickly determining the condition of matériel being considered for reissue, retrograde, or maintenance. As a result, equipment can be classified and retrograded promptly with less skilled personnel than would be required if full technical inspections were used. Some scrap may have been shipped out of country and some serviceable assets may have been scrapped, but equipment was moved at the same rate troops were withdrawn. Generally serviceable equipment was retained. Only borderline unserviceable items may have been misclassified. This was not a great price to pay to insure meeting troop withdrawal and equipment turn-in schedules.

CHAPTER VII

Service Support in Vietnam: Construction, Real Estate, and Communications

Construction and Real Estate

The construction aspects of the Vietnam war are described in this section only as an overview. A separate monograph has been written on this subject.

Base Development

Base development contingency plans prepared prior to the buildup in Vietnam recognized that operations would be conducted in a primitive area, almost totally devoid of logistics support capabilities, and that a vast construction effort would be required to build port facilities, Army airfields and heliports, storage depots, hospitals, communications sites, roads, bridges and base areas for tactical units. Also it was recognized that construction would be completed under adverse conditions of civil unrest, unpredictable warfare, and at a great distance from an industrial base.

The contingency planning for base development in Vietnam was directed by Commander in Chief Pacific. Headquarters U.S. Army Pacific was responsible for preparing the Army portion of the plan. Actual development of the Army base development plan for 1965 was delegated by Headquarters U.S. Army Pacific to Headquarters U.S. Army Ryukyu Islands. Headquarters Military Assistance Command, Vietnam, was responsible for co-ordination and control of logistic support within the objective area. As operations increased in scope, the planning responsibilities were transferred to Headquarters U.S. Army Vietnam. Thereafter, the planning system followed the established chain of operational control to the Joint Chiefs of Staff and of administrative and logistic control to the Department of the Army. Ultimate control on force structure and level of construction effort was maintained by Office of the Secretary of Defense without delegation.

The original planning developed by Headquarters U.S. Army

Ryukyu Islands was in great detail and identified deficiencies and problem areas. Provisions were made for management of the construction effort first by U.S. Army Ryukyu Islands and later by the 1st Logistical Command. As specified by Commander in Chief Pacific, planning was based on a relatively small in-country force level of 64,000 troops. The use of tents was envisioned for the first six months. The situation that developed was much different, both in size and nature of operation, than envisioned during planning.

Standards and criteria for construction were established by Military Assistance Command, Vietnam. Three standards of cantonment construction were prescribed. Each standard depended on the anticipated duration of occupancy of the activity. The three standards were field, intermediate and temporary. However, standards of living for troops were allowed to develop to a high degree.

The Commanding General U.S. Army Vietnam was authorized to construct to intermediate standards. Military Assistance Command, Vietnam, reserved the right to authorize temporary standards. In general temporary standards included pre-engineered metal or painted wood buildings, and modern utility systems. Intermediate standards permitted wood buildings with limited utility systems and field standard included tents or wood buildings with minimal utility systems.

Controls over construction were exercised by Military Assistance Command, Vietnam. Early in 1966 a Director of Construction was established at that headquarters in recognition of the magnitude of the military construction program. The Directorate of Construction was assigned directive supervision and authority over all Department of Defense construction commands and agencies except for those organic to major combat units. This authority extended to the direct assignment of specific projects to construction commands and agencies and to the adjustment of equipment, materials, and other resources necessary to meet priorities established by Commander U.S. Military Assistance Command, Vietnam. The Director of Construction was assigned the responsibility of supervising and coordinating the accomplishment of joint master base development plans.

Military Construction

From fiscal year 1965 through fiscal year 1971, Congress authorized approximately $1.387 billion of Military Construction, Army funds for construction in support of Southeast Asia. The majority of these funds, approximately $969 million, were provided for construction projects in Vietnam. From a relatively small Military Construction, Army program of approximately $40 million in fiscal year 1965, the funding program for South Vietnam peaked in fiscal year 1966 and 1967. During that period the basic, amended, and supplemental Military Construction, Army programs and Military Assistance Program transfers totaled approximately $707 million. The fiscal year 1968 and 1969 basic and supplemental programs totaled approximately $185 million. There were no fiscal year 1970 Military Construction Army funds programmed for South Vietnam because of the large unobligated balances from prior years. The Army proposed $40 million for South Vietnam in fiscal year 1971, but this was reduced by Congress to $27 million including $2 million in planning funds.

Although the basic Military Construction, Army programs for fiscal year 1965 through fiscal year 1971 (except for fiscal year 1970) provided construction funds for South Vietnam, the bulk of the funds were derived from supplemental appropriations (including amendments to the regular appropriations). The initial supplemental authorization was in fiscal year 1965 through a Joint Resolution by the Senate and House of Representatives and allowed a great deal of flexibility in carrying out the Presidential program in Southeast Asia. Subsequent supplemental authorizations were provided in lump sum amounts because of the continuing need for flexibility in the administration and execution of the construction program for Southeast Asia in order to adjust to changes in the military situation.

In addition to the Military Construction, Army funds, Congress provided Office of the Secretary of Defense with contingency funds for emergency construction which the Secretary of Defense could use to provide for unforeseen construction requirements which he considered vital to the security of the United States. These funds were released to the Services on an as-needed basis by Office of the Secretary of Defense upon notification to Congress, and provided the greatest degree of flexibility in meeting contingency construction requirements in support of Southeast Asia. Within the $969 million Military Construction, Army funds authorized for South Vietnam, the Secretary of Defense Contingency Funds amounted to $135.6 million. As of 31 December 1970, $895 million of the funds authorized had been obligated and the work in place totaled $808 million.

Prior to the 1969 Presidential decision to improve the Republic of Vietnam Armed Forces capabilities and start United States troop withdrawals, the major portion of the construction effort in South

Vietnam was to provide logistical facilities in support of United States combat operations. With the "Vietnamization" decision, Secretary of Defense Melvin R. Laird limited new construction starts to the following categories: facilities required in Vietnamizing the war to include South Vietnam Armed Forces modernization and improvement and Military Assistance Command, Vietnam, advisor facilities; Line of Communication program facilities such as roads, airfields, and ports; emergency facilities required for the safety, health, security, or in-country redeployment of the forces; necessary repairs to battle damaged facilities, and facilities required to support redeployment of U.S. units.

From 1969 on, an increasing percentage of the available Military Construction, Army funds were used for Army of Vietnam improvement and modernization projects such as maintenance depots, storage facilities, training centers, and communication stations.

Real Estate Management

The Pentalateral Agreement between the United States, South Vietnam, Laos, Cambodia, and France in 1950 provided the basis for mutual defense and established that a host country would provide land at no cost to a nation's forces. This agreement is general in scope so administrative agreements were necessary between Government of Vietnam ministries and the U.S. Embassy and U.S. Forces. Commander U.S. Military Assistance Command, Vietnam, was given the responsibility for real estate operations in support of military needs. He was authorized to further delegate authority in carrying out this responsibility.

The term of occupancy for using Vietnam bases was indefinite. Each U.S. request for real estate included the following statement: "Upon termination of use and occupancy of the area, Military Assistance Command, Vietnam, retains the option of removing or abandoning in place any structure or installation placed thereon." Leases were utilized by U.S. Forces to acquire privately owned buildings such as warehouses, office spaces, and billets which were required, but not made available by the Government of Vietnam. Rental payments were made from the requesting agency's Operation and Maintenance, Army funds. These payments were made in *piasters*.

Table 11 outlines the breakdown on U.S. Army Real Estate holdings, lease costs, and construction costs in South Vietnam for the period 1964–1970.

TABLE 11—REAL ESTATE HOLDINGS IN SOUTH VIETNAM

Fiscal Year	Cost of Construction to the U.S. Government (thousands of dollars)	Lease Costs (thousands of dollars)	Acres Under Army Control
64	3,044	614	366
65	5,139	2,152	370
66	21,700	24,180	73,095
67	222,360	26,289	125,676
68	364,956	14,641	184,159
69	545,190	12,879	197,754
70	651,162	11,333	186,750

Facilities Engineering

In Vietnam for the first time in the history of modern warfare, extensive facilities engineering services were provided in an active theater of operations. Troops were provided with facilities without having to be occupied with the accompanying problems of maintenance and operation of those facilities.

The Army relied almost entirely on a contractor, Pacific Architects and Engineers, to furnish facilities engineering support in II, III, and IV, and later in I Corps. Use of a contractor allowed engineer troops to be used for operational support and base construction. The contractor's organization was tailored to the particular installation supported. Using a contractor for a housekeeping type operation was consistent with the Department of Defense objective of minimizing the number of in-country support troops. The contract was worded so that Pacific Architects and Engineers furnished the required labor, organization, and management and the U.S. Government provided equipment, repair parts, tools, and materials on a nonreimbursable basis as well as quarters and messing facilities on an as available basis. At peak strength Pacific Architects and Engineers had a work force of over 24,000 employees.

On 1 July 1968 technical control of the Pacific Architects and Engineers contract passed from the 1st Logistical Command to the U.S. Army Engineer Construction Agency, Vietnam. Although the U.S. Army Procurement Agency, Vietnam retained administrative control of the Pacific Architects and Engineers contract, the contracting officer's representatives positions were filled by U.S. Army Engineer Construction Agency, Vietnam engineers who directed and supervised the contractor's efforts. (Chart 15) The three District Engineers at Saigon, Qui Nhon, and Cam Ranh Bay supervised the Installation Engineers located at the various bases

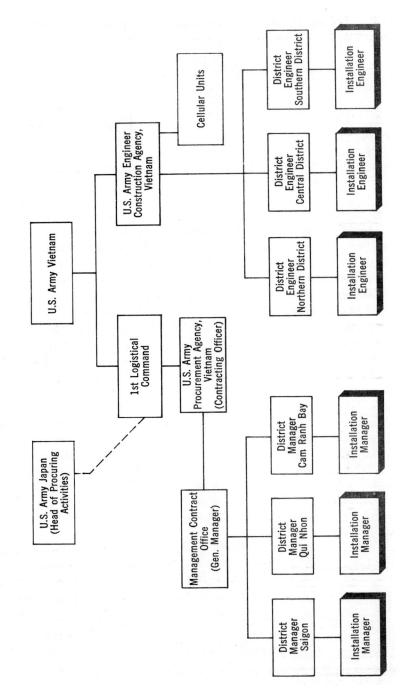

and provided technical support to the installation in which they were located.

Other real property maintenance support was furnished by the Vinnell Corporation, which operated and maintained high-voltage central power plants at several major installations.

One of the unusual features of the Vietnam conflict was the application of normal peacetime statutory and regulatory constraints which had a considerable effect on the facilities engineering program. The limitations on approval authority for the use of operations and maintenance funds on minor construction projects costing more than $25,000 and the strictures on approval authority for the alteration and repair of battle damaged facilities proved to be limiting factors in repairing the facilities, although the program was not hindered by a lack of funds to do the job.

The project approval limitation had substantial impact on the facilities engineering program. This was particularly true in the earliest years of the Vietnam buildup, when the bulk of facilities engineering effort (about 80 percent in fiscal years 1965 and 1966) was necessarily devoted to new construction.

Experience in Vietnam showed that utility requirement estimates were entirely too low. Planning data on standards of living were in need of revision. The heavy demands for electrical power, water, and sewage systems had not been foreseen and local commercial and municipal systems were incapable of providing any support.

Communications

The Army communications system in Vietnam evolved from a single half-duplex radio teletype circuit between Saigon and Clark Air Force Base, Republic of the Philippines in 1951 to a system involving 220 installations with 13,900 circuits during the 1965–1969 period.

To keep pace with these rapid developments, the 1st Signal Brigade was activated in April 1966. During 1967 its strength reached 19,700 personnel and contained all signal units not directly associated with tactical units. All strategic and tactical communication systems were connected through the resources of the brigade.

This extensive communications network, equipped with new standard tactical equipment, automatic message switching centers, and telephone exchanges required logistical support from the U.S. Army Vietnam 1st Logistical Command logistics system. For those fixed communications sites which were contractor operated the contractor was responsible for providing resupply. An unusual aspect of the resupply system for communications equipment was in the field of Communications Security distribution. Due to security and accountability requirements Communications Security equipment was shipped to Vietnam by means of the Armed Forces Courier Service which used Tan Son Nhut as the port of entry. From there in-country distribution had to be made through a special Communications Security logistics system. This required special and intensive management to marry up Communications Security equipment with the telecommunications equipment. There was another special resupply system established for the Satellite Communications System. Requisitions for Satellite Communications items were forwarded via a dedicated communications network to the Satellite Communications Agency located at Fort Monmouth, New Jersey. These requisitions were transmitted by leased teletype circuits directly to the prime contractor, Hughes Aircraft in Fullerton, California. Repair parts were then mailed directly to the communication facility via Army Post Office facilities. Items too bulky or which were prohibited from being shipped through mail channels were shipped to Norton Air Force Base, California and then sent by air freight to their destination. In a number of cases, a courier was provided to insure that parts did not become lost or misplaced when the aircraft arrived in-country.

Communications Support of Logistical Units

The logistical system in Vietnam was greatly dependent upon good communications and demanded a wide variety of transmission media to transfer logistical data between logistics headquarters, logistics support elements, and supported units. The communications subsystem in support of logistics activities consisted of the Defense Communications Agency managed system, the U.S. Army Vietnam managed Corps Area Communication System, the Southeast Asia Automatic Telephone System, and the manual switchboards that interfaced with the Southeast Asia Automatic Telephone System. Logistic activities were also provided use of the Automatic Secure Voice Communications network in South Vietnam. They were also provided access to the Corps Area Communication System communication center which interfaced with the worldwide Automatic Digital Network.

Logistics of Standard Signal Items

Common supply signal equipment items, with the exception of classified NESTOR (mythological designator used to identify a family of secure voice devices) common supply items, were requisitioned through a common supply channel—the 1st Logistical Command. The classified NESTOR items were handled through Communications Security logistical channels, however the 1st Logistical Command common supply channel was used to distribute NESTOR ancillary items (for example installation kits and cable assemblies) .

Logistics of Non-Standard Items

The logistic support of U.S. Army Strategic Communications peculiar items was performed entirely by the 1st Signal Brigade. This brigade was simultaneously a customer for, as well as the supplier, manager and operator of the peculiar items. Much of the logistics support of the non-standard, fixed plant items was provided through operations and maintenance contracts which offered the expertise and logistical channels necessary to operate and support the systems.

The Area Maintenance and Supply Facility concept was introduced to support both fixed and tactical systems. Under this concept two facilities were established in Vietnam to provide direct support and general support to the fixed communications electronics systems. Supply was accomplished on a major site basis, with each major site requisitioning for all its supported sites. The requisitions for all types of technical supply were submitted directly to an Area Maintenance and Supply Facility. Differentiation between defined common items and peculiar items of supply was made only at Area Maintenance and Supply Facilities. The Area Maintenance and Supply Facilities requisitioned common items from the theater depots and requisitioned peculiar items directly from the Continental U.S. National Inventory Control Point. Maintenance was provided on a direct support and general support basis from the major sites and Area Maintenance and Supply Facilities respectively.

Resources

Since no signal personnel were assigned to 1st Logistical Command, the Signal Office coordinated required work with the 1st Signal Brigade which had the major communications role in Vietnam. Prime factors in determining the configuration and composition of the communications system were subscriber requirements and densities. However, due to the nonavailability of mobile communications equipment capable of meeting the sophisticated requirements of a modern Army, the extensive use of fixed communications equipment was necessary.

System Effectiveness

The communications system was inadequate in early 1965 resulting in the loss of numerous requisitions. The needs of logisticians soon influenced the development of a responsive and reliable communication system. By the summer of 1968 dial telephone exchanges, secure voice terminals, and message and data transmission facilities had been placed at every major logistical installation in South Vietnam.

CHAPTER VIII

Service Support in Vietnam:
Subsistence and Miscellaneous

Subsistence

U.S. soldiers in Vietnam ate well. Ice cream and eggs to order were not uncommon items at fire support bases. Extensive use of large refrigerators, refrigerator vans, and helicopters permitted troops in the field to enjoy garrison type rations on an almost routine basis. Naturally these conditions were not available in 1965, but grew as logistics units arrived and facilities were established and improved.

In early 1965, the Headquarters Support Activity, Saigon, under operational control of the U.S. Navy, was responsible for supplying perishable and nonperishable subsistence to all units in South Vietnam except in I Corps which was supplied by Headquarters 3d Marine Amphibious Force. Headquarters Support Activity, Saigon submitted its requisitions directly to Defense Personnel Support Center in Continental U.S. Perishables were shipped by air on a 2–2–3 day cycle to upcountry units. Nonperishables were shipped by Landing Ship Tank (LST) on a monthly basis to units located in Vung Tau, Cam Ranh Bay, Nha Trang and Qui Nhon. The Navy continued to support all U. S. forces as the wholesaler until March 1966. At that time the responsibility for II, III and IV Corps was transferred to Headquarters, 1st Logistical Command.

When the 1st Logistical Command assumed the mission of subsistence support from the Navy, requisitions were centralized for II, III and IV Corps and submitted through 2d Logistical Command in Okinawa to the Defense Personnel Support Center. Later the system was modified and requisitions were placed directly on Defense Personnel Support Center. In November 1969, the system was further modified requiring requisitions to be placed through the Defense Automated Addressing System in order to integrate subsistence data with other logistics information at the Logistical Control Office, Pacific.

Originally field units subsisted primarily on B rations and

the MCI or meal, combat, individual (an individually packaged meal, which does not require refrigeration). Units in areas such as Saigon, Cam Ranh Bay and Vung Tau subsisted upon A rations including fresh fruits, vegetables and milk in accordance with the monthly Continental U.S. Master Menu.

This was later changed to a special thirty-day menu developed for use in South Vietnam. This menu required more refrigerator capacity than was available, and another menu, a twenty-eight-day cyclic menu was developed in late 1966 requiring less refrigeration.

Fresh fruits and vegetables were received from Continental U.S., Western Pacific, and in-country sources. Items which could not be successfully moved through the long Continental U.S. supply line were procured from Western Pacific and in-country suppliers.

In October 1967, the Sea Land Corporation began providing refrigerator cargo service to South Vietnam. Four C4J vessels arrived in Cam Ranh Bay every 15 days. Each vessel hauled 120 refrigerated vans and 530 general dry cargo vans. The 120 refrigerated vans were divided with 60 going to Saigon, 30 to Qui Nhon and 30 remaining at Cam Ranh Bay. Distribution was made to Saigon and Qui Nhon by a smaller shuttle vessel from Cam Ranh Bay. This system was used because of the costs to construct other land cranes to offload C4J vessels which do not have organic cranes. A T3, capable of carrying 93 refrigerated vans and 360 general cargo vans, was introduced to service the port of Da Nang.

To provide a wide range of dairy products, the A ration required three recombining milk plants to be built in Vietnam. A Foremost Dairy plant in Saigon began production in December 1965. Under a contractual agreement with the Army, Meadowgold Dairies constructed one plant in Cam Ranh Bay which began production on 15 November 1967 and another in Qui Nhon which began production on 4 February 1968. The cost was to be amortized and ownership transferred to the U.S. Government. By assuming the risk of the operations in Vietnam, the Army obtained the Meadowgold product at a lower cost. To augment the ice cream provided by the milk plants, additional small size ice cream plants were brought into country to provide ice cream as far forward as possible. The number of these plants reached a high of 40.

Because construction of permanent general warehouses was a slow process and generally accomplished only in largely populated areas such as Long Binh, Cam Ranh Bay and Qui Nhon, a large quantity of Class I items were stored in the open. The movement of subsistence to covered storage was not completed until early 1970.

Refrigeration was necessary for receiving, storing and issuing the perishable A ration components. Refrigeration was provided by use of 1,600 cubic feet pre-fab refrigerated units, permanent cold storage facilities, leased facilities, and floating storage.

The system of distributing subsistence supply encompassed sea, air and land transportation. Subsistence supply was affected by the long distances between depots and supported units and on occasion when the movement of perishable cargo was pre-empted by cargo with a higher priority. During the monsoon season support to isolated installations also taxed the available modes of transportation.

Subsistence support to other U. S. Forces and Free World Military Assistance Forces as well as open messes and civilian contractors resulted in an additional burden on Class I operations down through the lowest level of distribution. Support of Free World Military Assistance Forces required adjustment to the U. S. Army twenty-eight-day menu which included stockage of special items (for example, rice and kimchi) to meet their requirements.

In addition to the usual A, B and MCI ration, the tactical situation created a need for unique rations for use on patrol to augment the MCI ration. A lightweight ration, the Long Range Patrol Ration, was developed by Natick Laboratories which was a dehydrated, precooked type available in eight menus and highly acceptable to the troops. A special indigenous patrol ration was also developed to support personnel of the Free World Military Assistance Forces.

Other Support Services

Organization for Support Services

Support services include food service, graves registration, laundry and bath, labor, bakery, mess, medical, decontamination and property disposal. Food service elements were organic to each major headquarters and were responsible for monitoring food service activities in their subordinate organizations.

Graves registration support was provided by collecting points operated by divisional Supply and Transportation Battalions and by non-divisional Supply and Service companies. The collection points ensured that identification certificates were in order, the human remains were clean, documentation was correct, and personal effects were accurately recorded and safeguarded. The remains were then transferred to one of the two in-country mortuary centers at Da Nang or Tan Son Nhut. The personal effects depots consolidated the personal effects from the individual's unit, the collecting points, and those items removed at the mortuary and forwarded them to Continental U.S. for delivery to the next-of-kin.

Property disposal services were furnished on a geographic basis. Property disposal yards were established in each of the four Corps Tactical Zones. Sale of material from the yards was controlled by a central sales office working under the auspices of the 1st Logistical Command Headquarters, until 1 July 1970, when Headquarters U.S. Army Vietnam assumed responsibility for this operation.

The other support services, (laundry, bath, bakery, mess, labor and decontamination) were furnished on an area basis. Because Field Service Companies, Supply and Service Companies, Laundry Detachments, Bakery Detachments, and Mess Detachments were assigned geographic areas of responsibility, it was necessary to split some companies into platoon size units. The area concept also resulted in service units having non-service parent units. (Chart 16) Bath support was augmented by Army engineer construction and self-help programs.

Food Service

From July 1965 to February 1966, Class I supplies were automatically "pushed" to South Vietnam and the food consisted of B rations and MCI rations. The Push Packages were shipped from the various depots in Continental U.S. to the most convenient outloading ports. Because of the urgency of the situation, ships of opportunity were used (ships in port not fully loaded, but available for government use). This resulted in the rations arriving in South Vietnam and being offloaded at ports other than those called for in the operation plan. Also in many cases the ships did not carry balanced components of the B ration. This caused an imbalance between the availability of various food components and the nutritional need of the troops being supported. To worsen the situation, Push Package markings were often ignored and the components of the rations were issued and consumed by units near the port of discharge, causing an unbalanced diet. The Push Package concept was successful only on the first two increments. Even though the use of Push Packages was stopped in February 1966, it took until 1968 to phase out non-authorized

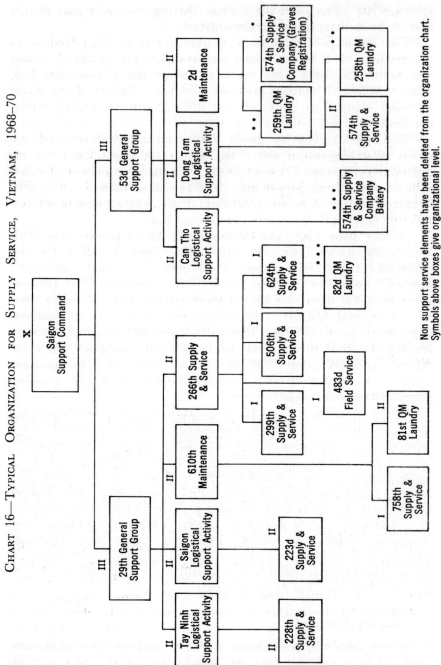

CHART 16—TYPICAL ORGANIZATION FOR SUPPLY SERVICE, VIETNAM, 1968–70

Non support service elements have been deleted from the organization chart.
Symbols above boxes give organizational level.

stockage list items from the system. During the early part of this period the food service program suffered.

The buildup of troops and conversion from MCI feeding to the feeding of B ration meats and components of the A ration was rapid. Attempts were made to follow the Continental U.S. Master Menu in certain areas of Vietnam (Saigon, Cam Ranh Bay and Vung Tau) but this was difficult due to limited refrigeration facilities.

The twenty-eight-day menu developed in 1966 reduced the strain on refrigeration assets. In August 1969, a refined twenty-eight-day cyclic menu was adopted. This menu consisted of 4,500 calories of food energy per man per day and contained a wide and balanced variety of meats, vegetables, fruits, cereals and beverages. Over 90 percent of the meals were served hot.

During June 1968, the "cantonment mess" project was initiated to upgrade dining facilities. This project called for the replacement of "field type" equipment with "garrison type" kitchen equipment in base corps dining facilities. The replacement equipment was to be the same type as that normally used in Continental U.S. It was not possible to use the cantonment equipment to the extent originally planned, however, due to limited electrical power, fuel and maintenance support. For these reasons, and for a need on the part of some units to maintain mobility, a number of units continued to use "field type" cooking equipment in base corps facilities.

When possible, for troops on patrol and other field missions, meals were prepared in base camp kitchens and delivered in insulated food containers. When such deliveries could not be made because of weather, enemy action or terrain either the MCI (a canned ration) or the Long Range Patrol Packet was provided. The latter consists primarily of dehydrated components. The Ration Supplement Sundries Pack was also provided when troops did not have access to a Post Exchange outlet. This pack contains such items as confections, tobacco including cigars and cigarettes, stationery, shoe laces and sewing kits. Originally it contained 16 items. The latest revision, based on the recommendations of U.S. troops in Vietnam, has 24 components.

Commissary Outlets

There were two commissary stores in Vietnam and both were operated by the Army. One was located at Saigon, and the other one at Long Binh. Access to the stores was limited to personnel not having an organized dining facility in their area.

This stringent policy was implemented in 1968 to offset large numbers of patrons crowding into minimal facilities to purchase limited amounts of retail subsistence items. By restricting use of the facility to personnel not having access to dining facilities, it virtually eliminated military patrons, but did provide commissary service to civilian government employees, contractor personnel, press representatives and other non-military personnel.

Care and Disposition of Remains

Early in 1961 the Commander in Chief, Pacific directed the U. S. Air Force to provide service support for deceased military advisory personnel in South Vietnam. This support was rendered by mortuary personnel from Clark Air Force Base, Republic of the Philippines. However, in 1963 a U. S. Air Force Mortuary was established at Tan Son Nhut. Its service was expanded in 1965 to include support to Free World Military Assistance Forces.

Later in 1965, as a result of an Army study on future mortuary support requirements, the Commander in Chief, Pacific directed that the mortuary mission be transferred to U.S. Army Vietnam effective 1 July 1966.

The following table depicts the Army fatality workload experienced during the period 1961 thru 1970:

1961 — 3	1964 — 146	1967 — 6,443	1970 — 4,906
1962 — 25	1965 — 1,081	1968 — 10,560	
1963 — 72	1966 — 3,719	1969 — 8,185	Total — 35,140

As fatalities increased it became difficult to control Summary Court disposition of personal effects. So, on 1 September 1966, U.S. Army Vietnam activated the Personal Property Depot at Camp Red Ball as a Division of the U. S. Army Mortuary, Tan Son Nhut. This depot was responsible for receiving, screening and shipping personal effects to the person entitled to receive them.

Due to the increase in combat activity and fatalities of U. S. Forces in the I Corps area, a stand-by mortuary at the Da Nang Air Base was placed in operation on 20 June 1967. In May 1967, the existing mortuary facility at Tan Son Nhut was determined inadequate and Commander U.S. Military Assistance Command, Vietnam, directed a study to relocate it. As a result of the study, a new facility was constructed on the Air Base. The mortuary activity was relocated to the new facility on 11 September 1968; on 16 December 1968 the Personal Property Depot at Camp Red Ball was relocated to a newly constructed facility adjacent to the new mortuary.

Mortuary

Viet Cong activities taxed the capacity of both the Tan Son Nhut and Da Nang mortuaries during the *Tet* Offensive in February 1968. During this period, technical guidance and additional identification capability was provided through temporary duty of qualified civilian personnel from the Office Chief of Support Services, Department of the Army and off-shore mortuaries located in Japan and Thailand. Embalmer capability was increased through temporary assignment of in-country qualified and licensed enlisted personnel to assist the civilian morticians in preparation of remains. These two mortuaries processed 2,291 remains during that month which was possible only through the complete co-operation of the military and civilian personnel concerned.

A plan for conducting a search and recovery program for remains of deceased persons in Vietnam was initiated as early as November 1968 with in-country graves registration units providing personnel for assignment to support this effort. The program was designated Operation Compassion. A central file bank for missing and "body not recovered" personnel for all Services was established at Tan Son Nhut Mortuary in support of this operation and for use in conducting searches upon cessation of hostilities.

Plans eventually materialized in the activation of the Joint Casualty Resolution Center located at Nakhon Phanom, Thailand and a Central Identification Laboratory, Camp Samesan, Thailand to conduct search, recovery and identification of remains in Southeast Asia.

Bath Services

The bath service support in Vietnam was provided to all U.S. and Free World Military Assistance Forces. During the early stages of the buildup most of the bath support was provided by fixed or improvised facilities. As the number of troops increased, Table of Organization and Equipment mobile bath units were introduced and were operating by June 1968. These units, augmented by fixed and improvised facilities, provided adequate hot and cold water shower support; however, most of the field expedient showers had to be operated using cold water only. Often most desirable locations for shower points could not be used for security reasons.

In December 1965, the total bath capability in South Vietnam consisted of 18 Table of Organization and Equipment mobile bath teams (with 8 shower heads each) having the combined capability of providing 126,000 showers per week—operating 16 hours per day (two 8 hour shifts). At that time all of the bath units were assigned to the 1st Logistical Command. The divisions and brigades contained no augmentations for bath units but received this support as required from supporting units of the 1st Logistical Command.

By July 1967, the bath service capability in the 1st Logistical Command had expanded to 60 bath teams, with a total of 69 authorized. These teams, working two 10-hour shifts per day, were capable of providing 420,000 showers per week. Troops billeted in urban areas had access to permanent shower facilities. Troops occupying base camps bathed in fixed showers which were constructed as part of the cantonment. When it was not possible to provide showers with mobile bath teams, collapsible canvas Austrailian shower buckets with a 5.87 gallon capacity provided additional capability. Decontamination teams equipped with a truck containing a tank and shower unit were also employed as the need arose. All of these fixed facilities were used to the maximum extent possible in order to free the mobil bath units for support to the forward areas (fire support bases and logistical support activities to which the combat soldier had access after combat operations).

Laundry and Dry Cleaning

Since almost all items of clothing and bedding used in Vietnam were made from materials that could be cleaned by laundering rather than dry cleaning, this portion will review the problems inherent in establishing laundry facilities.

In August 1965, mobile laundry units were requested to provide the additional requirements generated by the troop buildup. However, this request could not be filled due to a lack of equipment. During December 1965, there were fifty standard-B field laundry machines (two-trailer units) in the 1st Logistical Command. These units were capable of servicing only 3,075,000 pounds of laundry per month. The total requirement per month exceeded 7,000,000 pounds.

During the early stages of buildup all laundry service, except the small amount that could be handled by supporting units having mobile laundry equipment, was obtained from local nationals. Since there were very few local commercial firms that had any sizeable capability at that time and no Army-operated facilities, most of the laundry service was furnished by maids, houseboys, and post exchange concessionaires. Due to the wide dispersion of troops and as a matter of convenience, arrangements for these services were generally handled by the individual or the unit desiring the service.

During fiscal year 1968 and fiscal year 1969 increased utilization was made of contract laundries because of commanders desires for pressed fatigues for troops in base camps. Although the Vietnamese contractors provided service below acceptable standards, their services were necessary to cover the large shortfall from organic laundry capabilities. The extent to which the U.S. Army depended on contract laundry is shown by the fact that in fiscal year 1969, production rose to a high of 12.8 million pounds per month at a cost averaging $855,000 per month.

The mobile laundry equipment situation began to improve in December 1966 when the first of the new Standard-A machines arrived in Vietnam. These machines were mounted on single trailers and greatly increased the mobility of laundry units. By July 1967, Standard-A machines comprised 45 percent of the laundry equipment in country. During this period, however, only 22 percent of the required 18 million pounds of laundry per month was processed by field laundry units. Physical and tactical limitations, shortages of Standard-A machines, and inherent limitations of field laundries all contributed to the laundry support problem. The shortfall was resolved by reliance on local nationals, concessionnaires and contractors.

In August 1967, there were 115 Standard-A laundry machines in-country with a capability of laundering only 25 percent of the total requirement. From November 1967 through January 1968, additional new Standard-A machines arrived in Vietnam bringing the total to 127 machines. Production from these and an undetermined number of Standard-B machines totaled 11.8 million pounds or an average of 3.9 million pounds per month for this period. During 1968 and 1969 the Standard-B machines were completely phased out of the system. The production rate for field laundries during this period ranged from a low of 2.4 million pounds per month to a high of 4.2 million pounds per month, which was achieved in June 1969.

As the buildup continued additional laundry units were assigned and by June 1968 mobile facilities were established. During this same period local commercial laundries were being placed under contract to handle the workload which exceeded the capability of the mobile facilities operated by the Army. The available mobile units had the capability to process only about half of the total laundry requirement, and this was limited to washing and rough drying.

Therefore, these units were employed primarily in support of medical facilities, isolated units, combat task forces, and in areas where there were large concentrations of troops and a sizeable workload of organizational type items.

As the troop buildup continued, it became apparent that the laundry services could be provided more economically by fixed facilities operating under the staff supervision of the Army. Plans were formulated for construction of ten laundries and sites were selected.

Eight of the ten fixed laundries programmed for construction in fiscal year 1969 were cancelled. The cancellation resulted from a study in 1968 based on the factor of low priorities for this type of construction and lack of need for fixed laundries due to reduction of forces in South Vietnam. The remaining two were approved and programmed by U.S. Army Vietnam for construction in fiscal year 1971 at Long Binh and Cam Ranh Bay. Due to further reductions of our forces in Vietnam, these two were never built, and the US Army continued to rely on contract laundries, with no fixed laundries in the Republic of Vietnam.

Clothing

The clothing issue-in-kind system of supply (provided for in CTA 50–901) was placed in effect in Vietnam on 1 November 1965. After that time, enlisted men were deployed there with the minimum quantities of items of the uniform. Relatively high value clothing items were recovered through turn-in and subsequently rehabilitated for reissue. Clothing items that were not turned in, and those not required in Vietnam, were placed in storage at home or government storage to be recovered and used by the individual on his return from Vietnam.

In March 1966, the 1st Logistical Command established an Army clothing sales store in Saigon. (Prior to that time a joint clothing sales store was operated there by the Navy.) The initial stockage of this store consisted of clothing items for both male and female personnel; but, due to the limited demand for items of female clothing, these items were discontinued from stockage in October 1967. After this time, female military personnel obtained their items of the uniform by mail order from military clothing sales stores located in Japan and Okinawa. Initially, cash sales at the Saigon sales store averaged $60,000 per month. However, after officers and warrant officers were included in issue-in-kind under the provisions of CTA 50–901, the sales volume decreased to $13,000 per month (in fiscal year 1970).

Property Disposal

The Property Disposal Operation was a function of Military Assistance Command, Vietnam, until 1 February 1966. It was then passed to U.S. Army Vietnam, and in turn to the 1st Logistical Command. During the early years, property disposal operations were hampered by the lack of trained military personnel. This is understandable since there were very few operational spaces for property disposal officer personnel anywhere in the world prior to the buildup in Vietnam. Traditionally, property disposal operations only generate high interest at or near the end of armed conflicts; during other periods it is usually assigned a low priority, perhaps because of its position at the rail end of the life cycle of matériel.

Personnel shortages were evident and in 1968 actions were taken to overcome them. Additionally, resident and nonresident courses were established by the U. S. Army Logistics Management Center at Fort Lee for property disposal personnel. Resident courses consisted of the Defense Advanced Disposal Management Seminar, Defense Disposal Executive Development Seminar, and the Defense Disposal Management Seminar.

A mobile instructor team was organized and conducted on-site courses. Additionally, the Quartermaster School conducted special property disposal courses for officers, enlisted men, and civilian employees assigned to the propery disposal program. Personnel assigned to the disposal operation in Vietnam in 1966 and 1970 are compared in the table below:

PERSONNEL ASSIGNED TO PROPERTY DISPOSAL OPERATIONS
IN VIETNAM

Category	FY 1966	FY 1970
Officers and Warrant Officers	3	35
Enlisted Men	16	577
Department of the Army Civilians	3	15
Local Nationals	126	267
Total	148	894

Disposal operations were hampered by lack of an early country-to-country agreement. Such an agreement should have been consummated at the ambassadorial level early or before the buildup started specifying how the U.S. Army would conduct property disposal operations. An essential element would have been a stipulation that the host country would have no control over U.S. property sold for export. A country-to-country agreement was signed on 9 November 1968 but had this been accomplished earlier, a considerable number of delays would have been eliminated and a more efficient property disposal operation would have been established. Buyers were discouraged from bidding on property offered for sale because of difficulties in obtaining host country customs clearances, a lack of labor, a slowness of host government bureaus in processing buyer requests for export licenses, a shortage of shipping, and long delays in awaiting berthing space. Simply stated, many arduous and difficult problem areas were encountered by representatives of the business community when conducting business affairs in a combat environment.

The inventories of property disposal yards greatly increased during the enemy's *Tet* offensive of February 1968 and his offensive again in May 1968. The increase was due to two factors. First, a great deal of equipment was damaged or destroyed during this period and was added to the inventory. Second, buyers were unable to remove property from property disposal office yards on a timely basis as a result of increased harassment by the enemy. These inventories were not reduced to a manageable level until early 1969.

The quantities of property received and the quantities disposed of during the period fiscal year 1968–1971 are shown in Table 12. Also shown are the quantities on hand at the end of each of those fiscal years. There was a large increase in the quantity of scrap received during fiscal year 1970. There were several reasons for the increase. Scales were not available in the property dis-

TABLE 12—PROPERTY DISPOSAL OFFICE OPERATIONS
(1968–1971)

Fiscal Year	Usable Property (in millions of dollars)			Scrap (in thousands of tons)		
	Received	Disposed Of	On Hand At End Of FY	Received	Disposed Of	On Hand At End Of FY
1968	96	78	31	80	37	61
1969	84	90	25	74	99	36
		(1.6)			(1.7)	
1970	102	72	55	487	122	401
1971	117	136	36	162	303	260
		(2.3)			(6.3)	
Totals	399	376		848	608	

USABLE PROPERTY—FIGURES IN PARENTHESES REPRESENT DOLLAR RETURN TO GOVERNMENT. FIGURES FOR 1968 DOLLAR RETURNS ARE ESTIMATED. FIGURES NOT IN PARENTHESES IN THIS COLUMN REPRESENT ACQUISITION VALUE.
SCRAP—FIGURES IN PARENTHESES REPRESENT DOLLAR RETURN TO GOVERNMENT. FIGURES FOR FY 1968 DOLLAR RETURN ARE ESTIMATED. FIGURES NOT IN PARENTHESES IN THIS COLUMN REPRESENT THOUSAND OF TONS OF SCRAP DISPOSED OF.

posal yards to weigh the scrap as it was unloaded. An estimate was made regarding the weight which normally resulted in less weight being recorded than was actually unloaded. Also the property disposal office yard dropped scrap from their records when a contract was signed by a buyer rather than waiting until the buyer removed the scrap by a specified time, as prescribed in property disposal regulations. After this contract was invalidated, the scrap in many cases was not again picked up on property disposal office records. During 1969, a concentrated effort was made at the direction of the Commanding General, 1st Logistical Command to bring all the property disposal office records up to date. This resulted in a sizeable increase in the quantity recorded. Finally, the phase down of U.S. Army Vietnam resulted in marked increases in the amount on hand in the property disposal facilities.

With the introduction of weighing scales in fiscal year 1970, the guesswork surrounding scrap inventories was eliminated and severe peaks and valleys were brought under control. However, downward adjustments continued for approximately a year thereafter because buyers under term contract were reaching bare ground prior to fulfillment of contracts which were based on earlier inventory estimates.

The property disposal operation, an element of the 1st Logistical Command, was assigned to the Property Disposal Agency on 18 August 1970. The mission of the agency was to supervise the development and implementation of policies, directives, and regulations pertaining to receipt, control, issue, and sales of Department of Defense, non-Department of Defense, U.S. Federal Agencies, Free World Military Assistance Forces, and Military Assistance Program excesses, and U.S. Forces generated and salvage material. The Property Disposal Agency was a culmination of efforts to enhance property disposal capabilities through improved equipment and increased personnel allocation.

Military Assistance Program Excesses

Because of the large volume of excesses being generated and sent to property disposal areas in the Pacific Command area, a special procedure was developed to make maximum use of these assets by the Military Assistance Program. Military Assistance Program Excesses covers procedures for the transfer of items, both major and secondary, from Pacific Command property disposal offices to Pacific Command Military Assistance Program recipients. A feature of this program is the policy that recipients will move matériel and perform necessary rebuild at their own expense to the extent feasible, thereby saving Military Assistance Program accessorial and rebuild funds. By visual inspection of material in property disposal offices and by review of listings of available items, Military Assistance Advisory Group and recipient country personnel determine items which are appropriate to fill a valid programmed requirement. A message forwarded to Commander in Chief Pacific by a Military Assistance Advisory Group requesting approval of the Military Assistance Program Excesses transfer starts the process. Commander in Chief Pacific reviews this request to determine that items are of a category normally supplied thru the Military Assistance Program and that a valid program requirement exists. Upon approval, the Property Disposal Office, Military Assistance Advisory Group, Office of the Secretary of Defense and the Military Department are advised, and the transfer of the matériel effected. Table 13 displays quantities of property moved from Pacific Command Property Disposal offices under Military Assistance Program Excesses during a portion of 1969 through calendar year 1970, and also displays removals from January through March 1971. These quantities include removals from the entire Pacific Command area, but a majority was from Property Disposal office facilities in Vietnam.

TABLE 13—PROPERTY MOVED FROM PACIFIC COMMAND PROPERTY
DISPOSAL OFFICES UNDER MILITARY ASSISTANCE PROGRAM
EXCHANGE PROCEDURES

Pacific Command Military Assistance Program Recipient Countries	Period During Which Property Was Removed From Pacific Command Property Disposal Offices	
	Part of Calendar Year 1969 and All of Calendar Year 1970	January 1971 through March 1971
Taiwan	$31,149,212	$ 9,638,090
Korea	16,400,728	7,406,000
Philippines	1,615,808	468,799
Cambodia	——	2,567,809
Indonesia	——	373,368
Totals	$49,165,748	$20,454,066

Medical Support

In the Vietnamese and Korean conflicts 2.5 percent of U.S. personnel who were wounded and reached a medical treatment facility died. This represented a sizeable improvement over the percentages of World War II (4.5 percent), World War I (8.1 percent) and the Civil War (17 percent). However emphasis should be placed on the fact that these percentages represent only the percentages of wounded personnel who died after reaching medical treatment facilities. In the Vietnamese conflict a far greater percentage of wounded personnel reached these facilities alive than during any prior conflict. This was primarily due to the use of helicopter ambulances. These aerial ambulances were able to rapidly evacuate casualties wounded to such a degree that death would have resulted in prior wars before the evacuee could reach a medical treatment facility.

Medical service in Vietnam was as complete as that found anywhere in the world. It included not only medical evacuation and hospitalization but also medical supply and maintenance, preventive medicine, dental, veterinary and medical laboratory services, medical intelligence, and medical research and development activities.

Initially medical support was organic to the 1st Logistical Command mission. As the buildup progressed and the magnitude of the medical mission increased, responsibility for the medical function was transferred to the 44th Medical Brigade upon its arrival in Vietnam on 1 May 1966. At this time the 44th Medical Brigade was assigned to the 1st Logistical Command; but in August 1967 because of the increased medical mission, the 44th Medical Brigade was reassigned to Headquarters, U.S. Army Vietnam. In 1970, the 44th Medical Brigade and the Surgeons Office, Headquarters U.S. Army Vietnam were consolidated and designated the Medical Command.

As our troop buildup began, medical units of all types were phased in along with the tactical and logistical units they supported. Completely equipped hospitals staffed with well-trained specialists were soon located throughout Vietnam.

Cross-servicing, whereby one Service cares for the sick and wounded of another was used extensively. Navy hospital ships located off the coast of Vietnam were included in this operation. Aerial evacuation was used to transfer patients to these "floating hospitals." Service hospitals were so located that by 1968 any casualty evacuated by helicopter was within 30 minutes flying time of a hospital capable of providing definitive surgical care.

Stability of hospitals permitted semipermanent and in some cases permanent construction. Preoperative, operative, postoperative and other intensive care areas were air-conditioned. In addition to well constructed facilities, several of the surgical hospitals were equipped with the newly developed Medical Unit, Self-Contained, Transportable. This is a system of shelters and

equipment designed to provide the required medical surgical capability for patient care in the field under a wide range of environmental conditions, and it represents a vast improvement over
tent hospitals of the past. Modules can be combined to form any
desired field facility, or treatment facility, and can be transported
by CH–54 helicopters; although they are normally transported by
fixed wing aircraft. After the arrival of the first Army Medical
Department air ambulance unit in 1962, medical helicopter operations, called DUST OFF, evacuated large numbers of military and
civilian patients. Table 14 shows the number of patients moved by
these air ambulances through 1970.

TABLE 14—EVACUATION BY ARMY AIR AMBULANCES IN VIETNAM

Year	Patients*
Prior to 1965	12,000
1965	11,000
1966	65,000
1967	94,000
1968	208,000
1969	241,000
1970	197,871
Total Air Ambulance	828,871
Hoist Patients 1969 (est)	4,188
1970	4,428
Total including Hoist Patients	837,487

*Each time a patient is moved by helicopter, he is counted again. A significant number of the above evacuees are civilians.

The courage and dedication of the air evacuation crews and
medical teams was laudable. They continuously went into areas
under fire and their casualty rates were high.

Military Assistance Command Vietnam established a 30-day
evacuation policy and endeavored to keep 40 percent of hospital
beds empty at all times to take care of sudden surges of casualties that occurred from time to time.

During the period 1 January 1965 through 30 April 1971, 83
percent of the admissions to U.S. Army Medical Treatment
Facilities were due to disease and non-battle injury. Seventeen
percent were due to wounds.

Five groups of diseases accounted for the majority (65 percent)
of the admissions for disease. These were malaria, fevers of unknown origin, respiratory ailments, skin problems, and diarrheal
diseases. Malaria was exceeded only by wounds and non-battle
injuries as a cause of mandays lost from duty.

"Combat casualties" consisted of those personnel wounded as

well as those killed in action. During the period January 1965 through 30 April 1971, 15 out of each 100 combat casualties fell in the killed category and 85 were wounded. Of the 85 wounded, two died after reaching a medical treatment facility and 83 lived.

The Army Medical Service also provided medical support to Free World Assistance Forces in Vietnam. In addition, assistance was given to the Vietnamese military and civilian populations through various medical programs. U. S. military hospitals admitted and treated sick, wounded, and injured Vietnamese civilians on an emergency basis from the first.

Medical supplies were handled through medical depots and hospitals. This was separate from the supply system for other supplies. This organization produced a customer oriented logistics system that was responsive to the needs of the patient and provided sufficient quantities of supplies for professional use.

The 32d Medical Depot managed the in-country inventory for medical matériel. Upon arrival in Vietnam in October 1965, it was assigned to the 1st Logistical Command. On 1 May 1966 it became a subordinate element of the 44th Medical Brigade. The 32d Medical Depot submitted requisitions to the U. S. Army Medical Depot, Ryukyu Islands. That depot either filled them or passed them directly to the U.S. Army Medical Material Agency in Continental U.S. located at Phoenixville, Pennsylvania. The requisitions submitted to Continental U.S. by-passed the U.S. Army Pacific Inventory Control Point, Fort Shafter, Hawaii. The 32d Medical Depot consisted of a base depot at Cam Ranh Bay and, as requirements for support developed, advance depots were established at Long Binh, Qui Nhon, Chu Lai, and Phu Bai. Each depot performed an area distribution mission through which issues were made to combat divisions, hospitals, Free World Military Assistance Forces, and other Services based upon inter-service support agreements. With the help of NCR automatic data processing equipment, the 32d Medical Depot managed a $15 million on-hand inventory and maintained a 45 to 60 day level of medical supplies. (A more detailed Medical discussion will be found in the Medical Monograph.)

Unique Support Missions

Riverine Forces

This type of operation was reminiscent of campaigns during the Civil War when the U.S. Army conducted riverine operations along the James and Mississippi Rivers and in southern swamps.

This type of warfare was also used on Mindanao in the Philippines during World War II.

The initial Mobile Riverine Force, created in 1967, was composed of an Army Infantry brigade and a Navy Task Force integrated at each level of command. This composite force operated as a complete package, independent of fixed support bases. This type of force offered flexibility and greatly increased our operational capability in areas previously inaccessible to our forces.

Logistic support for these forces was established at Vung Tau. U.S. Navy LST and Army landing craft were used to carry the major part of resupply cargo to Dong Tam, which was the major base camp for riverine operations. Throughout the delta operation, transportation boat units (medium and heavy) played a major direct support role. Infantry troops were billeted aboard U.S. Navy barracks ships and were carried to combat by helicopter airlift and armored landing craft.

Existing Army and Navy supply procedures were found to be adaptable to riverine operations. A few problems developed in using equipment immersed at times in briny or dirty water, but the command emphasis placed on preventive maintenance during these operations helped to relieve these problems. Riverine operations were a good example of interservice rapport.

Support of XXIV Corps in I Corps

Prior to the 1968 *Tet* offensive, the predominant U.S. land forces employed in I Corps were U.S. Marines supported by U.S. Naval Support Activity, Da Nang. Prior to November 1967, the U.S. Army maintained support activities on a small scale at Da Nang for Army troops in I Corps. The number of troops was not sufficient to establish command headquarters as such, but our support activities maintained Army personnel in I Corps, in conjunction with the U.S. Naval Support Activity. The rapid influx of U.S. Army land forces during the *Tet* offensive required and equally rapid and extensive buildup of logistic forces and matériel. The requirement for an Army tactical headquarters to be established for the I Corps became apparent and the XXIV Corps came into being. Interim arrangements were used, as the Army established supporting facilities, in addition to the ones already there which received supplies from either Army or Navy sources. Eventually redeployment of Marines from I Corps and the phasing out of the U.S. Naval Support Activity, Da Nang caused detailed planning to begin in preparation for the U.S. Army to assume support responsibility for this Corps. A target date of

July 1970 was established. This action was the first of its kind anywhere in an active theater of operations. While other Army elements in Vietnam were reducing their scope of operations in line with the announced withdrawal policy, the logistic mission of the Army in I Corps was expanded.

Despite the problems generated by a lack of knowledge on the part of both Army and Navy personnel as to terminology and organization, the rapport achieved and maintained throughout the takeover, planning, and execution was probably the single most important contributing factor to its overall success.

GOER 8-TON CARGO CARRIER, ALL-TERRAIN, ALL-WEATHER AMPHIBIOUS
CARGO VEHICLE, ABOVE; GOER 8-TON CARGO CARRIER PROCEEDING
CROSS-COUNTRY THROUGH SWAMPY AREA, BELOW.

CH–47 CHINOOK HELICOPTER BRINGS IN SLING LOAD OF ARTILLERY
AMMUNITION DURING OPERATION BOLLING, ABOVE; AIR
DELIVERY BY FLYING CRANE OF AMMUNITION AND
ARTILLERY PIECE, BELOW.

DeLong Pier Complex at Vung Tau with View of Rock Causeway
and Sand Fill to be Used for Hardstand, above; Use of
Sea-Land Vans for Transportation of Ammunition, below.

UNLOADING OF SEA-LAND VANS BY CRANE OF CARGO SHIP
AT CAM RANH BAY

Off-loading of Sea-Land Vans by Use of Gantry Crane at Cam Ranh Bay, above; Civilian Contractor Han Jin Trucks Waiting to be Unloaded, below.

ARMY VESSEL LTC JOHN U. D. PAGE TIED UP AT SOUTH BEACH,
CAM RANH BAY

USS Corpus Christi Utilized as a Floating Aircraft Maintenance
Facility Anchored Off Coast at Vung Tau, above; Aerial
View of Vietnam Railway Service Repair Crews
Clearing Right of Way and Installing
New Track, below.

USE OF CONEX CONTAINER, ABOVE; LOADING LAUNDRY INTO DRYER
AT CAM RANH BAY, BELOW.

MAINTENANCE PERSONNEL REMOVING ENGINE FROM 5-TON TRUCK FOR
REPAIR, ABOVE; USE OF MAINTENANCE VANS IN A
MOTOR POOL OPERATION, BELOW.

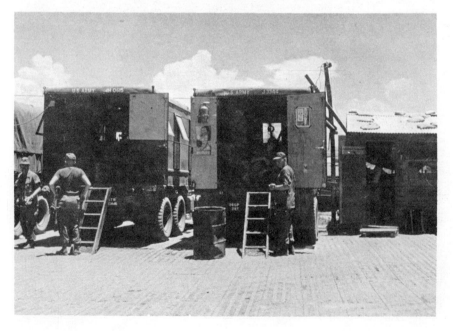

OPERATION OF ROME PLOWS IN CLEARING TREES AND UNDERGROWTH
FROM AREAS IN VIETNAM, ABOVE; LANDING CRAFT MECHANIZED
(LCM) ESCORTS BARGE LOADED WITH ROCK, FUEL, STEEL
GIRDERS AND OTHER ITEMS ON THE VAM
CO TAY RIVER, BELOW.

FLYING CRANE LIFTS 175MM GUN AT VUNG TAU

CHAPTER IX

Logistic Support of U.S. Advisors and Special Forces, Vietnam Armed and Pacification Forces, and Free World Military Assistance Forces

Logistic Support of U. S. Advisors

The logistic system available to supply the advisers assigned to Military Assistance Command, Vietnam, prior to the buildup was based on the concept of a small group of advisors centrally supported from Saigon. When an adviser arrived in-country, he reported to the Military Assistance Command, Vietnam, in Saigon, received a brief orientation, was issued the bare essentials of personal and field clothing, a weapon, a couple of magazines of ammunition, a mosquito net with bars, and eating utensils. He was then flown to his destination via Air Vietnam. Resupply of the adviser was the responsibility of the Vietnamese Army for ammunition, vehicles, and petroleum, oils, and lubricants, but such support was minimal. Since an adviser was required to either eat on the economy or buy his rations at the commissary or PX in Saigon, he was pro⌐ vided a cost of living allowance. He was provided an imprest fund to pay for equipment maintenance. However, in the early years of the Vietnam conflict, Saigon remained the umbilical cord of life for the adviser.

In April 1962, the Army established the United States Army Support Group, Vietnam, later designated United States Army Support Command, Vietnam.

Upon activation, this organization assumed some of the logistic functions previously performed by the Army section, Military Assistance Advisory Group Vietnam, but not the support of up-country compounds.

On 1 July 1962, the Headquarters Support Activity Saigon was established under a chain of command descending from the Commander-In-Chief of the Pacific Fleet but under the operational control of Commander U.S. Military Assistance Command, Vietnam. After this change adviser support improved. Under various interservice support agreements Headquarters Support Activity Saigon performed common item supply and service support functions for all U.S. advisers including such things as subsistence, clothing, PX supplies, and billeting services. From its inception, it was envisioned that Headquarters Support Activity Saigon responsibilities would be limited to peacetime functions or at the most to the situation that existed in South Vietnam during the 1962–1964 period.

In addition to Headquarters Support Activity Saigon, the U.S. Navy had its own logistic system in South Vietnam for the support of U.S. Navy personnel such as U.S. Navy advisers under the Naval Advisory Group, Military Assistance Command, Vietnam. The U.S. Marine Corps had a semi-separate logistics establishment for support of the U.S. Marine Corps. Also the U.S. Air Force vested most of its logistic responsibilities in its Headquarters, 2d Air Division.

At the beginning of 1965, the combined U.S. logistic support effort in South Vietnam was capable of supporting about 20,000 U.S. personnel. A small highly fragmented portion of this effort supported the U.S. advisory personnel. No one organization had full responsibility for logistic support. For example, the Headquarters Support Activity, Saigon and the Military Assistance Command, Vietnam, Headquarters Commandant operated parallel supply lines for different commodities in support of U.S. advisers. Four different systems furnished repairs, and each of the Services had its own medical supply system operating on a "stovepipe" basis to Continental U.S. As the advisory effort increased in keeping with the expansion of the Vietnamese forces, and as the logistic system to support U.S. combat forces took shape, a logistic system for support of the advisors evolved whereby supply support was furnished from three basic sources: Military Assistance Command, Vietnam; the Vietnamese Army; and U.S. Army Vietnam. The type of support drawn from each of these sources was as follows: organizational clothing and equipment and individual weapons with a basic load of ammunition were issued by the Military Assistance Command, Vietnam, Headquarters Commandant. Compound defense weapons and ammunition were obtained from the Vietnamese Army Administrative and Direct Support Logistics company in each province. In cases where weapons were not common to the Vietnamese Army, such as the M16 rifle and M60 machine guns, the weapons and ammunition were drawn from U.S. Army Vietnam. Subsistence was also drawn from U.S. Army Vietnam. Field ration messes were established where there were fifty or more men and a mess association was authorized where there were less than fifty men.

However, the expansion of the adviser effort often required the deployment, on short notice, of numerous seven or eight man detachments at district level. These small detachments were in many cases located in isolated positions, miles from the nearest support facility, and had to rely primarily on periodic air resupply. The formation and deployment of mobile advisory teams of four or five members also presented unique support problems. In the IV Corps Delta area, for example, where many of these teams were employed, small water craft were about the only satisfactory means of travel. Sampans and other small Vietnamese vessels were too slow to escape sniper fire and too small to carry the five man teams with the supplies and equipment necessary to support their mission. A decision was made to acquire commercial type U.S. manufactured boats known as "Boston Whalers." Approximately 200 of them were obtained. They were purchased through the ENSURE program (discussed in Chapter III). Three-fourths of these boats were used by mobile advisory teams and through their use team mobility was greatly improved.

Logistic Support of U.S. 5th Special Forces Group

The mission of the 5th Special Forces Group (Airborne) and its predecessor (U.S. Army Special Forces (Vietnam)) was to advise and assist the Vietnamese government in the organization, training, equipping, and employment of the Civilian Irregular Defense Group Forces.

The first Civilian Irregular Defense Group camp had been built near Ban Me Thuot in 1961. At the beginning of 1964, there were 25 of these border camps, a figure which would double by the end of the year. This network of strategically located fortified camps, each with an airstrip, proved to be invaluable reconnaissance and fire support bases for Vietnamese forces fighting the enemy main forces in the border areas.

Because of the sensitive nature of the 5th Special Forces Group missions and operations, many aspects of its logistic support were also sensitive. The distinguishing feature of the 5th Special Forces Group logistic support was the reliance upon a Quick Reacting Procurement System for certain special forces equipment. The Army Materiel Command expeditiously purchased and shipped commercial or other service matériel not available in the Army inventory but needed to support special warfare programs. The bulk of the 5th Special Forces Group everyday support, however, came from the U.S. Army Vietnam logistic system. Because of the limited organic maintenance capability of operating detachments and the volume of nonstandard items in the 5th Special Forces Group, maintenance of equipment was based on repair by replacement. Unserviceable items were evacuated, either in or out of country, to the appropriate level of a supporting maintenance activity.

An S-4 section of the 5th Special Force Group headquarters headed the internal logistic organization of the 5th Special Forces Group. Additionally, 5th Special Forces Group Logistical Support Centers (organic in-country support elements) provided operational logistic support to deployed Special Forces detachments and to the counterinsurgency program. The Logistic Support Center organization provided a cross section of logistic functions and capabilities with necessary interfaces enabling it to draw upon a broad range of non-organic support capabilities both from within and without Vietnam.

Logistic Support of Republic of Vietnam Armed Forces

U. S. Military Assistance to the Vietnamese Armed Forces commenced on 23 December 1950, while the French Indochina War was still in progress. With the end of that war and the departure of the French, the United States continued to supply the fledgling Republic of Vietnam with military matériel and equipment. President Eisenhower's commitment for their support was put into effect through the establishment of a Military Assistance Advisory Group.

In 1955 the mission of the Military Assistance Advisory Group was expanded to include organizing and training the South Vietnamese Armed Forces as well as providing them with equipment and other matériel. Then in 1961 President Kennedy approved requests for additional aid. Increased communist pressure continued to generate larger military requirements, and in February 1962, the Military Assistance Command was created for the purpose of improving command, control, and the support of the adviser program. The advisers, of course, advised the South Vietnamese Armed Forces in organizing and training their personnel and assisted them in acquiring necessary equipment.

The South Vietnamese Armed Forces increased in manpower from approximately 435,000 in 1964 to 623,000 by the end of 1966 and to over 1,000,000 by the end of 1970. The logistic adviser effort increased as the South Vietnamese Armed Forces personnel strength increased. On 20 July 1965, U.S. Army Vietnam was established to provide a control element for the U.S. Army Forces in Vietnam. On 1 September 1965, the logistic adviser functions and support of the field advisory program were transferred to U.S. Army Vietnam, with the exception of the staff advisory functions of the Military Assistance Command, Vietnam, staff. Effective 15 March 1968, the operational control of the logistic advisory effort for the South Vietnamese Army was transferred from U.S. Army Vietnam back to Military Assistance Command, Vietnam. Within Military Assistance Command, Vietnam, the Assistant Chief of Staff for Logistics, J-4, served as the principal advisor to Commander U.S. Military Assistance Command, Vietnam, on all matters relating to the logistic systems which supported the counterinsurgency operations in South Vietnam and provided advice to the South Vietnamese Armed Forces on logistics, including matériel systems development, organization, plans, policies, and operations.

The Director of the Logistics Advisory Directorate (J-46) was the principal adviser to the Assistant Chief of Staff, J-4, on all matters relating to the South Vietnamese Armed Forces logistics system and advised and assisted logistics elements of the South Vietnamese Armed Forces in providing effective, responsive, and economical logistic support. To accomplish this mission, the J-46 directed the logistic advisory organization shown in Chart 17. In addition to the advisory effort provided by the Logistics Advisory Directorate, the advisors listed below also assisted the South Vietnamese Army in logistics at various levels:

Advisor Positions	Responsible Organization or Agency
Corps G–4 Advisors	Corps Senior Advisor
Division G–4 Advisors	Division Senior Advisor
Division Logistical Support Battalion Advisors	Division Senior Advisor
Sector S–1 and S–4 Advisors	Province(Sector) Senior Advisor
Sector Administrative & Direct Support Logistic Advisors	Province(Sector) Senior Advisor
Medical Advisors	MACV Command Surgeon

Improvisations were often required in order to accomplish the advisory effort in a timely fashion, within the available resources. The following are two examples of improvisation in organizational concepts that were employed:

1. Due to the need for a sizeable increase in adviser strength and since considerable delay was expected in acquiring fill from Continental U.S. sources, an experimental concept using Mobile Advisory Teams was tried in IV Corps in October 1967. Nineteen teams, consisting of five U. S. personnel, and one Vietnamese

CHART 17—LOGISTICS ADVISORY DIRECTORATE

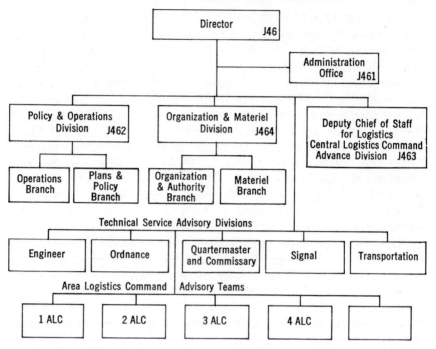

interpreter, were deployed. One team was assigned to each province and one to each South Vietnamese Army division.

2. Based on results experienced by the Mobile Advisory Teams, Mobile Advisory Logistic Teams were designed. They were structured along much the same lines as the Mobile Advisory Teams. The teams were allocated one to each Area Logistical Command; except in the III and IV Corps, where, due to higher troop density, one additional team was allocated. The Mobile Advisory Logistic Teams mission was to provide on-the-spot administrative, supply and logistic training and assistance to depots, administrative and direct support logistic companies, and Regional and Popular Force units.

The U. S. advisory elements, though predominantly U. S. Army, included members from the other Services. These elements received common support from the component commander in whose area they were located.

All logistic advisers were carefully selected to assure that each one was fully qualified. The outstanding accomplishments of the advisers is evidence that this selectivity has paid off. Logistic advisers made a major contribution to bringing the South Vietnamese Armed Forces to the level where Vietnamization could begin.

Until 24 March 1966, the South Vietnamese Armed Forces was generally equipped with U. S. equipment and matériel through the Military Assistance Program (Grant Aid). At that time the funding system was changed to a Military Assistance Service Funded program. Military Assistance Program type requisitioning and programming techniques, however, continued to be employed. For secondary items and consumables, the South Vietnamese Armed Forces submitted requisitions through Military Assistance Command, Vietnam, to the U.S. Army Materiel Command International Logistical Center at New Cumberland, Pennsylvania for Continental U.S. items, or to the U. S. Army Depot, Japan for off-shore procurement, and Military Assistance Program peculiar items. (*Chart 18*) There was an exception for medical items. Requisitions were placed on the Medical Depot in Okinawa for these items. Major items were "pushed" in accordance with delivery schedules furnished by Military Assistance Command, Vietnam. Ammunition was controlled by Commander in Chief U.S. Army Pacific. This supply system remained in effect until 1970. After this time, South Vietnamese Armed Forces Base Depots forwarded requisitions for secondary items and consumables to the 2d Logistical Command in Okinawa. If the 2d Logistical Command was unable to fill the requisitions from their on-hand assets, they forwarded the requisitions to the appropriate Continental U.S. supply source.

An additional source of equipment became available to the South Vietnamese Armed Forces when the phase down of U. S. Forces began in 1969. At this time U.S. Army Vietnam began publishing listings of items of equipment that became surplus to its needs and that it could therefore make available to the South Vietnamese Armed Forces. After this, if South Vietnamese Armed Forces base depots received requisitions for items that they did not have on hand, they would check the U.S. Army Vietnam surplus listings. If the item was available from this source, they would request the item from U.S. Army Vietnam instead of the 2d Logistical Command in Okinawa. The system was later automated, and by 30 June 1971 more than $70 million in U.S. Army Vietnam excess consumables and more than $50 million in major items had been transferred.

A constant effort was made to upgrade weapons and equipment used by the South Vietnamese Armed Forces. The matter of weapons was particularly critical, because the enemy had begun introducing modern communist-bloc weapons, including the highly effective AK47 automatic rifle as early as 1964. By 1967, all enemy units were equipped with this weapon, which had a much higher rate of fire than any of the U.S. World War II weapons with which South Vietnamese troops were armed.

The M16 automatic rifles, long sought for issue to the South Vietnamese forces, began to arrive in April 1967, but in quantities that would equip only the airborne and Marine battalions of the General Reserve. After strong recommendations on the part of General Westmoreland, an accelerated schedule of M16 shipments was approved in the fall of 1967, and by mid-1968 all regular infantry maneuver battalions had received the new weapon.

The United States Military Assistance Command established a Distribution and Allocations Committee in the fall of 1968. The committee was established to allocate, and control the distribution of critical matériel that was either in South Vietnam or due in country in an effort to accelerate the approved South Vietnamese Armed Forces improvement and modernization programs. The committee reviewed the mission requirements and asset positions of the United States Forces, South Vietnamese Armed Forces and Free World Military Assistance Forces and recommended allocation and distribution actions in support of the military effort in South Vietnam. Items considered by the committee were in actual or potential short supply. It included items managed under the Closed Loop Program, U.S. Marine Corp Rebuild and Evacuation Program, and the U.S. Air Force Repairable Asset Management System. A data base was established for each item to include amount on hand, depot assets, and maintenance float.

The continued improvement in the South Vietnamese Armed Forces modernization program led to the termination of the committee in June 1970, at the request of Commander in Chief Pacific.

In 1967 Military Assistance Command, Vietnam, and the Vietnamese Joint General Staff took action to expand the South Vietnamese Armed Forces commissary system in order to improve the diet of Vietnamese servicemen and their dependents while reducing the prices they had to pay for subsistence items. The U.S. contributed a one-time grant of $42 million for food items, which when sold provided self-regenerating funds from which stocks could be replenished. Sales of the new items began in September 1967. By the end of the year, revenues exceeded a million dollars, covering the cost of overhead, construction equipment, and further expansion. By the end of June 1968, 201 retail outlets were in operation serving troops and dependents throughout Vietnam.

During June 1969, Presidents Nixon and Thieu met at Midway Island. They discussed, among other subjects, increased logistical support to the South Vietnamese Armed Forces. Subsequently the "MACV Morale Study" recommended Military Assistance Service Funded support of canned meats and shortening for 1.1 million South Vietnamese servicemen during a two year period at an estimated cost of $42.7 million. A plan was prepared incorporating these recommendations. The U.S. Agency for International Development representative reviewed the plan in March 1970 and recommended that the plan be lengthened to a three year period with no increase in Military Assistance Service Funded support. This latter plan proposed 100 percent of the necessary Military Assistance Service Funded subsistence supplement support be furnished during the first year, 70 percent the second year and 30 percent during the final year. The plan envisioned a projected three year expansion of South Vietnam's farm and garden program and canning industry coupled with a rising economy permitting the government of Vietnam to attain self-sufficiency in furnishing adequate subsistence to its armed forces. In April 1970, General Abrams, Commander, Military Assistance Command, Vietnam approved the plan for submission to the Department of Defense.

The Secretary of Defense approved the plan with certain stipulations including: a fund limitation of $42.7 million, that Department of the Army not release funds until Commander U.S. Military Assistance Command, Vietnam, approved a distribution plan, and that Commander U.S. Military Assistance Command, Vietnam, review and concur in a South Vietnamese Armed Forces distribution plan prior to submission of requisitions. The distribution plan was approved by General Abrams on 8 September 1970. It required both units and depots to stock subsistence supplements. Each troop unit and organization would draw an initial issue based on the payroll strength plus a safety level. The safety level was 10 percent for hospitals, training centers, and military schools and 3 percent for all other units. The depots were authorized to stock the ration supplements with a forty-five day operating and fifteen day safety level. The ration supplement included canned fish (mackerel, salmon, tuna, sardines), meats (beef chunks, beef and gravy, luncheon meat, ham chunks, port sausage), poultry (chicken, turkey) and shortening. The items were issued to authorized personnel at fixed rates per individual.

The South Vietnamese Armed Forces logistic organization

(*Chart 18*) had a system that worked moderately well, but required improvements throughout the entire spectrum before attaining complete logistic self-sufficiency. Changes in the conduct of the war increased South Vietnamese Armed Forces logistic support requirements at an accelerated rate. The Vietnamization program intensified the efforts of improving and modernizing the South Vietnamese Armed Forces logistics system toward self-sufficiency. Major factors which affected the South Vietnamese Armed Forces logistic capabilities were as follows:

1. Rapid increases in the South Vietnamese Armed Forces combat force structure required commensurate increases in the logistics support base.

2. The introduction of modern sophisticated weapons and support equipment in significant densities into the South Vietnam Armed Forces inventory enlarged the scope and complexity of the logistics support requirements. Large inventories of aircraft, helicopters, boats, vehicles, weapons, and communication assets required extensive supply storage, distribution, maintenance, evacuation, and disposition systems to support them. Basic to those systems were the requirements for technically-trained military and civilian personnel and modern depot facilities. Although additional logistic personnel were subsequently authorized, efforts to fill authorizations with trained qualified personnel were slow to achieve desired results. Competition for civilian labor between U.S. Forces, civilian firms, and the South Vietnamese Armed Forces left the latter short of technically trained and skilled civilians. Depot repair capabilities and physical facilities also were inadequate to support requirements generated by the Improvement and Modernization Program. The rapid expansion of territorial forces placed a tremendous burden on the Administrative and Direct Support Logistical companies.

To accelerate the development of South Vietnamese Armed Forces logistics self-sufficiency, a Logistics Master Plan concept was prepared which combined several individual logistic plans, programs, projects, and studies, each designed to improve the South Vietnamese Armed Forces logistical system. The elements of the Logistic Master Plan were as follows:

1. *The Combined Logistics Offensive Plan* was basically a short range plan designed to foster a positive aggressive logistic offensive spirit in the conduct of logistic operations. The plan identified problems, designated agencies responsible for solving the problems, and established the completion date for each problem outlined in the plan.

CHART 18—SOUTH VIETNAMESE ARMED FORCES ORGANIZATION FOR LOGISTICS

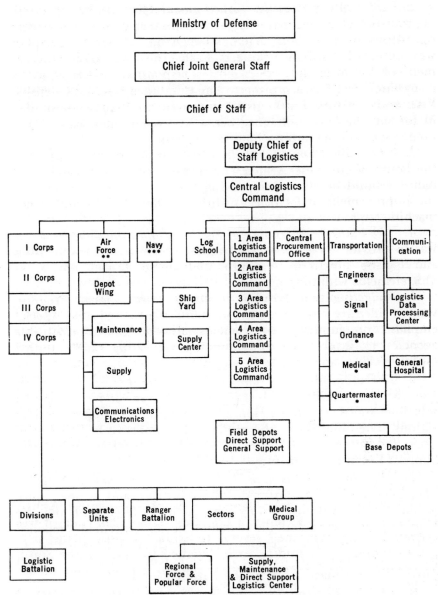

*Provides Common Secondary Item Supply Support to the ARVN, VNAF, and VNN.

**Provides Logistic Support Peculiar to Aircraft.

***Provides Logistic Support Peculiar to Naval Vessels.

2. *The Country Logistics Improvement Plan* was a long range program which listed major objectives for improving the logistic operations of the South Vietnamese Armed Forces. The plan was composed of specified projects. Each project identified Government of Vietnam and U.S. agencies responsible and assigned a completion date for each project. The Combined Logistic Offensive Plan and the Country Logistic Improvement Plan were similar in format, the basic difference being that the former was a short range plan and the latter a long range plan.

3. *The Base Depot Upgrade Plan* was intended to upgrade the South Vietnamese Armed Forces Engineer, Signal, and Ordnance rebuild depots by improving the depot structure through the improvement of facilities, utilities, technical skills and depot machine tools.

4. *The Plans for Turnover of Facilities and Functions Program* was to provide for the orderly transfer of United States facilities and logistic functions to South Vietnamese Armed Forces, as U.S. elements withdrew.

5. *Budgeting and Funding Concept Improvement Program* was to identify master plan programs which required special emphasis on funding requirements and designate responsible agencies to insure that programming budgeting, and funding aspects received appropriate attention.

6. *The Administrative and Direct Support Logistical Company Study* identified problems and their causes, recommended solutions and designated action agencies responsible for corrective actions. The objective of this study was to improve logistic operations and support capabilities of the Administrative and Direct Support Logistical companies.

7. *The South Vietnamese Armed Forces Automated Materiel Management System* outlined the objectives and general provisions for an Automated Logistic System Development and the sequence of events for implementation and assigned responsibilities to applicable agencies. This program was designed to provide the South Vietnamese Armed Forces with an automated capability to manage assets at the national level.

8. *The On-The-Job Training Program "PROJECT BUDDY."* In 1968, it was recognized that the time was rapidly approaching when, depending on the ability of the Vietnamese forces to take over the job of policing and defending their own nation, our U.S. strength in Vietnam would be withdrawn.

In January 1969, the 1st Logistical Command piloted a program called Project BUDDY with the approval of Headquarters

U.S. Army Vietnam and Military Assistance Command, Vietnam. Project BUDDY was designed to teach the South Vietnamese Army to assume responsibilities in the logistics area by providing on-the-job training in logistics skills and management. While such training had been going on for years, there was no previous requirement for a formal on-the-job training program.

On 13 October 1969, a Military Assistance Command, Vietnam, directive was published for on-the-job training which was applicable to all of its subordinate and component commands. It established a combined effort by Military Assistance Command, Vietnam and the South Vietnamese Armed Forces to identify skills in need of improvement and to provide South Vietnamese Armed Forces personnel with on-the-job training in these skills. On-the-job training consisted of numerous programs, varying in length from a few days to six months, and in scope from an upgrade of an individual's current skill to a qualification in a new Military Occupation Speciality. This training was conducted for both South Vietnamese Armed Forces officers and enlisted personnel.

Operation BUDDY was a good program but after October 1969 was not used to its full advantage. The middle management people at Military Assistance Command, Vietnam were more concerned with the prerogatives of their advisers and not enough with training the South Vietnamese Armed Forces. As a result, only 9,300 had been trained under this program by the end of fiscal year 1970.

9. *South Vietnamese Army Ammunition Improvement Plan.* This plan provided for the improvements necessary to give the South Vietnamese Armed Forces a capability to completely support their current and anticipated ammunition storage, inventory management, surveillance and maintenance requirements.

Logistic Support of South Vietnamese Pacification Program

Pacification is the process of establishing or reestablishing effective local self-government within the political framework of the legitimate central government and its constitution. It includes the provision of sustained and credible territorial security and the genuine, voluntary involvement of the people as well as the initiation of self-sustaining and expanding economic and social activity. Some obvious areas where military forces can assist the pacification effort are the opening of roads and waterways and the maintaining of lines of communication, important to both economic and military activity.

The objectives of pacification are not difficult to describe but the attainment of those objectives involves cultural and social forces not so easy to understand and certainly not easy to manage. Some of the means and organizations through which the U.S. logistic system assisted the pacification program of the Republic of Vietnam were as follows:

Logistic support of the Vietnamese Regional and Popular Forces was included in the U.S. Military Assistance Service Funded program. Supplies were issued to these forces by South Vietnamese Army Sector Management and Direct Support Logistic Centers.

The Peoples Self Defense Forces were provided certain designated items of supply through the same channels as were the Regional and Popular Forces above.

Logistic support of the Rural Development Cadre was generally funded through the U.S. Agency for International Development system in accordance with the Agency for International Development and Department of Defense Realignment Program. Except for ammunition, petroleum, oils, and lubricants and maintenance support which was provided by the South Vietnamese Army, support was generally provided through provincial warehouses operated by the Agency for International Development. However, at times U.S. Army Vietnam provided requested support on a reimbursable basis.

Supply support and funding for the Civilian Irregular Defense Group was provided through the U.S. 5th Special Forces Group Counterinsurgency Support Office. The 5th Special Forces Group placed the necessary requisitions on the U.S. Army Vietnam depots. The Civilian Irregular Defense Group has since been phased out and its activities absorbed by the South Vietnamese Army Regional and Popular Forces organization with support being provided through the South Vietnamese Army supply system.

Support of refugees has been provided by the Government of Vietnam, U.S. and other voluntary agencies. U.S. Agency for International Development was the basic administrator of this program for the U.S.; however, U.S. troop support was provided on an as required basis, and included building temporary shelters, latrines and other utility items. Support normally provided under the U.S. and Government of Vietnam programs included an immediate rice allowance for 7 days of 500 grams per day per person and 3 cans of condensed milk per family. The rice allowance could be extended for up to 30 days. Resettlement or return to village assistance was provided next, and included a rice allowance of 15 kilograms per person per month. A housing construction allowance of 7,500 Vietnamese dollars and ten sheets of metal roofing was also provided after the enemy's *Tet* and May offensives of 1968. Together these offensives left 13,000 civilians dead and 27,000 wounded, created over one million refugees and destroyed or damaged over 170,000 houses.

On 2 February 1968, at the height of the *Tet* crisis, President Thieu announced the formation of a Central Recovery Committee to direct and coordinate the activities of all government agencies both civilian and military, in expediting civil recovery. This force received full and immediate support from all U.S. agencies, civil and military. The resulting project was known as Project Recovery.

Fortunately when the enemy struck again in May 1968, the Central Recovery Committee was still organized and again served as the catalyst for Government of Vietnam and U.S. action. By mid-May Project Recovery could point to a record of considerable achievement. The Central Recovery Committee provided care for a peak number of 750,831 evacuees that had been made homeless as a result of the *Tet* Offensive. By mid-May, only 286,000 *Tet* refugees remained and 140,000 of these had been created after 5 May 1968. Over 33,000 metric tons of food, 66,000 tons of construction materials, and 5,000 tons of miscellaneous clothing, blankets, and other items were released from Saigon and regional warehouses. Relief and resettlement allowances amounting to over 483 million Vietnamese dollars were paid to nearly 60,000 families. Almost 580,000 bags of cement and 634,000 sheets of roofing were distributed to approximately 64,000 families.

Another support program was introducing refugees to techniques for improving yields of agricultural crops, particularly vegetables. Handicraft projects were also organized and small industries were developed. Food-for-work projects were also started, utilizing food made available under Public Law 480, Title II.

The lines of communication program has directly benefited civilians and local economies by providing improved roads for transportation of people and goods. The total Military Assistance Command, Vietnam, Lines of Communication improvement program called for the upgrade of 4,075 km of road. As of 15 May 1971, over 60 percent of this work had been completed. More than 1,700 km of the work was done by U. S. Army troop effort and the remainder by the U.S. Navy, South Vietnamese Army, or by contractor personnel.

Another program that benefited the Vietnamese people was the assistance by U. S. agencies in restoring the Vietnamese Railway System. This program had a dual goal objective. The first was to provide transportation assets that would move great tonnages at low cost, and the second was to renew an economical means of travel for the Vietnamese people between their homes and the larger market areas. Overall planning for railway restoration began in June 1966. It was a joint effort by the Government of Vietnam and U. S. agencies. All reconstruction efforts were co-ordinated through three standing committees, composed of members of Military Assistance Command, Vietnam, Government of Vietnam, U.S. Agency for International Development, and the Joint General Staff, with primary responsibility resting with the Joint Committee on Rail Restoration.

The rail system suffered extensive damage during World War II and the French Indochina War; but, with U.S. Agency for International Development assistance, it was rebuilt between 1954 and 1959. Then in 1960, the system came under attack again when the Viet Cong began a concerted and continuing campaign towards its destruction.

Evidence of the accomplishments of the restoration program is witnessed by the fact that the system entered 1968 with only 475 km of operational railroad, but early in 1970 the system consisted of 1,109.3 km of meter gauge main line from Saigon to Dong Ha in I Corps and approximately 130 km of branch line trackage.

A Medical Civic Action Program was conducted by Military Assistance Command, Vietnam, through the use of U.S. Forces and directed toward improving the local health environment, to include treatment and education of civilians in basic sanitation methods and other preventive health measures. This program was funded through US Military Service channels, with subsequent charge made to the Agency for International Development and Department of Defense realignment program based on a flat charge per treatment rendered.

A Military Provincial Hospital Assistance Program was created to furnish expendable medical supplies in support of the Ministry of Health hospitals and health service facilities. Medical care under this program included care to the population in general, paramilitary personnel, and civilian war casualties. The U.S. Army provided personnel as augmentation teams to assist the Government of Vietnam Ministry of Health in various hospital facilities. In addition, the U.S. Army provided half of the funding support for this program.

Requisitions to obtain supply support of this program were

forwarded to the U.S. Army Medical Depot in Okinawa. Supplies were shipped to the Ministry of Health Medical Logistic Center, Phy Tho, Saigon, and issued through the Ministry of Health logistics system.

The Government of Vietnam National Police Field Forces were provided supplies and equipment through U.S. Army channels. Army funds were utilized and requisitions were submitted through U.S. Army channels by Military Assistance Command, Vietnam, Civil Operations Revolutionary Development Command, Vietnam.

Commodity support was provided to upgrade in-country port and waterway facilities. The program was funded by U.S. Agency for International Development with subsequent reimbursement from Army funds. Supplies were basically obtained through Agency for International Development channels with the U.S. Army providing technical assistance as well as supplies on an as required and as available basis.

Logistic Support of Other Free World Military Assistance Forces

Upon the introduction of Free World combat forces into Vietnam in 1965, the U.S. assumed the preponderance of logistic support for the Free World Military Assistance Force units. These units came from the Republic of Korea, Thailand, Republic of the Philippines, Australia, and New Zealand.

With the exception of Australian and New Zealand forces, the other Free World Military Assistance Forces had been Military Assistance Program supported. Thus, many items of their equipment had to be replaced by items normally issued to U.S. Forces to make them supportable by the U.S. logistic system.

The role of these units upon deployment to Vietnam was generally not determined until the eve of deployment, thus delaying until the last moment a determination of their specific equipment requirements. Of particular significance in alleviating equipment and supply shortages earlier than would have been otherwise possible was the conversion of Free World Military Assistance Force support from Military Assistance Program to Military Assistance Service Funded Program. In this connection Military Assistance Service Funded has application only to local forces in Vietnam, Laos, and Thailand and third country forces in Vietnam. It should be noted, however, that the funding for the support of Australian and New Zealand forces has been accomplished by financial agreement involving no appreciable cost to the U.S.

Generally Office of the Secretary of Defense and the Joint Chiefs of Staff approved the Free World Military Assistance Forces force structures to be supported by the United States. Military Assistance Command, Vietnam approved the Table of Organization and Equipment and Table of Distribution and Allowances in co-ordination with the Allied governments concerned. U.S. Army Regulation 795–10, "U.S. Army Materiel and Service Support for RVNAF/FWMAF," governs the funding and requisition procedures for the Free World Military Assistance Force. Major item losses suffered by U.S. and Free World forces were reported to U.S. Army Major Item Data Agency through the AR 711–5 Army Equipment Status Reporting System. This agency then developed loss factors for replacement planning for the preparation of Army Materiel Plans and for use by the staff planners in developing and executing the Procurement of Equipment and Missiles Army portion of the Army budget.

General supplies (Classes II, IV, VII and IX except missile peculiar items), ammunition, petroleum, medical supplies, memorial services (mortuary, cremation, etc), laundry and bath services, procurement services, and terminal and water transportation services were normally provided to Free World Military Assistance Forces through U.S. Army Vietnam or U.S. Navy logistic system in the same manner as the supplies and services were provided to U.S. Forces. Two areas where exceptions existed were maintenance and subsistence. The U.S. system provided limited maintenance support to the Free World Military Assistance Forces. This support was furnished for selected items only and was to provide a back-up support to the allied maintenance system. Aviation maintenance support was provided to Australian, Thai, and Korean Forces. Reports were furnished to U.S. Army Pacific on aviation maintenance for funding and data collection purposes.

The Directorate of Food, Headquarters, 1st Logistical Command, monitored the four U.S. Army Support Commands who requisitioned, received, accounted for, issued, and supervised the Class I support for all Free World Military Assistance Forces in South Vietnam. The Directorate of Food was responsible for funding and monitoring local procurement and contract services support of dairy products, bread, fresh fruits and vegetables, and ice.

Initially, the U.S. government agreed to provide subsistence support to the Republic of Korea forces in Vietnam but did not specify a "Kimchi Ration." The Republic of Korea forces in

Vietnam received either the MCI or the A ration. The agreement was amended in 1967 to provide one meal of the Korean Combat Ration daily. This special ration was developed in Vietnam, with assistance from a U.S. country team and the U.S. Army Natick Laboratories. The majority of the items in the ration (including the Kimchi) were indigenous to Korea. Thus the Republic of Korea Forces in Vietnam were provided one meal of the A ration, one meal of the MCI and one meal of the Korean Combat Ration. Australian and New Zealand forces were furnished the standard A ration supplemented with marmalade and local purchase items. The Philippine forces were furnished the standard A ration with additional rice in lieu of some of the potatoes. The Thailand forces were furnished components of the standard A ration supplemented by local purchase. They were also supplied with coconuts, morning grass, lemon grass and ginger root. (The South Vietnamese Armed Forces were provided with components of the A ration supplemented with indigenous items. They were also provided the MCI and the Long Range Patrol Packet).

The 32d Medical Depot was responsible for the medical supply support of the Free World Military Assistance Forces.

The U.S. Army provided limited maintenance support to the Free World Military Assistance Forces except in I Corps, where the U.S. Navy provided the service until mid-1970, when the Army also assumed the responsibility for that area. This support was furnished for selected items to provide back-up support to the allied maintenance system.

Agreements were made to provide aviation maintenance support to Australian, Thai, and Korean forces operating in Vietnam. This worked smoothly with reports furnished to U.S. Army Pacific for funding and data collection purposes. Standardized and simplified reporting reduced confusion and administrative workload in the field. Support of the Free World Military Assistance Forces was excellent.

A mission of the U.S. Army memorial activities in the Republic of Vietnam was to receive, process, identify and evacuate the remains of deceased Free World Military Assistance Forces. As part of the 1st Logistical Command's mission of providing this mortuary service cremation facilities were established for the Republic of Korea Forces. Initially, cremation services were provided by contract with Tobia Mortuary of Saigon. Two crematory units of the type used in civilian funeral homes in Continental U.S. were procured and became operational in June 1967. Remains of other Free World Military Assistance Forces forces were processed through the mortuaries in the same manner as U.S. personnel and then evacuated to their countries.

The U.S. Army provided laundry and bath service support to Free World Military Assistance Forces in II, III, and IV Corps from the time of their arrival; service to I Corps began in 1970. Laundry service was supplemented by contract laundries where requirements exceeded organic Army capability.

The mission of the terminal and water transportation system was to operate deep and shallow draft ports, and logistics over the shore sites in South Vietnam and to provide intra-coastal and inland waterway lighterage services. The mission also included receiving, documenting, loading, discharging, and transhipping Free World Military Assistance Force and Agency for International Development cargo as it moved through the water terminals.

The U.S. Army Procurement Activity also provided procurement support to the combat support elements of the Free World Military Assistance Forces along with Military Assistance Command, Vietnam; U.S. Army Vietnam; and elements of the other U.S. military services.

Free World Military Assistance Forces were trained primarily by sending small numbers of selected personnel to schools in the Continental U.S. and by our military assistance advisory personnel in their own countries. In South Vietnam, the Free World Military Assistance Forces received informal training as required. U.S. units providing combat service support to these forces instructed their key personnel on the use of U.S. matériel and systems, and in turn received orientation on the supported Free World Military Assistance Forces procedures. This cycle was repeated as necessary when new replacements arrived in either unit.

Vietnamese Rebuilding Home with Lumber Donated Through
TARP Program in Bien Hoa, above; Dam Built to Improve
Irrigation System in the Village Rice Fields in
Thuy Phu, Vietnam, below.

MALT Team Head Confers with American Advisor and
Local S–4 of a Vietnamese Supply Maintenance
District Support Logistical Company.

CHAPTER X

Worldwide Impact of Vietnam on Logistics Readiness

Impact on Active Army

The diversion of new production assets and withdrawal of equipment from the major Army commands in 1965–1966, to support high priority requirements in Southeast Asia, had a predictably adverse impact on the worldwide logistics readiness posture of the Army. For example, by June 1966, only 35 percent of Continental Army Command's active Army units were meeting logistics goals in equipment on hand and 25 percent were meeting equipment status goals. A similar posture existed in other commands. U.S Army Pacific (less U.S. Army Vietnam) had only 40 percent of the Active Army units meeting equipment on hand goals and 18 percent meeting equipment status goals. At the same time, U. S. Army South reported only 46 percent equipment on hand and 50 percent equipment status; U. S. Army Alaska reported 64 percent equipment on hand and 50 percent equipment status; and U. S. Army Europe reported 66 percent for equipment on hand and 50 percent equipment status. Similarly the majority of our major combat units outside of Vietnam were C–3, marginally ready; or C–4, not ready. For example, both the 2d and 7th Infantry Divisions in Korea were C–4.

Because of the ever-growing demands of combat, worldwide logistics readiness was not able to show substantial improvement during the next two years. In the latter part of 1968, the Army initiated an intensive management program, designed to overcome reported shortfalls. Procedures were established to intensively manage mission essential items required at unit level, working through each major command headquarters. These procedures provided pinpoint management of resources, refinement of unit authorizations and redistribution of assets. Readiness Improvement Programs, developed in conjunction with each command involved, are now a major element of the Logistics Offensive. In 1969 the intensive management procedures began to take effect as reductions in high priority requirements by the forces in Vietnam allowed the application of available assets to other commands.

The Army's logistic readiness posture has reflected almost continuous improvement worldwide since that time. During September 1970, the Army reached its highest levels in equipment on hand and equipment deployability since the drawdown for Southeast Asia began. During this period, over 90 percent of all reporting units met or exceeded logistic goals for equipment on hand, and 69 percent for equipment deployability. These levels were maintained throughout the remainder of fiscal year 1971 with only temporary fluctuations.

Impact on War Reserve Stocks, Operational Projects Stocks, and POMCUS Stocks

In addition to redistributing assets from units not in the combat zone, it was necessary to draw upon Pre-Positioned War Reserves, Operational Project Stocks, and POMCUS Stocks (Prepositioned Materiel configured to Unit Sets) in order to meet the unprogrammed requirements in Vietnam. War reserve stocks in the Pacific were used to support early deployments to Vietnam. Later there was a considerable drawdown worldwide to meet increased requirements for Southeast Asia.

In February 1966, to further increase assets available for use in Vietnam, Department of the Army instructed all major commands to make a special review (in addition to the regular annual review) of all their operational projects. Any matériel not absolutely essential would be made available to meet requirements in Vietnam. Equipment which had been configured in unit sets in the Western Pacific area was also included in this drawdown.

Full recovery from the drawdowns of these Pre-positioned War Reserves, POMCUS, and Operational Projects Stocks had not been achieved by mid-1971.

In March 1970, a study labeled **PROJECT STRAT REQUIREMENT** was initiated by the Duputy Chief of Staff for Logistics, to validate and recommend for revision, as necessary, methods and principles used in the determination of theater war reserve and automatic supply requirements. The purpose was to verify the accuracy of requirements determination, so that both prepositioned matériel overseas and post D-day automatic supply are responsive and effective in meeting the needs of combat forces in wartime. The study was completed in September 1970 with recommendations which, when fully implemented, will improve the range and quantity of items included in theater war reserves and automatic supply planning. Simultaneously with **PROJECT STRAT REQUIREMENT**, a special review of worldwide operational projects was conducted. The main objective of this review was to revalidate command operational project requirements, eliminating stocks which were not truly mission essential. This review resulted in a reduction in requirements of $272,774,000. The study was approved by the Army Chief of Staff on 1 February 1971 and action has begun on the implementation of its recommendations.

Impact on Reserve Components

The Reserve Components suffered a major setback concerning receipt of modern equipment during the Army's buildup for the conduct of large scale operations in Vietnam. During the period fiscal years 1965–1968, the delivery of equipment to the Reserve Components was in token quantities because the limited supply was required to fill higher priority requirements. Deliveries during this four year period amounted to approximately $460 million. In addition to the inadequate equipment deliveries, the Reserve units were tapped as a source of equipment to be withdrawn and redistributed to active Army claimants. These withdrawals amounted to approximately $209 million. Major items withdrawn from the Reserve Components to fill urgent Vietnam requirements included over 200 aircraft, 460 40-mm guns, 50 M88 Recovery Vehicles, and approximately 650 3/4-Ton Vehicles. Since fiscal year 1966, Office of the Secretary of Defense has monitored and maintained approval authority of all equipment withdrawals from the Reserve Components to meet active Army requirements.

Chart 19 portrays the general impact that the Vietnam buildup had upon the Reserve Components. It displays by fiscal year the various inventory changes in billions of dollars. These changes reflect the value of equipment issued minus the value of obsolete equipment turned in. It is significant to note that during fiscal year 1964 the Reserve Component inventory was approximately $2.18 billion and because of the requirements generated by commitments in Southeast Asia, the inventory did not show improvement over the fiscal year 1964 level until mid fiscal year 1969.

The phasedown of U.S. operations in Southeast Asia permitted an accelerated delivery of equipment to the Reserve Components. Beginning in fiscal year 1969, equipment deliveries to the Reserve Components increased at a noticeable rate. Deliveries were valued at approximately $150 million in fiscal year 1969 and at $300 million in fiscal year 1970. As of the end of the 3d Quarter of fiscal year 1971, equipment valued at approximately $590 million had been allocated for delivery against an estimated allocation

CHART 19—RESERVE COMPONENT EQUIPMENT INVENTORY CHANGES

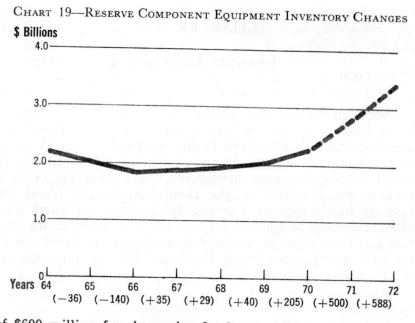

of $600 million for the entire fiscal year. These deliveries have improved the equipment readiness of the Reserve Component units, but there still remains much to be done considering that the units have on hand about 61 percent of the equipment required for the conduct of effective premobilization training. Principal deliveries during fiscal year 1970 included a significant number of new tactical vehicles and radios, sufficient M14 and M16 rifles to permit the complete modernization of the Reserve Component rifle inventory, preferred aircraft including the CH–54 and UH–1D, and the first M60 tanks.

To further improve the equipment situation of the Reserve Components, Department of the Army in fiscal year 1971 developed a maintenance program which permits the Office of Reserve Components to select critically required items for overhaul and subsequent issue to the Reserve Component units. It is anticipated that during the fiscal years 1971–1974 equipment valued at $1 billion will be provided under this program. This will be in addition to new items issued under normal distribution programs.

CHAPTER XI

Lessons Learned

Although no one can predict the future, the likelihood of being involved in another limited war seems to be high. Since the advent of the nuclear age, limited wars and insurgency operations have been both frequent and common. Since World War II, the U. S. Army has gone through the Korean War, the Lebanon landing, the operation in the Dominican Republic, and was involved in Vietnam for a decade, being there in strength since 1965. A number of lessons have emerged from the Vietnam years that can be applied in similar future campaigns. These can be grouped under three broad headings: Personnel, Equipment, and Policies and Procedures.

Personnel Lessons Learned

1. A twelve month tour is too short if a logistic system is to operate at near peak efficiency. When casualties (combat and non-combat) are considered, about 10 percent of the personnel change every month. On the other hand, if other benefits merit a fixed short combat tour policy, then in-theater personnel turbulence must be held to a minimum by strictly limiting the number of assignment changes for each individual during his tour.

2. The Continental U.S. training base is overly civilianized. The small pool of trained and experienced military people in maintenance operations, ammunition operations, storage and warehousing operations, and supply management is incapable of providing the number of skilled personnel needed when a force buildup starts. Either depots and installation logistics facilities should increase their military strengths or Continental U.S. civilians in these facilities should be used to support an overseas buildup until the Continental Army Command school system can turn out the required number of trained military men and women. An additional benefit that would result from using more military in Continental U.S. logistical installations would be that there would be assignments in Continental U.S. where skilled overseas returnees could employ their expertise.

3. There is a need to improve driver training programs in Continental U.S. Poorly trained drivers add to maintenance

workloads and cause the overseas commanders to divert personnel resources to establish driver training programs. Continental U.S. training should include operating in combat type conditions.

4. Units of the Reserve Components called to active duty performed well. The decision to rely on draftees or regulars instead of calling up reserve units meant that valuable logistics skills were not put to use. The few National Guard and Reserve units that were used in the Da Nang area during the summer and fall of 1968 were very good. Brigadier General James W. Gunn, Commanding General, US Army Support Command, Da Nang remarked that ". . . these units proved to be outstanding in every respect. They were composed of mature officers and men who arrived in-country with 100 percent of their TOE strength and equipment. They were for the most part well educated and highly motivated and skilled. . ."

5. Replacement centers in combat zones should assure that every individual has a set of readable fingerprints in his 201 file. The prompt and current identification of the dead is a must.

Equipment Lessons Learned

1. The use of DeLong Piers in Vietnam showed that new ports can be created quickly or existing ones expanded in a relatively short time. As a contingency for any possible future conflict in undeveloped areas, these piers should be stockpiled in several geographic areas.

2. Cross-country petroleum pipelines can be used in insurgency type operations. Their use reduces the number of trucks required, thereby shortening convoy lengths. However, there is a price to pay in fuel losses as the enemy is given an opportunity to easily interdict the supply system and local inhabitants can readily pilfer a valuable and useful commodity. Using pipelines in insecure or partially secure areas means the acceptance of higher fuel losses in order to save other resources. Pipeline knowhow disappears in peace time. We must have people who can inspect the equipment in storage and determine what is needed to make it work. Pumps in storage for twenty years just won't work—even if they do they are probably not nearly as reliable or efficient as ones developed in the interim. There is a need for better surveillance and updating procedures.

3. Logistic management has become increasingly dependent on automatic data processing and high-speed digital data transmissions, both within the contingency area and between Continental U.S. and overseas locations. Therefore, logistic contingency plan-

ning must be explicit as to communications requirements and heavy transportable self-contained equipment must be developed to provide prompt availability of high-quality circuits, automatic switches, and terminal equipment to tie into the automatic digital network.

4. Containerized shipments reduce port congestion and handling time and upon offloading the containers can be used as a substitute for covered storage facilities. There is a need for container ships to have self-supporting gear for off loading in early combat and at both shallow draft locations and deep water ports. Containerized shipments should be used to a maximum in the early stages of an operation and especially so in an underdeveloped area.

5. There is a need to standardize intermodal container sizes. They should not be so large that port or city congestion will preclude their use or that they will be incapable of being lifted by heavy lift helicopters.

6. Dry battery supply and storage—We must assure that there is adequate refrigerated storage space for dry batteries.

7. Fresh foods can be provided to the combat soldier on a regular and routine basis. This requires a lot of refrigeration equipment and use of helicopters, but is worth it in terms of morale and combat effectiveness.

8. Armored vehicles of the V100 type (the M706 Armored Car) should be available in adequate numbers to provide convoy security. The field expedient of "hardening" (armor plating) assigned cargo type vehicles prevents the most effective use of these vehicles—hauling cargo.

9. The 5-ton and 2½-ton trucks with dropsides make loading and unloading with forklifts an easier and faster operation.

Policies and Procedures Lessons Learned

1. We must recognize early in any similar operation that requirements for an expanding force will increase faster than will the ability of manufacturers to produce the needed items. The declaration of a national emergency will lessen the degree of the shortfall, but a shortfall will exist for some period of time. Therefore, special management actions, to include withdrawing assets from low priority organizations for redistribution to the high priority ones, controlling the allocation of new assets in short supply, and programing retrograde, repair, and reissue should be instituted early. Shortages can be tolerated easier in the low

priority units than in units in combat, but readiness levels also have to be watched and the impact of overall shortages minimized.

2. The logistic organization is over-structured and too imbalanced toward functionalism with too little weapons systems or commodity orientation. Beginning at the Department of the Army and progressing out toward the theater of operations, consolidation and elimination of superstructures must take place. The Deputy Chief of Staff for Logistics at Headquarters Department of the Army and at Army Materiel Command, for example, are functionally duplicating command management of logistics without specific weapons systems or commodity intelligence at either level. Further study is needed to determine which echelons of command management can be eliminated or changed to facilitate logistic support of a theater of operation such as Vietnam. The role of an intermediate headquarters is questionable in the direct chain between the source of logistics intelligence data and matériel and the supported logistic echelon in the zone of combat operations. A component commander required to furnish major logistic support to ground forces in a contingency operation must be provided with a logistic management capability, vested in an officer whose rank and logistic experience are appropriate to the ultimate scope of the logistic operation. This senior logistician and his staff must participate in prior planning for contingency operations and be deployed to the area concurrently with the forward echelon of the headquarters of the combat forces.

3. While separate pipelines for Medical, Signal, Aviation and Special Forces logistics worked, and usually worked well under the environment existing in Vietnam, it is doubtful that we can afford more than one pipline into a theater of operations in future conflicts. This is particularly so where the pipeline is of great length both in geography and time and where the pipeline is subject to enemy action.

a. Since initiation of accelerated action in the Republic of Vietnam the mobile National Cash Register 500 automatic ledger posting machine has been installed as the standard direct support or general support stock control and accounting system in Army non-divisional combat service support units. This system was initially developed to fill the urgent need of support units in Republic of Vietnam during 1965–1966. Due to exceptionally successful deployment in Republic of Vietnam, the system was adopted for Army-wide installation. In addition, divisional support units in Republic of Vietnam utilized this standard system for supply applications. Division Logistics System, using the mobile UNIVAC

1005 card processor was developed during this same time frame for use by divisional support units.

b. As a "spin off" from development of the standard combat service support system for support of the Army in the field, a Quick Reaction Inventory Control Unit has been added to the Army Force Structure. This unit is to be readily available for overseas deployment to provide immediate in-theater stock control and supply management to provide a base for orderly development of theater level support operations. The Quick Reaction Inventory Control Unit is currently being trained at Fort Lewis. If conditions dictate that several separate pipelines are required, it is possible to operate these unique systems within the structure of the Quick Reaction Inventory Control Unit. The Quick Reaction Inventory Control Unit is a combination of people, organizations, automated and manual machines, and procedures to provide effective combat service support to a task force.

c. The primary lesson learned during the buildup, that central logistic system design, development and control was required, has been applied in the expansion of responsibilities for standard systems development in Headquarters Department of the Army, Office of the Deputy Chief of Staff for Logistics and its Class II activity, Logistics Doctrine Systems and Readiness Agency. This latter expansion has not yet come to complete fruition, but control of military standard support, such as Military Standard Requisitioning and Issue Procedures, Military Standard Transaction Reporting and Accounting Procedures, Military Standard Transportation and Movement Procedures and logistic data elements had been initiated. Functional proponent participation in standard operating systems design and development has been implemented.

4. There is a need to establish standards of living for troops early in a campaign. Once the standards have been decided on, they should be binding on all troops of all services. From these standards flow the requirements for real estate, construction materials, utilities, real property maintenance, post, camp and station property authorizations, as well as some engineer unit requirements. Also affected by the troop standards of living is the extent to which Post Exchanges are to be established and stocked. For logisticians, this is particularly important because PX supplies also consume port, shipping and in-country transportation space. Army and Defense contingency planning should include alternative plans for different standards of living. In the absence of such criteria, every unit will establish its own standards, usually high; and

constantly strive to upgrade them. This places excessive demands on an already busy logistic system.

5. Security in Vietnam type operations is a larger consideration for logistical units than in wars characterized by front lines and relatively secure rear areas. Convoys need to have protection, both ground and air. Installations need personnel and sentry dogs for local security. They also need equipment such as night lighting devices and sensors to support the local security forces. Stock levels should be as small as possible to present less lucrative targets. The huge excesses that developed in Vietnam were costly in men and dollars to dispose of or retrograde. The shipment of unneeded matériel from the Continental U.S. in future conflicts should be avoided.

6. Automatic data processing equipment and computers are needed. The intelligent and coordinated use of this equipment and its associated technology can provide the basis for an efficient and flexible logistic system.

7. The concept of common supply support is usually sound for selected items, but it cannot be imposed without considerable advanced planning both as to the items to be commonly supplied and the conditions and situation in the area concerned. The most profitable areas for the application of common supply support included subsistence, selected items of petroleum, oils, and lubricants and construction matériel. There is a need and an ongoing effort (Department of Defense Study Group) to develop criteria defining the commodities or items and conditions under which common supply support should be applied.

8. The use of contractors to augment or supplement the military forces is feasible and workable. Where contractors are to be supported by the Army logistical system, they can be better supported by depots than by direct support units. The Army supply system can obtain demand data for nonstandard commercial parts. However, the determination whether to support contractors from the Army's supply system or to have the contractor provide his own support should be the result of a careful analysis. The cost effectiveness and responsiveness of each method should be evaluated.

9. A combined military and commercial petroleum distribution system is workable. However, a need exists to have a petroleum, oils, and lubricants Contracting Officer in country to deal with local commercial petroleum firms.

10. The concept of Push Package is sound. Implementa-

tion procedures have been revised to provide fewer items based on equipment densities.

11. Preventive maintenance programs are basic to achieving higher operational rates on equipment. Command attention is a continuing need.

12. The use of commercial equipment on military projects is feasible and efficient. This is particularly applicable to large scale engineer efforts such as the Line of Communications road construction program. The Vietnam experiences showed that when standardized items of critical military construction and utility equipment are not available or appropriate, a program should be established to standardize available commercial items.

13. An adequate intra-theater airlift capability must be planned for. Plans for air transporting 10 percent of the anticipated cargo and 65 percent of the total monthly forces should provide an adequate initial capability.

14. The equipment required for the operation of a property disposal activity should be planned for and made a part of the approved Table of Distribution and Allowances and Table of Organization and Equipment. Country to country agreements should be made at the ambassadorial level to insure that the host country does not have control over U.S. equipment being sold to out of country purchasers.

15. A number of policies evolved from the process of phasing down forces in Vietnam under the Keystone Programs. Seven of these follow:

a. Redistribution of assets generated from deactivations and redeployments must be controlled through the existing wholesale distribution system to assure adequate cancellation of outstanding requirements.

b. A maintenance facility must be established to repair assets turned in by deactivated units. These assets must be brought to an issuable condition.

c. All redeployment and deactivation planning must include comprehensive instructions on disposition of all matériel forecasted to become available.

d. The workload associated with preparation, preservation and packaging of retrograde matériel must be recognized, and augmentation Tables of Organization and Equipment must be developed to provide the required staffings.

e. Doctrine developed to support deployment of forces from the Continental U.S. to overseas areas is not adequate for redeployment of forces from the combat zone back to the Continental

U.S. The biggest deficiency is the failure to recognize that the assistance of the Continental U.S. Post Engineer, Post Signal, Post Medical and Post Maintenance facilities are not available in the combat zone.

f. The sanitation and entomological requirements imposed on retrograde matériel from Vietnam actually determined the speed with which retrograde could be accomplished.

g. Organic divisional support elements are incapable of providing normal mission support to the division in combat for a period up to as long as the last 30 days prior to their redeployment. This logistics support must be provided by non-divisional support elements exclusively.

16. Loss of several Ammunition Supply Points to fire and enemy action justifies the need to find a better method of storing ammunition in a combat zone. Covered storage would have provided a significant decrease in losses caused by burning debris resulting from explosions.

17. Financial management must receive concurrent attention and priority with logistics management. Further, when this occurs, effective and efficient matériel management can follow. This was proved by our experience in Vietnam. Vietnam experience has proved that financial management techniques, when utilized to an appropriate degree, could be useful tools in the effective and efficient management of matériel in combat areas. Financial management systems for Operations and Maintenance funds supporting combat operations are most effective when they are mechanized, require a minimum change from the normal Service system, and provide for the distribution of matériel cost to appropriate cost accounts. The Services, when planning contingencies, should outline appropriate financial management systems for Operation and Maintenance funds supporting operations in the combat areas.

18. An adequate transportation capability, with a proper balance between sealift and airlift resources, is essential to the deployment and successful support of forces deployed in an overseas area. Since the bulk of matériel must be transported by surface means, an adequate and responsive sealift must be in-being. Such a capability is dependent on a modernized Military Sea Transportation Service nucleus fleet backed by access to the resources of an equally modern U.S. merchant marine. A responsive and adequate airlift must be available to support initial deployments, to provide for follow-on movement of personnel, items designated for normal movement by airlift, and for high-priority matériel. The growing capability of U. S. civilian and

military airlift emphasizes that the services must develop and test boldly engineered logistic systems to exploit the advantages inherent in this mode of transportation.

19. Provisions should be made for a Traffic Management Agency to be established prior to any type of projected operations. The Traffic Management Agency should have operational control of the transportation assets that are available for common-user service. Using an agency such as Traffic Management Agency means a sizeable reduction in the waste of transportation resources.

20. The attendant maintenance and supply requirements associated with unnecessarily sophisticated or complex equipment and weapon systems may outweigh the value of the dubious operational improvements. For purposes of illustration:

a. Why multi-fuel engines? Concentration of fuel distribution may have been more economical. b. Did we need communications retransmission capability in tanks? c. Did we train sufficient marksmen to justify precision rifles? d. Would not light weight cheaply constructed mass fire weapons serve better than expensive maintenance significant items? e. Must vehicles be waterproof for their occasional submerging? f. Would light weight plastic flotation bags serve better?

Salvage and Scavenger

1. Battle damaged or abandoned American equipment provided the innovative Viet Cong with a source of raw materials. The following provided some illustrations:

a. 155-mm shells were used as mines to destroy tank or personnel carrier tracks.

b. High-powered American rifle shells were adapted to "water pipe" guns by expanding the bullets with coins with holes in them. Inaccurate as the weapon may be, a hit is devastating.

c. 155-mm shells and others of similar size have been successfully used as mortars.

Battlefield Policing

Total destruction of abandoned equipment appears necessary. There is considerable evidence that the soldier is overly equipped and discards items on the march.

Appendix

Commanders of 1st Logistical Command, Vietnam
1965–1970

Colonel Robert W. Duke	1 April 1965–1 January 1966
Major General Charles W. Eifler	1 January 1966–12 June 1967
Major General Shelton E. Lollis	12 June 1967–11 August 1967
Major General Thomas H. Scott, Jr.	11 August 1967–1 August 1968
Major General Joseph H. Heiser, Jr.	1 August 1968–22 August 1969
Brigadier General Hugh A. Richeson	22 August 1969–1 September 1969
Major General Walter J. Woolwine	1 September 1969–26 June 1970

Glossary

AVEL	Aviation Materiel Management Center
AMMC	Aviation Electronics
DS	Direct Support
FAMF	Floating Aircraft Maintenance Facility
FWMAF	Free World Military Assistance Forces
GS	General Support
GSGP	General Support Group
JP–4	A Kerosene-base Fuel for Turbine Engines
LCM	Landing Craft, Mechanized
LCU	Landing Craft, Utility
LST	Landing Ship, Tank
MCI	Meal, Combat, Individual
POL	Petroleum, Oils, and Lubricants
RVNAF	Republic of Vietnam Armed Forces
TOE	Table of Organization and Equipment
TRANS	Transportation

Index

☆ U.S. GOVERNMENT PRINTING OFFICE : 1976   O—209–238